THE BANKING CRISIS OF 1933

The Banking Crisis of 1933

by Susan Estabrook Kennedy

UNIVERSITY PRESS OF KENTUCKY

332.1

FOR AUSTIN LOVELL ESTABROOK

AND DOROTHY OGDEN ESTABROOK

CONTENTS

ACKNOWLEDGMENTS

ALTHOUGH the shortcomings of this manuscript remain mine alone, I should like to thank several of the many persons who contributed to its more creditable aspects.

I am grateful for the efficiency and courtesy of countless librarians and archivists at the Library of Congress, the National Archives, the Herbert Hoover Presidential Library, the Franklin Delano Roosevelt Memorial Library, the Michigan Historical Collections of the University of Michigan, Columbia University, the University of Virginia, Yale University, Princeton University, and the Federal Reserve Board. The offices of the secretary of the Treasury and the Comptroller of the Currency were particularly accommodating. Special thanks are due to Miss Elizabeth Mason of the Columbia Oral History Collections and Mr. William B. Liebman, curator of the Herbert H. Lehman Papers, both of whom were exceptionally helpful. The late Mrs. Eugene Meyer and her daughter kindly permitted me the use of Governor Meyer's memoir; and the late Judge Ferdinand Pecora and his son granted me access to his oral history recollections.

Four gentlemen deserve more than this inadequate acknowledgment of their many contributions to this study and to my career in history. Robert Karl Windbiel introduced me to the profession and convinced me to begin the work which has culminated in this manuscript. Eric L. McKitrick began my training in graduate research, contributing a sense of the perspective of the discipline. William E. Leuchtenburg oversaw each phase of the writing of the doctoral dissertation which formed the basis for this study, consistently offering constructive and incisive criticism. And Stuart Bruchey, after adding analysis and suggestions which improved the text significantly, supervised its final presentation for defense with a measure of enthusiasm and compassion for which there can be no repayment.

My family gave even more than their usual generous support. E. Craig Kennedy, Jr., my husband, may appreciate "The Banking Crisis of 1933"—as I do—as the occasion of our meeting; he knows that he has my thanks for sharing our first years of marriage with Messrs. Hoover and Roosevelt. My mother, Dorothy Ogden Estabrook, typed the manuscript many times, always believing that it would one day be completed in this form. And my father, Austin Lovell Estabrook, who did not live to see it finished, nonetheless gave it purpose by his constant pride in it and in me. Its dedication to my parents can only indicate the large measure of my debt and my gratitude.

Susan Estabrook Kennedy

CHAPTER I

Prosperity and Depression

ON WEDNESDAY morning, December 11, 1930, the New York State commissioner of banks closed the Bank of United States in New York City, locking up over $286 million belonging to more than 400,000 persons. Confused and disillusioned depositors had had no warning that a combination of inadequate supervision and criminal mismanagement had so jeopardized their small savings, and concerned citizens now wondered about the safety of deposits in other banks. Some even speculated that the collapse of the "Bank of United States" implied that the government's own bank had failed.

The Bank of United States had been chartered under the laws of New York State by a garment manufacturer and was run by his son Bernard Marcus and another manufacturer, Saul Singer. The younger Marcus and Singer consolidated the bank's position by mergers until by mid-1929 it formed a complex of fifty-seven branches throughout New York City with $314,720,000 in resources and deposits of $220 million in some 440,000 accounts, most of them small savings and thrift deposits. In addition, the same men controlled the affiliated Bankus Corporation, the City Financial Corporation, and the Municipal Financial Corporation, as well as three safe deposit companies, more than twenty subsidiary real estate corporations, and an insurance company. Over these, Marcus and Singer exercised virtually sole control and did not bother their disinterested board of directors with details of operations; the board appeared satisfied with their management—especially with the granting of $2,578,632 in uninvestigated loans to board members. The directors probably did not know about, and certainly did not question, purchases by Marcus and Singer of the bank's own stock in order to drive up prices, even when the speculators overextended themselves dangerously and fell back upon questionable banking practices to cover their dealings. During the summer of 1929, for example, they bought more than 80,000 units at $202 each, and when high-pressure sales techniques failed to unload these shares on depositors and friends, they were forced to arrange sale to the affiliates which they controlled. By August of that year, Marcus and Singer had purchased 118,000 units and loaned the affiliates $11 million from the bank's deposits to rebuy the certificates. The two men had been equally extravagant in real estate transactions on behalf of the bank, tying up over $25 million in properties which could not be liquidated easily.

When the New York State Banking Department sent in its examiners for the regular semiannual review of the bank's books, the examiners reported to Superintendent of Banks Joseph A. Broderick that many of the bank's $70,314,432 in real estate holdings were frozen, that loans to affiliates should be reduced, that the bank should not borrow from the Federal Reserve in order to lend to its subsidiaries, and that loans whose only security was the bank's own stock should be removed; reports on the affiliates were even more critical. Superintendent Broderick met with Marcus and Singer to recommend a change in policy and personnel but did not press his demands when he learned that the managers had a solution at hand.

Marcus and Singer had decided to cover their difficulties as they had in the past—through merger. Consequently, in August 1929 they opened negotiations with J. and W. Seligman and Company for the purchase of 115,000 units of Bank of United States stock to carry with it membership on the bank's board of directors. Although this deal did not go through, they continued stock and real estate speculations, made even more loans to affiliates, and sought to improve their cash position by drawing in new depositors. Their only retrenchment measure, as they awaited the next state audit, was a rearrangement of their books to make $12 million in affiliates' loans appear to have been paid. At the annual stockholders' meeting early in 1930, Singer informed the investors, without details, that their holdings were in excellent condition, for which he received a vote of thanks and no questions.

In March 1930, Marcus and Singer began to work for a merger of the Bank of United States with a large trust company. Subsequently, they also planned to combine with two other state banks and one national bank (Manufacturers Trust Company, International Trust Company, and Public National Bank and Trust Company). When consulted, Superintendent Broderick refused to approve or disapprove these deals until completion but suggested that the new management should be of the highest order and should include a real estate expert who belonged to none of the old institutions; he further stipulated that the new bank must be admitted to the New York Clearing House Association. The Federal Reserve Bank in New York, also concerned with the mergers, withheld involvement pending the next examination.

On September 15, 1930, the examiners of the Reserve Bank and the state banking department issued their latest report on the Bank of United States. Capital had been completely wiped out, they said; liabilities exceeded assets by $2,920,606.27. The stock was selling at $40 per unit, causing $15,991,380 in depreciation on the companies' own holdings. Of loans totalling over $37 million, they judged some $9 million doubtful, $14 million slow, and the other $14 million subject to some criticism. Marcus, however, kept this information secret from the directors and issued a public financial statement on September 24, claiming capital of $25,250,000, a surplus of $10 million, and undivided profits of $7,156,375.16.

Merger negotiations continued. On November 10, however, the other parties to the four-bank combination advised Marcus and Singer that they could not pursue an agreement in the face of current market conditions. Another effort to save the bank (involving J. P. Morgan and Company, National City Bank, Central Hanover Bank and Trust Company, Lehman Brothers, and the Bankers Trust Company) had already failed. On November 22, the trust company merger collapsed when the company insisted on the right to withdraw if general conditions deteriorated further before an agreement was approved. The following day, through the efforts of Broderick's office and the Federal Reserve Bank, the four-bank deal was revived, but during the next ten days little progress was made, and finally one party submitted new and impossible conditions, killing the plan. Panicky efforts to find another merger or to support the Bank of United States with fresh capital from other New York banks all proved abortive.

When the public became aware of the bank's difficulties on December 10, runs developed. Armored trucks rushed cash to the beleaguered branches, but the demand continued throughout the day. Undiscouraged by rain or police, frantic depositors stood in long lines to retrieve their savings. Fearing that the wave of withdrawals might spread to the savings banks or beyond the city, Broderick and the Federal Reserve men argued until 3 a.m. with officers from Morgan, Chase, National City, Guaranty Trust, Irving Trust, Chemical, Corn Exchange, and other large New York banks to try to arrange salvation for the Bank of United States. The best the bankers could offer, however, was a 50 percent guarantee of depositors' money. Broderick therefore informed the directors that the Bank of United States would have to be closed to protect its remaining assets from the run which would inevitably resume if it opened in the morning.

On December 11, then, creditors found the branch doors of the "Pantspressers' bank" shut. More than three-fourths of the 440,000 depositors had accounts of less than $400; many were Jewish immigrants, unemployed in the wake of the stock market crash and ensuing depression. At best, after long legal battles to obtain stockholders' assessments, the creditors received about half the value of their claims. A jury later found Superintendent Broderick innocent of charges that he had neglected his duty in failing to close the bank sooner. But bank President Bernard K. Marcus and Vice-president Saul Singer went to Sing Sing prison for the rearrangement of their affiliates' loans during the winter of 1929–1930.

Justice arrived late and offered small comfort, however. In light of the collapse of the City Trust Company a year earlier and extensive probes and recommendations for state banking reform, the failure of this vast banking complex highlighted the fact that neither New York State nor the Federal Reserve had prevented a recurrence.[1]

1. M. R. Werner, *Little Napoleons and Dummy Directors: Being the Narrative of the Bank of United States* (New York: Harper, 1933); Eugene Meyer,

The closing of the Bank of United States illustrated that combination of inept management, government timidity, and impersonalization of finance which had brought down more than 5,000 banks during the 1920s and would topple another 5,000 in the first three years of the Great Depression. It also showed up two fatal flaws in the American banking structure: first, a need for fundamental reform of bank organization, operation, and supervision; and second, the unique relationship between credit and finance, on the one hand, and public confidence and fear on the other.

The banking system of the United States, like its other forms of business enterprise, developed in a haphazard manner. Many Americans suspected powerful financial institutions, preferring local control or none at all and great freedom of opportunity to make money with a minimum of restraints. These groups resisted any single, strong, coordinated approach to the problem of providing citizens with banking facilities. Others took the opposite line, advocating either central banking or an extensive system of large and stable banks with close national supervision. For a century and a half, the country could not make up its mind which of these alternatives should prevail.

Confusion reigned from the beginning. Even before the Founding Fathers could act on Alexander Hamilton's suggestion of a central bank in 1791, four states had granted bank charters; others issued licenses during the lifetime of the First Bank of the United States. In 1811, antibank politicians allowed the First Bank to pass out of existence, but five years later Congress launched a Second Bank of the United States, largely to cope with debts resulting from the War of 1812. Although neither of these banks was a true central bank, they did perform a limited number of central

Columbia Oral History Collection (hereafter cited as COHC), p. 604; Henry Bruère, COHC, pp. 142–44; Jackson Reynolds, COHC, pp. 145–49; Frederick Lewis Allen, *The Lords of Creation* (New York: Harper, 1935), pp. 328–30; Norman Thomas, "The Banks of New York," *Nation* 132 (11 Feb. 1931): 147–49; Frederick Powell, *Depositors Paid in Full* (New York: Arbitrator, 1931); Daniel R. Fusfeld, *The Economic Thought of Franklin D. Roosevelt and the Origins of the New Deal* (New York: Columbia University Press, 1956), pp. 535–38; Bernard Bellush, *Franklin D. Roosevelt as Governor of New York* (New York: Columbia University Press, 1955), pp. 120–22; *New York Times,* 12 Dec. 1930, 4 Nov. 1932, 8 Feb. 1933.

banking functions, and the Second Bank might have become such an institution (as did the Bank of England) had it survived.[2] But when President Andrew Jackson vetoed recharter of this bank, central banking of any sort vanished from the United States for eighty years.

Meanwhile, state-licensed institutions proliferated. Bankers, as well as other businessmen, took advantage of Jacksonian concerns for free incorporation and easy credit. As late as the 1890s, a South Dakota court held banking a strictly private business in which the proprietor had an absolute right to own and operate his bank without supervision or control by any governmental authority.[3] Franchises were often easy to obtain; in some states in the early twentieth century, banking boards were not permitted to refuse charters to new institutions. Minimum capital requirements for banks were small, in some cases less than $25,000. And controls remained lax. Particularly in the Midwestern and North Central states, the country was overbanked and banking was undersupervised. Competition and profit-seeking encouraged freewheeling methods, reckless lending policies, and too-frequent speculation.[4]

At the same time, bank-issued currency added to fiscal confusion and instability. In 1864 Congress passed a national banking law with the intention of taxing most of the circulating notes of state banks out of existence and producing a more uniform national currency. In effect, the act reduced the number of state-chartered banks and established a rival system of national banks under the authority of the federal Comptroller of the Currency, although it neither prohibited states from licensing banks nor established a central bank for the entire country. Under the National Banking Act, five or more persons could form a corporation to carry on banking business; their articles of association would be filed with the Comptroller, who would issue a federal charter and supervise operations. These bankers had to have at least $50,000 capital in towns of less than 6,000

2. Harold Barger, *The Management of Money: A Survey of the American Experience* (Chicago: Rand McNally, 1964), pp. 22–23.

3. *State* v. *Scougal*, 51 N.W. 585 (1892). The case invalidated a law requiring state charter or franchise of banking corporations. The decision still stood in 1933.

4. For details of chartering from 1880 to 1930, see Gerald C. Fischer, *American Banking Structure* (New York: Columbia University Press, 1968), pp. 126, 184–98.

inhabitants and progressively higher amounts in larger places (towns of 6,000 to 50,000 required $100,000, and cities over 50,000 needed $200,000). Moreover, national banks were required to keep a portion of their deposits in cash in their own vaults or in other national banks in "redemption" (later called "reserve") cities. Country banks had to maintain 15 percent of their assets as reserves; those in redemption cities had to hold 25 percent in cash.

The National Banking Act was only partially successful, however. State banks dropped in number from 1,492 in 1862 to 1,089 in 1864, 349 in 1865, 297 in 1866, and 247 in 1868, the lowest figure since 1857; national banks increased from 467 in 1864 to 1,294 in 1865 and 1,634 in 1866. But by 1933, only one-third of the nation's banks (then 18,000) were national; they held approximately two-fifths of total banking resources ($56 billion).[5]

Americans also failed to embrace large-scale and unified banking. By 1900, only 87 banks of all kinds operated branches; this number increased to 530 in 1920 and 751 by 1930 (compared with 2,523 in 1960). Like national banking, branching was concentrated in large cities, primarily on the east coast.[6] Middle America suspected the power of large single banking interests, although some areas, particularly California, the Northwest, and around Chicago, permitted the rise of bank holding companies, group banks, and chain banking.[7] The McFadden Act of 1927 sought to eliminate any branch banking in the United States, allegedly to rescue the nation from Eastern aggression. In contrast, Great Britain, France, and Canada concentrated commercial banking in a few large institutions with

5. Board of Governors of the Federal Reserve System, *Banking and Monetary Statistics* (Washington, D. C.: National Capital Press, 1943), p. 6.
6. Arizona, California, Delaware, Maryland, North Carolina, Rhode Island, South Carolina, Vermont, and Virginia permitted statewide branch banking. Georgia, Indiana, Iowa, Louisiana, Maine, Massachusetts, Mississippi, Montana, New Jersey, New York, Ohio, Pennsylvania, Tennessee, and Wisconsin allowed branching in limited areas. Alabama, Arkansas, Colorado, Connecticut, Florida, Idaho, Illinois, Kansas, Minnesota, Missouri, Nebraska, Nevada, New Mexico, Texas, Utah, Washington, and West Virginia prohibited branch banking. Kentucky, Michigan, New Hampshire, North Dakota, Oklahoma, South Dakota, and Wyoming had no legislation on the subject.
7. Marquis James and Bessie Rowland James, *Biography of a Bank: The Story of Bank of America N.T. and S.A.* (New York: Harper, 1954); Virgil Willit, "The Banks Go Chain-Store," *American Mercury* 20 (June 1930): 144–52. For the development and organization of a banking group, see below, Chapter 4.

many branches and suffered no failures, while Japan and Norway abandoned unit for branch banking in order to escape epidemic failures.

Thus a majority of this country's banks lacked internal strength and could count on little support if they experienced difficulties. Between 1864 and 1896, 328 national and 1,234 state banks failed; one-fourth of these closings occurred in the western grain states. Rising prices and general industrial prosperity kept bank mortality figures low between 1897 and 1919, although 102 institutions (19 national and 83 state banks) went down in 1908 following the panic of the previous year.[8] During that crisis, banks had suspended cash payments, indicating that bankers needed a systematic method of mobilizing reserve funds to provide needed currency, since the Treasury could not supply the volume of money required to prevent panics.

The desire for an elastic currency, therefore, lay behind the next major piece of national banking legislation; like the 1864 act, however, the 1913 law would affect commercial banking structure as well. Debate over the money question eventually focused on a plan for currency secured by commercial assets, but the country could not afford to return to the chaos of bank-issued currency which had existed before the Civil War. The new system, therefore, required a central bank. This novel idea roused immediate and hostile opposition; the Democrats particularly—following the philosophy of Jackson and of Woodrow Wilson's New Freedom—disliked centralization, which might easily lead to the eclipse of state charters and independent banking. Therefore, the Federal Reserve Act, passed on December 23, 1913, created neither a European-style central bank nor a single system of federally-chartered institutions headed by a unitary government bank. The act merely built upon the existing composite structure: national banks had to belong to the Federal Reserve System; state banks might join or not as they chose; and the directing board oversaw only a twelve-part decentralized supervisory agency. This system was regarded by its foun-

8. Board of Governors, Federal Reserve System, *Banking and Monetary Statistics*, p. 283; Cyril B. Upham and Edwin Lamke, *Closed and Distressed Banks: A Study in Public Administration* (Washington, D. C.: Brookings Institution, 1934), p. 4.

ders as a passive agent to coordinate banking reserves in time of emergency, not as an active force for monetary stabilization.[9]

At the same time, the structure provided only a partial supervision of banks, since none but national institutions could be compelled to join and the powers of the Federal Reserve Board were limited to exacting those requirements specified in the law. The remainder of the System's "authority" rested on influence and leadership—the expectation that it could point out a proper direction for commercial banks through its changes of discount rates and open-market operations, and that they, in turn, would alter their own policies to conform to the general good. Member banks were under no compulsion to follow these leads, however. In practice they accepted suggestions of the Federal Reserve Board and district banks when it suited their own purposes and profits, and rejected any which did not, regardless of the effect on the System as a whole. The 1920s offers an excellent example of this selective cooperation.

Men hailed the 1920s as the New Economic Era in which America had permanently shattered the old patterns of rise and decline and entered an age of endless prosperity. Politicians and business leaders overcame the problems of postwar readjustments with the weapons of technology, concentration of industry, consumer credit, and a government benevolent to business; they chose to avoid or postpone an economic contraction by accelerating manufacturing, services, and sales. The Committee on Recent Economic Changes, established by Herbert Hoover's Conference on Unemployment, reported in the spring of 1929 that acceleration, rather than structural change, accounted for the great economic development of the decade. Although no major new product had been devised since the war, per capita production increased significantly, largely through the application of power to the old industries and through industrial reorganization. American products found a ready market in the demolished economies of Europe, while at home advertising and credit sales stimulated consumer purchasing.[10]

9. Barger, *Management of Money*, pp. 35–46.
10. George E. Mowry, *The Urban Nation, 1920–1960* (New York: Hill and Wang, 1965), pp. 6–7; William E. Leuchtenburg, *The Perils of Prosperity, 1914–1932* (Chicago: University of Chicago Press, 1958), pp. 7, 189–90; Robert

Americans welcomed good times, enjoying the idea of quick riches obtained with a minimum of physical effort; the public now believed that economic rather than political institutions governed society, and that economic power was less oppressive than political power had been. Government did nothing to disabuse the nation of this new attitude. By the end of the Harding administration, an alliance between government and business had become firmly fixed, and the Republican party wholeheartedly accepted a concept of society based on the union of these two interests. A generation of historians criticized Republican presidents, especially Calvin Coolidge, for this deference to business, but as a prominent economist later pointed out, conditions *were* good: production and employment were high and rising, wages were not up much, but prices remained stable, and while many were still poor, more were comfortably well off or richer than ever before.[11]

Therefore, while not everyone was "in the market," more men than ever before eagerly invested in stocks, bonds, and real estate, refusing to be discouraged even by the spectacular collapse of the Florida land boom in 1925. In the early 1920s stock prices were low but yields favorable; during the second half of 1924 they began to rise, continued up in 1925, dropped in 1926, and entered a steady climb in 1927. A host of new men invaded Wall Street, competing with established houses and capturing popular imagination. In many cases the old brokers had to follow the lead of the new, abandoning their traditional role as guardians against excess. The stock market in the 1920s seemed less a long-range register of corporate prospects and more a manipulator's playground.[12] An

Sobel, *The Big Board: A History of the New York Stock Market* (New York: Macmillan, 1965), pp. 36–37, 39, 41–42, 45, 229–30; Ogden L. Mills, "Recovery or Bust," speech, Indianapolis, Indiana, 25 Oct. 1934, Mills Papers, Library of Congress, box 140; Herbert Hoover, *The Memoirs of Herbert Hoover*, 3:14–15.

11. John Kenneth Galbraith, *The Great Crash: 1929* (Boston: Houghton, Mifflin, 1954), pp. 6–12, 76–77. See also Leuchtenburg, *Perils of Prosperity*, p. 242; John Tipple, *Crisis of the American Dream: A History of American Social Thought, 1920–1940* (New York: Western, 1968), p. 21.

12. Ferdinand Pecora, *Wall Street Under Oath: The Story of Our Modern Money Changers* (New York: Simon and Schuster, 1939), p. 5; Giulio Pontecorvo, "Investment Banking and Security Speculation in the Late 1920's," *Business History Review*, 32 (Summer 1958): 166–91; Galbraith, *Great Crash*, pp. 12–14, 17–19, 79–83, 152–55; Robert Sobel, *The Great Bull Market: Wall Street in the 1920's* (New York: Norton, 1968), pp. 59–76, 96–112.

enchanted public poured money into a mechanism it neither could nor wanted to understand. "Hot tip," "buy on margin," "paper profits," "speculation"—all these meant only a dazzling prospect of immediate untoiled-for wealth. Franklin Roosevelt said later that the American public was playing Alice in Wonderland and expected the poorhouse to vanish like the Cheshire cat.[13]

Government policies, particularly in the Federal Reserve System, encouraged this spirit of expansion. Among the reasons for the establishment of the Federal Reserve System had been the hope that the agency might control the volume of credit available to industry, commerce, agriculture, and banking. The twelve Reserve banks had autonomy over credit policies of the member banks of their respective districts, and they expected to influence those operations by changing the discount rate or by buying and selling securities in the open market. Open-market operations could change bank reserves. When Reserve banks bought securities, they paid by checks drawn on themselves; sellers then deposited those checks in their accounts in commercial banks, which sent them on to the Reserve banks for credit to their reserve accounts, thus increasing both their deposits and their reserves. Reserve bank sales of securities did the opposite, shrinking member banks' reserve accounts. Commercial banks made loans against these reserves; hence, any addition to or subtraction from their reserve accounts expanded or limited their lending power. On the other hand, changes in the discount rate meant raising or lowering the interest which member banks would have to pay on loans from the Reserve banks to get cash or replenish reserves. Thus a Reserve bank could encourage expansion of bank loans by lowering the discount rate to the point where a bank would profit by loaning out the money it borrowed from the Reserve bank.[14]

In practice, the System suffered from a surprising lack of coordination in these policies. The Federal Reserve Board engaged in an unresolved tug-of-war with the governors of the twelve banks for dominance of the System. At the same time, it deferred to the

13. Franklin D. Roosevelt, *Looking Forward* (London: Heinemann, 1933), pp. 217–28.

14. Sobel, *Big Board*, pp. 199–200; Ogden L. Mills, speech, Harvard Business School Club, 28 May 1935, Mills Papers, box 141; Ross M. Robertson, *History of the American Economy*, 2d ed. (New York: Harcourt, Brace and World, 1964), pp. 501–11.

New York Reserve Bank, particularly during the tenure of Benjamin Strong as its head. One critic, Clinton W. Gilbert, said that although J. P. Morgan and Company with its associates and satellites had failed to induce Congress to create a central bank instead of the Federal Reserve, they captured control of the System within ten years and for practical purposes transformed it into a central bank for their own use. Gilbert further charged that Governor Strong acted for Wall Street in dominating the Council of Governors and had no difficulty in overshadowing the men who headed the Federal Reserve Board during the 1920s. For its part, the Board repeatedly refused to use what powers it had to hold down credit expansion and speculation; System policies, such as they were, actually encouraged inflation of credit while they evaded any curtailment of the runaway markets.[15]

Although guidelines were established in 1923 for limiting credit to productive use, the Federal Reserve abandoned them within two years. In 1925 it yielded to business demands for reduced discount rates and responded to appeals from European central banks for bolstering of their monetary reserves. Governor Strong lobbied with particular effectiveness for help to England in its return to the gold standard. Strong had formed important contacts with European central bankers, especially in England and France, in 1917 while he was arranging World War I financing; several—notably Montague Norman of the Bank of England—became his close friends. As the American leader in international finance during the postwar period, Strong became convinced of the usefulness of international central bank cooperation. Since the United States government would not take the initiative in promoting reconstruction and stabilization abroad, Strong took it upon himself to arrange American support for England's return to the gold standard by U.S. gold credits, loans from the House of Morgan, and a lowering of interest rates in New York to below the London rate in order to attract international balances to London and to divert international borrowing from London to New York. He later did the same for Belgium, France, Italy, Poland, and Rumania.[16] Protests from such sources as Secretary of

15. Gilbert, *The Mirrors of Wall Street* (New York: Putnam's, 1933), pp. 9–10, 13–16, 18–26; Robertson, *History of American Economy*, pp. 498–501; Sobel, *Bull Market*, pp. 54–58; Galbraith, *Great Crash*, pp. 32–47; Barger, *Management of Money*, p. 362.

Commerce Herbert Hoover and the *New York Times* effected a brief abandonment of this easy credit early in 1926,[17] but the Federal Reserve again accommodated the Bank of England, the Reichsbank, and the Bank of France by its open-market purchases and the lowering of the discount rate. Federal Reserve banks began open-market operations to inflate credit in July 1927, and in August they lowered the discount rates from 4 to 3½ percent. By these maneuvers they injected $5 billion in reserves into the System, raising outstanding Reserve credit to $1,592,000,000.

These mechanisms, geared to international stabilization, affected local channels of credit as well. During the 1920s general prosperity and the Federal Reserve's "easy money" policies made more money available to commercial banks for lending. But the old recipients of such funds no longer needed them. The surge of business and financial activities following the war meant that large industrial corporations, formerly the heaviest users of commercial bank loans, could now operate and expand out of their own undistributed profits; they no longer depended on the commercial banks. Yet those same banks had even more money available to them to make loans. Therefore, bankers turned to types of long-term investments which were less safe (because they were not self-liquidating) and to the financing of speculative activity, including stock market and real estate investments. In 1915 commercial banks had put 53 percent of their loans into commercial ventures, 33 percent into securities, and 14 percent into real estate; by 1929, the percentages had shifted to 45, 38, and 17, respectively. At the same time, the banks increased their own real estate and other investments from 29 to 40 percent. Brokers' loans on the New York Stock Exchange rose 24 percent.[18] These last proved particularly dangerous.

A later economist noted that "one of the paradoxes of spec-

16. Lester V. Chandler, *Benjamin Strong: Central Banker* (Washington, D. C.: Brookings Institution, 1958), pp. 89–96, 147, 188–89, 247–56, 258–62, 303–22, 332–422.

17. Hoover, *Memoirs*, 3:5–10; *New York Times*, 1 Jan. 1926; Eugene Lyons, *Herbert Hoover: A Biography* (Garden City, N. Y.: Doubleday, 1964), pp. 212–13.

18. Board of Governors of the Federal Reserve System, *All-Bank Statistics, United States, 1896–1955* (Washington, D. C.: G.P.O., 1959), pp. 34–35; Milton Friedman and Anna Jacobson Schwartz, *A Monetary History of the United States, 1867–1960* (Princeton, N. J.: Princeton University Press, 1963), pp. 244–45.

ulation in securities is that the loans that underwrite it are among the safest of all investments. They are protected by stocks which under all ordinary circumstances are instantly salable, and by a cash margin as well. The money, as noted, can be retrieved on demand."[19] Moreover, a partisan of the Federal Reserve Board tried to argue that the lowering of the discount rate to 3½ percent had not caused speculation, attributing the increase in discounts to "a normal seasonal increase" and striking off the total increase in Reserve credit against gold exports and the decline in money in circulation.[20] The Federal Reserve bulletins and annual reports, however, noted "a continued rapid growth in the volume of member bank credit used in investments and loans on securities,"[21] and even defenders of the System were forced to admit that it was responsible for inflation in 1927 and 1928.[22]

Individuals bought securities "on margin" by putting down a fraction of the cost of their stocks with the intention of paying the rest at a later date, often out of the profits of a future sale. Brokers extended these loans to their clients for the unpaid balances of their accounts. In order to do so, the brokers themselves borrowed the money in the "call loan market," sometimes from the commercial banks and in 1928 and 1929 increasingly from corporations and other nonbanking sources which wanted to get in on the profits by using their free funds. Large brokerage houses such as J. P. Morgan and Company and Kuhn, Loeb and Company frowned on the use of the call money market, but other firms participated eagerly and usually

19. Galbraith, *Great Crash*, p. 26; Marcus Nadler and Jules I. Bogen, *The Banking Crisis: The End of an Epoch* (New York: Dodd, Mead, 1933), pp. 3–4; Smead to Adolph Miller, 30 Apr. 1929, memorandum on changes in banking, loans, and investments between July 1927 and April 1929, Federal Reserve Board files; Hoover, *Memoirs*, 3:10–14; Theodore G. Joslin, *Hoover Off the Record* (Garden City, N. Y.: Doubleday, Doran, 1935), p. 25; William Starr Myers and Walter H. Newton, *The Hoover Administration: A Documented Narrative* (New York: Scribner's, 1936), p. 12; Rixey Smith and Norman Beasley, *Carter Glass: A Biography* (New York: Longmans, Green, 1939), pp. 296–301; George Soule, *Prosperity Decade: From War to Depression, 1917–1929* (New York: Holt, Rinehart and Winston, 1947), pp. 154–56.

20. Charles Sumner Hamlin to Carter Glass, 9 Oct. 1928, Glass Papers, University of Virginia, box 64.

21. Federal Reserve Board, *Annual Report, 1927*, p. 11; Chester Morrill to French Strother, 13 Sept. 1932, Federal Reserve Board files.

22. J. M. Daiger, "Did the Federal Reserve Play Politics?" *Current History* 37 (Oct. 1932): 25–32; Charles Sumner Hamlin, Diary, Library of Congress, 1 July, 24 Aug., 27 Sept. 1932.

found banks to accommodate them. When they did not, General Motors, Cities Service, Sinclair Consolidated Oil, Bethlehem Steel, and Standard Oil of New Jersey, among other corporations, generously offered millions out of their own securities' profits, surplus earnings, undistributed profits, and even operating expenses.

Once committed to this kind of lending, the banks found it hard to reverse themselves; they could not suspend credit for speculation without also cutting off funds for the legitimate needs of production and trade. Therefore, they continued to accommodate small investors and large brokers. Many bankers were not blind to the argument that if they did not supply call money, the corporations would, with a consequent diversion of profits.[23] Some banks even had special coordinates, "investment affiliates," to handle their securities business. Not only did the bank itself make loans to investors and brokers, but the affiliate bought and sold stocks and bonds —an activity forbidden by law to the parent bank.[24]

In 1928, when the European emergency had passed and American bank lending had expanded significantly, the Federal Reserve Board decided to check speculation. In February 1929, therefore, the Board urged the Reserve banks to adopt a policy of "direct pressure" in order to "restrain the use, either directly or indirectly, of Federal Reserve credit facilities in aid of the growth of speculative credit." The Board assumed that by merely asking it could influence member banks to restrict the use of credit in the stock market while keeping it available for productive purposes. But the New York bank, long an opponent of this policy, felt that the time for it had passed; it preferred to use open-market purchases and the discount rate, which could bring about more "direct pressure" than the Board plan. Accordingly, the New York bank frustrated the Board's plans during much of 1929. Member banks also withheld cooperation; in one spectacular gesture, the National City Bank of New York offered $25 million in the call money market for brokers' loans.[25]

23. M. R. Werner, *Privileged Characters* (New York: McBride, 1935), pp. 443–44; Sobel, *Big Board*, pp. 255–57; Sobel, *Bull Market*, p. 29.

24. For the history of one of these double organizations, the National City Bank and the National City Company, see below, Chapter 5; Eugene Meyer, COHC, pp. 682–86; Hoover, *Memoirs*, 2:107; Soule, *Prosperity Decade*, pp. 156–57; Pontecorvo, "Investment Banking," pp. 167–91.

25. *Federal Reserve Bulletin*, Feb. 1929, pp. 2–3, 93–94; Federal Reserve Board, *Annual Report, 1929*, pp. 2–3; *1928*, p. 229; summary of criticisms by

The Federal Reserve Board itself was powerless to force the New York bank to accept the Board's view of the credit situation; nor could it compel member banks to carry out its policies. So long as a financial institution met the membership and reserve requirements, it had satisfied the obligations specified in the Federal Reserve Act of 1913 and need pay no further deference to the central board in Washington. Beyond that, a banker could operate his institution as he chose. As for the character of bankers in the 1920s, Carter Glass said that in some cases they were no more than "little corner grocerymen calling themselves bankers—and all they know is how to shave a note."[26] Another critic noted that "many of the bankers were, in common with their customers, sometimes careless to the point of criminal negligence, and sometimes ignorant to the point of imbecility."[27]

Although many banks supported the boom, not all enjoyed unmixed prosperity. Despite a rise in the number of commercial banks from 27,000 to 31,000 between 1914 and 1921, the nation had fewer than 25,000 by 1929. Only a small portion of this reduction came through mergers; 5,411 banks failed during the 1920s, and suspensions averaged one per day in the early 1930s. This rate of bank failures far outstripped that for other businesses after 1921.

Fundamental problems in the banking structure underlay these suspensions. Of the 5,411 banks which closed, 88 percent had assets under $1 million; 40 percent started with less than $24,000. Thus, the vast majority of failed banks were small institutions. Similarly, nearly 90 percent of the banks which went under were located in small, rural communities, primarily in the West North Central and South Atlantic states, where staple agriculture was depressed. These regions were also overbanked, having 25 percent of the country's population and 38 percent of its total banks. Moreover, two and one-half times as many state as national banks failed, and four-fifths of

H. Parker Willis, 2 May 1929, Federal Reserve Board files; George Leslie Harrison, memorandum of conversation with Roy A. Young, 25 Jan. 1925, Harrison Papers, Columbia University; *New York Times*, 28, 29 Mar. 1929; Hamlin, Diary, 16, 27 Oct. 1925, 1 May, 28 July 1929, 4 Jan., 14 Feb., 28, 29 Mar., 21, 23, 24, 28 May, 5, 7, 12 June 1929; "Improper Use of Bank Credit: 1929," Federal Reserve Board files.

26. Quoted in Caroline Bird, *The Invisible Scar* (New York: McKay, 1966), pp. 97–98.

27. *Privileged Characters*, p. 436.

the failures occurred in states which prohibited branch banking. Those same areas traditionally opposed large banks and centralization of the banking structure, including the Federal Reserve System. Of the 9,285 banks which suspended between 1921 and 1931, 7,587 –85 percent of the total–did not belong to the Reserve System.[28]

Hence, many of the banks which failed had no one to protect them from unwise operating policies and no one to rescue them when their ventures turned sour. Unitary banks, chartered with minimal capital, often without adequate reserves, were trapped when Midwestern land prices collapsed early in the 1920s and the Florida land boom broke in 1925; banks which supported agriculture suffered from the depression which devastated farming throughout the period; others, anxious to cash in on the boom, offered reckless bonuses and interest rates to attract customers away from their competitors or loaned every available nickel without a thought to their cash position should a run occur. Moreover, the small nonmember had no parent or sister institution to supplement its liquidity when it needed ready cash. Unlike a branch bank, it could not diversify credit risks, mobilize additional resources, or draw on more than the local store of management talent. Nor could it depend upon the benefits of Federal Reserve membership for rediscounts to supply extra cash. Finally, when one country unit bank could not meet its depositors' demands, its failure undermined confidence in other banks, starting an epidemic run which frequently pulled down all

28. Federal Reserve Board, *Annual Report, 1933*, pp. 3–4; J. F. T. O'Connor, *The Banking Crisis and Recovery under the Roosevelt Administration* (Chicago: Callaghan, 1938), pp. 94–95; Eugene Smolensky, *Adjustments to Depression and War, 1929–1945* (Atlanta: Scott, Foresman, 1964), pp. 41–43; Jesse H. Jones, with Edward Angly, *Fifty Billion Dollars: My Thirteen Years with the RFC (1933–1945)* (New York: Macmillan, 1951), pp. 13–14; Eugene Meyer, COHC, pp. 680–82; 496–97; Ray B. Westerfield, "Defects in American Banking," *Current History* 34 (Apr. 1931): 17–23; J. M. Daiger, "Bank Failures: The Problem and the Remedy," *Harper's Magazine* 162 (Apr. 1931): 513–27; *Commercial and Financial Chronicle*, 1 Apr. 1933, p. 2156; Guy Greer, "Why Canadian Banks Don't Fail," *Harper's Magazine* 166 (May 1933): 722–34; C. D. Bremer, *American Banking Failures* (New York: Columbia University Press, 1935), pp. 31–36, 42–44, 46–54, 109–11; Thomas W. Lamont, in "Should America Adopt a Unified Banking System?" *Congressional Digest* 12 (Apr. 1933): 108, 110; Board of Governors, Federal Reserve System, *Banking and Monetary Statistics*, pp. 283, 297; "Summary Report of the Federal Reserve Committee on Branch, Group, and Chain Banking," Mills Papers, box 59; Adolph Miller Papers, Federal Reserve Board, box 6; Fischer, *Banking Structure*, pp. 29–32, 42–49, 56–64; Pecora, *Wall Street under Oath*, pp. 237–38.

the banks in the neighborhood, the sound along with the weak.

In spite of these defects in financing the boom, prosperity lasted until 1929. Construction activity, new private investment, employment, and consumer spending—the usual indicators of rise and decline—hit a peak in 1927 and then slid downward. Hindsighted economists see that productivity increased much faster than either wages or consumption in the 1920s and had to reach the saturation point, particularly in consumer durables; agriculture was depressed throughout the period. For contemporaries, however, continued rise of the stock indices told of a new era, and for the last two years of prosperity the stock market and its paper profits concealed the underlying flaws in the economy.[29]

In 1929 the artificially extended rise came to an abrupt end. Some, including Joseph P. Kennedy and Bernard Baruch, withdrew in time, but most did not. In October 1929 the long-delayed slump set in, activating all of the weaknesses which years of optimism had permitted to develop. The great bankers could not sustain the market, and small investors, involved too deeply for either their resources or their understanding, gave way to panic. Millions in cash and paper disappeared overnight. The greatest cost, however, was to the mind and heart of America. The confidence of the New Economic Era dissipated with the plummeting trade indices. An oppression of the spirit, more devastating than any economic decline, overwhelmed the nation.

The 1929 stock market crash began a depression more terrible than any in United States history. Collapse of the stock market, on top of the decline in construction, employment, and consumption of durables, set off a further drop in production, wholesale prices, personal income, and the stock of money. Between 1929 and 1933, net national product fell by more than one-half in current prices, more than one-third in constant prices, and more than one-third in

29. Rexford Guy Tugwell, "Flaws in the Hoover Economic Policy," *Current History* 35 (Jan. 1932): 525–31; Soule, *Prosperity Decade*, pp. 278, 287–88; Nadler and Bogen, *Banking Crisis*, pp. 5–9; Robertson, *History of American Economy*, pp. 630–34; James Couzens to William J. Norton, 8 Nov. 1926, quoted in Harry Barnard, *Independent Man: The Life of Senator James Couzens* (New York: Scribner's, 1958), p. 193; *New York Times*, 5 June 1929; James E. Palmer, *Carter Glass: Unreconstructed Rebel* (Roanoke, Va.: Institute of American Biography, 1938), pp. 209–10.

monthly wholesale prices.[30] But America did not return to "normal" after the liquidation of inflated values was completed. Business failed to revive after the first panic as it had in earlier depressions; the worst became yet worse. Just as the 1920s seemed an endless upward movement, so the Great Depression went beyond all expectations of decline. America's optimism lasted as long as the depression seemed a righteous and selective punishment of speculators, but it deteriorated as lengthening contraction touched the entire country without moral distinctions. The nation awakened roughly from its dream of prosperity; the years of fantasy had left it badly prepared to meet harsh reality. Individuals now felt impotent in a complex economic apparatus they could neither understand nor control. In contrast with the exhilaration of the 1920s, the despair of the 1930s drove America face to face with its most basic assumptions, forcing it to reconsider a way of life presumed perfect.[31]

One of the most devastating blows to national confidence was the increasing tempo of bank failures. In 1928, 491 banks suspended operations; in 1929, 651; thereafter the figures skyrocketted: 1,352 failures in 1930, 2,294 in 1931. Although no banking panic immediately followed the stock market crash, in November 1930 a contagion of failures started in Nashville and spread to Missouri, Indiana, Illinois, Iowa, Arkansas, and North Carolina. Gripped by fear, depositors rushed to convert their time and demand deposits into cash; the runs which followed pulled down 256 banks with deposits of $180 million in November and 353 with over $370 million in deposits the next month. On December 11, the Bank of United States in New York City closed, the largest commercial failure in American history. Another spate of runs began in March 1931 and reached a high point in June, attacking the Midwest, Pennsylvania, and New York in particular, intensifying with the collapse of the major European central banks.[32]

30. Friedman and Schwartz, Monetary History, pp. 299–331.

31. Tipple, Crisis of the American Dream, p. 14; William E. Leuchtenburg, "The Great Depression," in The Comparative Approach to American History, C. Vann Woodward (New York: Basic Books, 1968), pp. 296–300; Matthew Josephson, Infidel in the Temple: A Memoir of the Nineteen-Thirties (New York: Knopf, 1967), pp. 2–3, 14, 23, 25–27, 34–39, 44–46, 48, 57–76.

32. State of New York, Annual Report of the Superintendent of Banks, 31 Dec. 1930, Part 1, p. 46; Friedman and Schwartz, Monetary History, pp. 308–15, 342–44; Commercial and Financial Chronicle, 22 Nov. 1930, p. 3247;

Bankers faced a triple threat between 1929 and 1931. First, depositors caught in the depression withdrew funds for living expenses or joined in massive drains when they felt their deposits were threatened by real or imagined banking troubles. Second, assets deteriorated as the stock market continued to drop. With the shrinkage in values of the securities in their own portfolios or held as collateral for loans, banks had less liquid funds to meet depositors' withdrawals; in order to obtain cash, they frequently had to sell off securities at current low prices. Third, Federal Reserve policy did not include supporting the prices on government securities to counter the depressed bond market.[33] To meet these difficulties, some bankers consolidated and merged, but most defended themselves by increasing liquidity.

Surrounded by the hulks of institutions which had failed, bankers tried to convert assets into cash to be ready to meet renewed runs. Cash assets comprised 14 percent of total holdings in 1929; by 1933 the overall figure had risen to 18 percent, and some New York banks achieved beter than 60 percent liquidity. In the same period, banks shifted assets from loans to investments and bought more easily convertible government securities for their own portfolios. Banks in the large metropolitan centers in particular built up their cash reserves, in some cases to three times normal. In fact, by the end of 1931, bankers had called in loans, converted to cash, and pursued deflationary policies to the point where they felt themselves caught in the relentless economizing.[34]

By protecting themselves rather than by helping others fight the depression, bankers abdicated leadership in their communities and threw away prestige with both hands. The same men who had claimed credit for prosperity refused to accept responsibility for ad-

Reynolds, COHC, pp. 143–45; Federal Reserve Board, *Annual Report, 1930*, p. 17; Myers and Newton, *Hoover Administration*, pp. 6–7, 35; *New York Times*, 1, 2, 8, 29 Jan., 6, 7, 16 Feb. 1935; Robertson, *History of American Economy*, pp. 518–20.

33. Reynolds, COHC, pp. 141–43, 149–50; Friedman and Schwartz, *Monetary History*, pp. 351–57; Nadler and Bogen, *Banking Crisis*, pp. 104–06.

34. Board of Governors, Federal Reserve System, *All-Bank Statistics*, p. 35; Friedman and Schwartz, *Monetary History*, pp. 449–61; Magnus W. Alexander to George Leslie Harrison, copy to Owen D. Young, 9 Aug. 1932, Correspondence of the Secretary of the Treasury, NA: RG 56, box 10; *Commercial and Financial Chronicle*, 10 Jan. 1931, pp. 184–85; 21 Mar. 1931, p. 2074.

versity and rejected the opportunity to maintain confidence in themselves and their institutions. Their retrenchment seemed a confession of inability to care for the nation's material well-being, a failure which appeared worse after an era of unlimited economic power. In addition, well-publicized embezzlements and suicides among the great of finance led both private citizens and public spokesmen to doubt the competence of their former demigods.[35] Throughout the 1920s and until 1931, the nation had looked to its bankers first to ensure prosperity and then to lead others out of the depression; thereafter, however, the bankers seemed scarcely able to help themselves. Loss of confidence in the leaders of finance, moreover, made the depression harder to fight and increased the burden on those left in command.

35. Hoover to George Leslie Harrison, 22 Mar. 1932; Harrison to Hoover, 22 Apr. 1932, Harrison Papers, box 8; Tipple, *Crisis of the American Dream*, pp. 168–69, 31–32, 159–60; *Father Coughlin's Radio Discourses, 1931–1932* (Royal Oak, Mich.: Shrine of the Little Flower, n.d.), pp. 20–21.

CHAPTER II

Hoover's Solutions

OF THE MEN available to cope with the depression, the new president, Herbert Hoover, appeared most capable. Hoover had taken office with the statement that the nation would have to deal only with "problems of progress to higher standards."[1] When Coolidge prosperity ended seven months later, however, Hoover held unimpeachable credentials for the job of recovery. He had more than achieved his boyhood goal—"to earn my own living without the help of anybody"[2]—and might guide the nation to do the same.

Already a successful consulting engineer before the outbreak of World War I, he was called upon by the American consul in London to organize relief for Americans stranded there during the August 1914 banking holiday. Later he supervised relief services for much of Allied Europe. At home, he served the Wilson administration as food czar, heading such popular win-the-war efforts as "Meatless Mondays." After the war, he joined the Harding cabinet as secretary of commerce, escaped the scandals of 1923, and continued in office under President Coolidge with a commendable record as administrator and humanitarian, showing special concern for flood victims. Several times during the 1920s he warned against the speculative markets and had the doubtful satisfaction of seeing his dismal predictions come true shortly after he became president. But as engineer, self-made millionaire, administrator, and world-renowned humanitarian, Hoover brought to the presidency a training and reputation which seemed excellent preparation for his difficult task of fighting the financial contraction.

On the other hand, Hoover lacked a political background and personality. Before 1929 he had never held elective office, yet some said that he could not have lost in his bid for the presidency in 1928, running on Republican prosperity and against Rum, Romanism, and Al Smith of Tammany Hall. He remained unschooled in popular politics and leadership, however. Although he realized that the president had a powerful weapon in his role as "educator," he never mastered the technique of using it and never sparked enthusiasm beyond his own circle of associates. Walter Lippmann called Hoover "indecisive in the face of conflicting wills which are the living tissue of popular government." He concluded that Hoover was not really a weak man, but that he had not mastered the politician's art.[3] White House usher Ike Hoover claimed that the president only sent for people "whom he knew in advance would agree with him."[4] And Eugene Meyer, whom Hoover appointed to head the Federal Reserve Board, added that the president "always had to be in on everything. He had to feel important."[5]

Despite the lack of an effective political personality, Hoover chose to combat the depression by means which depended almost exclusively upon exciting a popular response. He beleived that the American system was fundamentally sound, that the economy remained essentially healthy, and that conditions would correct themselves aided by nothing more than the voluntary cooperation of businessmen, bankers, workers, and consumers. A compelling appeal by some influential personage, probably the president, would unite these groups to overcome panic and revitalize credit and consumption. Hoover began immediately, summoning leaders of the various sectors of the economy to agree "to maintain business progress."[6] He chose these tactics rather than calling a special session of Congress (which he said would "disturb the healing processes now un-

1. Hoover, State Papers, 1:12; Hoover, Memoirs, 3:38–40, 471, 475; Myers and Newton, Hoover Administration, pp. 18–19.
2. Quoted in Joslin, Hoover Off the Record, p. 6.
3. Lippmann, "The Peculiar Weakness of Mr. Hoover," Harper's Magazine 140 (June 1930): 1–7.
4. Irving Hood Hoover, Forty-Two Years in the White House (Boston: Houghton Mifflin, 1934), p. 232.
5. Meyer, COHC, pp. 693–95.
6. Carl N. Degler, "The Ordeal of Herbert Hoover," Yale Review 52 (Summer 1963): 573.

doubtedly going on in the economic situation"[7]) or pushing for concrete structural changes in the economy.

Between November 15 and November 21, 1929, Hoover met with leaders of industry, agriculture, and labor. The result of these conferences was a series of joint statements offering encouragement, agreeing to maintain wage rates, and planning renewed business progress. He also asked state governors to initiate public works projects to stimulate construction and employment, worked through the United States Chamber of Commerce, and established the National Business Survey Conference. In some of these appeals he was successful, as for example in convincing the American Legion to forego a cash veteran's bonus in 1931. He also issued statements on the fundamental soundness of the economy, including the first and second annual messages to the Congress on the State of the Union, the 1930 annual Chamber of Commerce dinner address, and the address to the annual convention of the American Bankers Association in the same year.[8]

Hoover regarded the depression as a crisis in confidence. Declining values and banking failures could not be explained in purely economic terms, he felt, and both situations would correct themselves as soon as people regained their faith. "One of the duties of the time," he recalled later, "was to maintain confidence of our people in the future. With the powerful spiritual and economic strength of the United States, this could only be a passing phase in the life of the nation."[9] Repeatedly he told the country that its banking and economic systems remained strong, that the stifling paralysis of credit stemmed only from an unjustified lack of confidence. At every upturn, he reported that the depression had ended,[10] but as each message proved false Hoover's credibility slipped, a decline all the more detrimental since he had based his fight on public trust.

Hoover did not totally reject action; he recognized that government had assumed a new role in the industrial economy and did not believe that the depression should simply be permitted to run its

---

7. Hoover, *State Papers*, 1:565.
8. Hoover, *Memoirs*, 3:83; Myers and Newton, *Hoover Administration*, pp. 120–21; Hoover, *State Papers*, 1:133–67, 428–31, 289–96, 375–84.
9. Hoover, *Memoirs*, 3:32–33.
10. Hoover, press statement, 6 Oct. 1931, *State Papers*, 2:4–7; third annual message to Congress, 8 Dec. 1931, ibid., pp. 46–51.

course. He did, however, see the proper role of the president as leader and guide rather than as interventionist and activist. Accordingly, Hoover confined himself to working through established channels.[11] He suggested remedies, called conferences, worked for cooperative agreements, and spoke for reforms.

In dealing with the banking situation, each of his State of the Union messages requested changes in the "feeble and badly organized" structure. In December 1929 he urged a joint study of banking; in June 1931 he asked for reforms of the Federal Reserve System; in October 1931 he requested ideas from the American Bankers Association. And he repeatedly suggested such revisions as universal Federal Reserve membership, statewide branch banking by national banks, separation of banks from their stock-selling affiliates, and limitations on long-term credits by commercial banks. Nothing came of any of these proposals during his term in office, and in fact Hoover put them forth only gratuitously. He did not press for any fundamental changes, nor did he endorse others' efforts to secure reforms.[12]

The president also labored under the apprehension that full information might excite public panic.[13] Therefore, he sacrificed potential support by keeping the public in the dark about events and policies, possibly forgetting that unaided speculation about "secret" dealings might cause greater worry than even the worst truths.

It is ironic that Hoover, who fought the battle for confidence, dissipated much of the nation's confidence in himself. Several factors contributed to his downfall. First, the country lay wounded in the ruins of a prosperity created by Republicans and bankers.[14] Second, although the president constantly predicted an imminent end to depression, hard times persisted. Third, neither Hoover nor the bankers nor the businessmen seemed able to cure the nation's ills by

11. Hoover, Memoirs, 3:29–32; Hoover, "The Real State of the Union," Further Addresses upon the American Road: 1938–1940 (New York: Scribner's, 1940), p. 62; Leuchtenburg, Perils of Prosperity, pp. 251–52; Joslin, Hoover Off the Record, p. 2.

12. Meyer, COHC, pp. 539–40; Hoover, Memoirs, 2:308–09; Lyons, Herbert Hoover, p. 279; Hoover, State Papers, 2:108–11, 137–39.

13. Hoover, Memoirs, 3:104; Tipple, Crisis of the American Dream, p. 164; Richard Hofstadter, The American Political Tradition and the Men Who Made It (New York: Knopf, 1948), p. 286.

14. James Truslow Adams, "Presidential Prosperity," Harper's Magazine 161 (Aug. 1930): 257–67.

fighting on the psychological level. And fourth, having chosen to scotch the depression in the minds of men rather than in their hands and pocketbooks, Hoover lacked the personality to carry on the battle. So critics charged:

> Mellon pulled the whistle,
> Hoover rang the bell,
> Wall Street gave the signal,
> And the country went to hell.[15]

President Hoover blamed Europe for the Great Depression on two counts: first, because of Federal Reserve inflation of credit to aid European countries before 1928; and second, because of "an economic hurricane" in 1931. Hoover admitted that the United States was "due for some economic readjustment" after the speculative orgy of 1928–1929, but he felt that domestic difficulties alone did not account for the severity or length of the crisis. Instead he believed the World War and Europe's "internal policies" had caused the depression.[16] Moreover, by the spring of 1931, the United States had improved its economic position, only to have progress arrested by failure of the Central European banks. The new contraction which followed endangered trade and international payments and came close to forcing the United States off the gold standard.

The international financial structure built up in the wake of World War I with the aid of American investments proved adequate during the inflationary 1920s but could not survive the depression. Germany's elections in September 1930 indicated a rejection of the Versailles reparations and unsettled an already nervous international money market. American and French financiers began to withdraw short-term loans from Central Europe. (American banks had advanced $1.2 billion to $1.5 billion on short-term paper, much of it to Central Europe. The loans had been placed on the assumption that they were normal advances on goods in export trade; much of

15. Quoted in Victor L. Albjerg, "Hoover: The Presidency in Transition," *Current History* 39 (Oct. 1950): 213–19.
16. Hoover, *Memoirs*, 3:vi, 4. Milton Friedman has argued that fixed rates of exchange between different national currencies (the gold-exchange standard) established in 1929 "ensured a world-wide decline in income and prices after 1928"; in other words, an international contraction. Friedman and Schwartz, *Monetary History*, pp. 359–62.

the money, however, was invested in capital improvements.[17]) On March 20, 1931, Germany and Austria announced that they were forming a customs union to promote trade and counteract the depression. France and the nationals of the Little Entente protested, and France pulled short-term funds out of Austria, hoping to break up the customs union plan.

Prices fell around the world and anxiety mounted. In the United States, industrial stocks fell ten index points in the ten days after March 25, 1931; by the end of April they had fallen 20 percent. Europeans bought fewer American commodities and sold American investments, so that the American markets reflected falling prices in Europe. Hoover was so concerned that on April 27 he referred to the European situation in a confidential speech at the Gridiron Club, warning that despite an apparent upturn the country should be prepared for more difficulties.[18] He also consulted with his cabinet, the diplomatic corps, Federal Reserve Board members, and prominent bankers.

In May, Louis Rothschild's Kreditanstalt in Vienna applied to the Austrian government for assistance; the bank financed almost two-thirds of Austrian industrial production and held 70 percent of total bank assets. The government tried to help, but the bank could not withstand foreign withdrawals and domestic runs; its gold reserves fell dangerously low. Temporary loans, including $14,070,000 from the Bank for International Settlements and a group of central banks including the American Federal Reserve System, were insufficient. When Austria applied to the League of Nations for permission to contract a foreign loan, France demanded that Austria renounce the customs union as a condition, but Austria refused. England defied France and made a loan out of its own resources, but again, the buttressing was insufficient.

By the end of May, trouble had spread to Germany, and business failed to show expected seasonal increases. In a desperate attempt to save the Berlin Reichsbank, the German government announced a 25 percent increase in taxes and a 10 percent decrease in in expenses. But Germany had already suffered external and internal runs with each new rumor from Austria, reducing the liquidity of

17. Myers and Newton, *Hoover Administration*, pp. 74–75.
18. Hoover, *State Papers*, 2:558.

the German banks and jeopardizing the mark. The German banks would not cooperate with one another, even in the face of great runs; many closed and panic spread. Like Austria, Germany got nowhere in the face of French pressures.

Meanwhile, Hoover had begun to counterattack. On May 6, even before the German situation had become critical, he called in the American ambassador to Berlin to discuss the withdrawal of foreign loans, restriction of credit, and flight of capital. The ambassador relayed Chancellor Bruning's fears that the financial crisis might precipitate a communist or Nazi revolt. Although gloomy reports from Vienna, Budapest, and Berlin were reflected in the American markets, Hoover rejected the idea of an emergency session of Congress: "We cannot legislate ourselves out of this depression," he said. While Chancellor Bruning pleaded with England for money and President von Hindenburg appealed to the United States, Germany experienced new disorders. To meet the economic and political crisis, therefore, Hoover summoned Republican leaders and suggested that the nations join in a one-year "moratorium" on all war debts.[19] On June 20, Hoover made the proposal public, calling on all creditor nations to agree to a year's postponement "of all payments on intergovernmental debts, reparations and relief debts, both principal and interest." In the next two weeks he fought French objections, and on July 6 announced that all governments concerned had accepted the moratorium principle.[20]

Although Hoover's moratorium was applauded both at home and abroad, the agreement did not stop banking troubles in Germany and Hungary. Capital continued to flow to France and the United States. Therefore, Hoover proposed a "standstill" whereby all banks in the nine or ten countries which held German short-term bills would agree not to present them for payment for a stipulated time. He believed this policy would be more effective than drop-in-the-

19. Hoover, *Memoirs*, 3:61; Myers and Newton, *Hoover Administration*, p. 82; Henry Stimson and McGeorge Bundy, *On Active Service in Peace and War* (New York: Harper, 1948), pp. 204–05; Bascom N. Timmons, *Portrait of an American: Charles G. Dawes* (New York: Holt, 1953), pp. 305–07.

20. Hoover, *Memoirs*, 3:61–80; Myers and Newton, *Hoover Administration*, pp. 76–109; Joslin, *Hoover Off the Record*, pp. 87–88; Hoover, *State Papers*, 2:591–93, 595–96; *Commercial and Financial Chronicle*, 27 June 1931, p. 4636; "At Last!" *Business Week*, 1 July 1931, p. 40; *New York Times*, 29 June 1931.

bucket loans. France, in a political play, now accused the United States of not cooperating, but an economic conference in London rejected the new French insistence on loans in favor of Hoover's latest suggestion. They agreed to the standstill on July 23; the next day France began withdrawing gold from England.[21]

With Germany temporarily out of danger and the threat shifting to England, Hoover moved to aid London. Federal Reserve banks in New York and other cities agreed to buy $125 million in prime commercial bills from the Bank of England; the Bank of France, still making gestures, did the same. On August 26 the new Nationalist ministry in London told the United States that these funds had been exhausted; it got another $400 million. Continued heavy withdrawals of gold by France and the Netherlands, however, so undermined British holdings that on September 21 the Bank of England defaulted on gold payments. European commodity and security markets closed; prices dropped everywhere. "It was," said one reporter, "a blow which shook the *spirit* of the world."[22]

Would the United States be next? Some countries (Italy, Greece, Germany, Austria, Hungary, and Chile) protected themselves by restricting trade and raising tariffs. Others (Denmark, Sweden, Norway, Colombia, Bolivia, and India) felt it would be safer to abandon the gold standard, as England had done. And a few of the more stable nations, led by Belgium and France, secured their own positions by withdrawing portions of their gold balances from the United States and earmarking more gold for future shipment home, thus reducing American reserves. Before 1931, foreign governments and central banks had deposited $1.5 billion at interest in American banks, but on September 22, 1931 alone, France withdrew $120 million in gold from New York. From September 16 to September 30 the gold stock declined by $275 million; another $45 million went during October, returning the gold stock to its 1929 level.[23]

21. Hoover, *State Papers*, 1:600; Myers and Newton, *Hoover Administration*, pp. 76–109; Hoover, *Memoirs*, 3:61–80.

22. Lawrence Sullivan, *Prelude to Panic: The Story of the Bank Holiday* (Washington, D. C.: Statesman Press, 1936), p. 1; Meyer, COHC, pp. 646–62; Myers and Newton, *Hoover Administration*, pp. 110–16, 118–23; Jackson Reynolds, COHC, pp. 150–51.

23. George Leslie Harrison, memorandum of conversation with Governor Norman of the Bank of England and Sir Ernest Harvey, 2 Oct. 1931, Har-

Against these depredations the Federal Reserve System raised the rediscount rates sharply, and the New York bank convinced the directors of the Bank for International Settlements that central bankers must oppose any future attacks on the dollar. For a time, in November and December, the foreign runs slackened.

The rush from abroad to convert dollar balances into gold frightened American depositors, however, and they began to withdraw currency from their banks. Changes in the rediscount rates doubled their anxiety. By November 7, 1931, almost half a billion dollars had gone into hiding.[24] One government official illustrated the extent of hoarding by the story of a South Dakota farmer and his wife who decided to buy a large farm which the bank had foreclosed on and was selling for $12,000. The couple looked at the farm, agreed to take it, and returned to the banker two days later to pay for it. They offered a tin can filled with money—$10,000. When the cash was counted and found to be insufficient, the surprised farmer said to his wife, "Well, Mama, I guess you brought the wrong can."[25]

Bank runs and failures increased spectacularly: 522 commercial banks with $471 million in deposits suspended during October 1931; 1,860 institutions with deposits of $1.45 billion closed between August 1931 and January 1, 1932. At the same time, holdings by the 19,000 banks still open dropped appreciably through hoarding and deterioration of their securities. Hoover countered with an antihoarding education campaign which resulted in considerable redeposits of currency during 1932, but the program did not work quickly enough to correct the dangerous undermining of America's gold supply by domestic and foreign withdrawals.[26]

Hoover had two alternatives for dealing with the banking problem: unrestrained liquidation, which would bring down more

rison Papers, Columbia University, binder 45; Federal Reserve Board, *Annual Report, 1931*; ibid., *1932*; Friedman and Schwartz, *Monetary History*, pp. 315–16; Mills, "The Financial Crisis and the Reconstruction Finance Corporation," speech, Providence, R. I., 19 Aug. 1932, Mills Papers, Library of Congress, box 138.

24. Mills, "Financial Crisis"; Sullivan, *Prelude to Panic*, p. 44, chart.

25. Jones, *Fifty Billion Dollars*, pp. 14–15.

26. Friedman and Schwartz, *Monetary History*, pp. 315–22, 345–47; Reynolds, COHC, pp. 154–55; Hoover, *Memoirs*, 3:82–83, 119–20; Myers and

small and weak banks, or some rescue action. Had he been the laissez-faire conservative many have painted him, he would have had to select the former course, but in line with his own ideas of modified progressivism, he chose the latter, appealing to the banking community to free $1.5 billion in resources of "apparently a million people" by means of a "vigorous effort at voluntary organization" under the leadership of the Federal Reserve System. His secretary of the Treasury pointed out that the administration "sought to provide additional credit for commerce and industry and to arrest the fearful process of deflation by putting the credit of the Reconstruction Finance Corporation back of our commercial and banking system; through the open market policy of the Federal Reserve System, and by the emergency powers granted to Federal Reserve Banks."[27]

Hoover's first proposal, voluntary action by the bankers, exceeded the strict requirements of both his own and the Federal Reserve's functions, but he requested only leadership from the government and assumed that action would come from the private and commercial banks. Accordingly, he sent a letter to Governor Eugene Meyer of the Federal Reserve Board on September 8, 1931; Meyer distributed copies of the plea to the twelve Reserve banks the following day.[28] At this point, the president did not include any call for a new government agency to assist the banks, although Meyer and others had urged him to revive the War Finance Corporation. The WFC had been created in 1918 to meet wartime financing problems; after the war it continued in operation, expanding to fight the agricultural depression of the 1920s until its liquidation in 1929. Meyer, who twice served as its managing director, and other former members hoped that a similar agency might solve the problems of 1931, but the president did not yet believe in such positive federal action.[29]

Newton, *Hoover Administration*, pp. 118–25; Herbert Bayard Swope to Hoover, 16 Oct. 1931, Herbert Hoover Archives, Stanford, President's File 5; Nadler and Bogen, *Banking Crisis*, pp. 111–12.

27. Ogden L. Mills, "The Road to Recovery and the Road to Ruin," speech, Toledo, Ohio, 26 Oct. 1932, Mills Papers, box 177.

28. Joslin, *Hoover Off the Record*, p. 133; Myers and Newton, *Hoover Administration*, pp. 116–17, 124–25.

29. "The RFC," *Fortune* 21 (May 1940): 47. According to Gerald D. Nash, the idea for a Reconstruction Finance Corporation came from these arguments by Meyer for a revived WFC, not from the Hoover administration;

Instead, on September 14, 1931, just before the British collapse, Hoover proposed to the Federal Advisory Committee and a group of prominent bankers from across the country, a National Credit Corporation, "a central pool of credit of $500,000,000 with powers to borrow another billion, to be administered by their own committee to rescue banks throughout the country which were under pressure."[30] [Discretionary, independent banker action still seemed to Hoover the best approach to relief of depositors.]

After Britain abandoned gold, further liquidations convinced the president that he must bring greater pressure on the bankers. Still resisting Meyer's suggestion that he summon an emergency session of Congress to reestablish the WFC, he called a secret meeting of New York bankers for October 4 at Treasury Secretary Andrew Mellon's Washington apartment. Hoover had conferred with Mellon, Undersecretary Ogden Mills, and Governor George Leslie Harrison of the New York Federal Reserve Bank before he invited the thirty or forty bankers, insurance men, and heads of building and loan associations to the meeting. This time he chose not a national delegation but New Yorkers, feeling that the financial capital of the nation would have to assume leadership. Those attending included representatives of J. P. Morgan and Company, the Chase National Bank, the National City Bank, and major life insurance companies.[31]

Hoover opened the conference with a devastating set of statistics: during the past nineteen months, bank suspension had immobilized $1,831,000,000; another $800 million had been hoarded. "It is perfectly apparent," the president said, "that these events have resulted in pressure which must of necessity not only have affected prices, and restricted business activity to a very severe extent, but which also have severely impaired the confidence of the public and bankers as well." He then repeated his suggestion of a national corporation "to furnish full credit to industrial concerns and to other

Nash claimed further that only the support of a Democratic Congress gave Meyer sufficient leverage to persuade Hoover to accept the plan. Nash, "Herbert Hoover and the Origins of the Reconstruction Finance Corporation," *Mississippi Valley Historical Review* 46 (Dec. 1959): 455–68.

30. Hoover, *Memoirs*, 3:84–85; memorandum, 14 Sept. 1931, Hoover Papers, Hoover Presidential Library, West Branch, Iowa, Official File (hereafter cited as OF), 230–D; Joslin, *Hoover Off the Record*, pp. 113–34.

31. Joslin, *Hoover Off the Record*, p. 135.

banks under pressure" in order to free frozen deposits and revive public faith.

Hoover asked the bankers to spearhead resistance to this contraction of credit by themselves establishing the organization he proposed. Possibly acting through the clearing houses, they could set up a corporation with $500 million capital, to be raised by a 2 percent contribution of the member banks, and with authority to borrow another billion dollars. This fund, he believed, could be used for two purposes; to rediscount bank assets which were not eligible for Federal Reserve loans, in order to prevent bank failures; and to make loans against the assets of closed banks to assure early dividends to depositors, thus reviving business and relieving destitute families. Hoover felt that the project should cover the entire nation, but New York "must of necessity assume both the initiative and the major burden" of combating the "degenerative vicious cycle" caused by Europe's troubles and domestic fear. Thus he continued to rely on banker-controlled measures, although he did propose supporting action by Congress, including a recreated WFC "if necessity requires."[32]

After Hoover and Mellon left the meeting, Meyer promised the bankers that he would continue to work for a government agency to replace the National Credit Corporation if the financiers would make a gesture of trying the voluntary association. Many of the participants accepted this as a guarantee that the government would act, and on that note they adjourned, saying they would meet in New York the next morning to develop a plan for the new corporation.[33]

Meanwhile, President Hoover asked key members of Congress to meet him at the White House two days later "to consider an urgent national matter." Like the bankers' conference, he demanded absolute secrecy; he believed that the current difficulty was another crisis in confidence and wanted no word of the gathering to add to public anxiety. Hoover himself kept up a facade of regular

32. Hoover, prepared statement, 4 Oct. 1931, and Hoover to Harrison, 5 Oct. 1931, George Leslie Harrison Papers, Columbia University, box 8; Hoover, *Memoirs*, 3:85–88; Myers and Newton, *Hoover Administration*, pp. 127–29; "Developments in President Hoover's Program to Stabilize Credit," *Congressional Digest* 10 (Dec. 1931): 300; Henry Bruère, COHC, p. 147.
33. Reynolds, COHC, pp. 151–52.

activities to avoid public suspicion. Reluctantly he left Washington on October 5 for a World Series baseball game in Philadelphia, only to find that some senator or congressman had leaked the story of the October 6 meeting to the press. Reporters pursued the president to the game, where he issued a noncommital confirmation but refused details. A secretary said later that the president "stood no better chance of having certain influential members of Congress, with whom he had to confer, keep a confidence for him, even though the fate of the nation might depend upon it, than would the pastor of a country church if he told the women's sewing circle that he was about to elope with the blond choir singer, but would not want them to say anything about it until after the marriage had taken place."[34]

When the thirty-two congressional leaders did meet, Hoover told them that the bankers were in the process of devising a credit organization, but he asked for action by Congress if private efforts "did not suffice." Most of those present assumed that a government finance corporation was inevitable, and the joint statement following the meeting called for "unity of action on the part of our bankers and cooperative action on the part of the government." Simultaneously, Harrison in New York and Hoover in Washington announced that twenty-four bankers had agreed to implement the president's plan for a National Credit Corporation. While the bankers agreed on a loan fund to prevent bank failures, they refused to make loans against assets of closed banks or loans to provide liquidity to institutions facing "insolvency through depreciation of bond or real estate values," a blow for New York, Boston, and Philadelphia. And they rejected as impractical the president's request for a pool to support the railroad bond situation.[35]

Eleven days later, the National Credit Corporation, chartered under the laws of Delaware, met in New York to elect directors and begin business. Banks joined the NCC by subscribing 2 percent of their deposits to its capital fund; they could then obtain loans on

34. Joslin, *Hoover Off the Record*, pp. 136–39; Hoover, *Memoirs*, 3:88.
35. Robert W. Morse, "President Hoover's Plan to Check the Depression," *Current History* 25 (Nov. 1931): 263; Harrison to Hoover, 7 Oct. 1931, Harrison Papers, box 8; Hoover, *Memoirs*, 3:88–93, 115; Myers and Newton, *Hoover Administration*, pp. 129–33; *New York Times*, 9 Oct. 1931; Mills, statement for newsreels, 7 Oct. 1931, Mills Papers, box 137; Harrison's statement reprinted in *Federal Reserve Bulletin* 17 (Oct. 1931): 553.

their sound assets which were not eligible for rediscount at the Federal Reserve banks, thus avoiding sales of slow holdings in a depressed market. Its first loans, to save banks in California and Louisiana, began a flow of $153 million to 575 banks; *Literary Digest* heralded the NCC as "Hoover's Golden Torch to Thaw Frozen Assets."[36]

Success for the NCC depended almost entirely on bankers' willingness to make loans. Economist Rexford Tugwell summarized the principle: "To be safe, a credit pool must be conservative; to be effective, it must be generous."[37] Bankers, however, felt that free lending would mean "taking the $500,000,000 out of the larger liquid banks, and tying it up in the character of loan that . . . cannot be quickly and readily liquidated."[38] Ogden Mills and George Leslie Harrison pointed out that the purpose of the NCC was at least partly psychological. "What is credit but confidence?" said Mills. Bankers, however, feared that the "unreasoning withdrawal of deposits" might ultimately reach their institutions; consequently, their first thought was self-protection.[39] Their caution was understandable; in September 1931 when President Hoover had asked Andrew Mellon to contribute a million dollars to save the Bank of Pittsburgh, Mellon refused. How could the administration expect more from outside bankers than from its own members?[40]

Moreover, the structure of the association itself worked against easy lending. Banks had to notify all members in their districts if they were in trouble and submit their books for examination; this review by their competitors made many reluctant to approach

36. *Literary Digest*, 17 Oct. 1931, pp. 5–6; "Emergency Pool to Help Banks May Serve to Stop Deflation," *Business Week*, 14 Oct. 1931, pp. 5–6; "Bank Pool Organized, Begins Raising $500-Million Funds," *Business Week*, 21 Oct. 1931, p. 5; Myers and Newton, *Hoover Administration*, p. 135; Mills, statement, *Commercial and Financial Chronicle*, 10 Oct. 1931, p. 2366; Paul M. Atkins, "The National Credit Corporation," *Review of Reviews* 85 (Jan. 1932): 48–49, 68.

37. Tugwell, "Flaws in the Hoover Economic Policy," *Current History* 35 (Jan. 1932): 530; Tugwell, *Mr. Hoover's Economic Policy* (New York: Day, 1932), p. 15.

38. U. S., Congress, Senate, Subcommittee of the Committee on Banking and Currency, *Hearings: Creation of a Reconstruction Finance Corporation*, 72d Congress, 1st Session, 1932, testimony of Melvin A. Traylor, p. 176.

39. Ibid., pp. 54–55, 68.

40. Henry L. Stimson, Diary, 22 Sept., 5, 6 Oct. 1931, Stimson Papers, Yale University.

the NCC for help. If they did seek aid, regional groups would not be anxious to provide it since members had to assume joint liability for any loans approved. Bankers in the NCC were no more generous in evaluating their colleagues' collateral for loans than they had been before the organization existed. Perhaps they did not understand: "I think everybody *apprehended* what was coming," recalled Henry Bruère of New York's Bowery Savings Bank, but "nobody foresaw it." Two critics later dismissed the NCC as "nearsighted and doomed to failure from the beginning," a sad little trick to alleviate depositors' fears.[41] Bankers accepted Tugwell's criterion for safety but not for effectiveness.

Another wave of bank failures—358 in December 1931 and 342 in January 1932—left President Hoover with little choice but federal action, since the NCC had loaned less than one-third of the funds available. As late as November 15 he had hope that he would not have to ask Congress for more than an easing of eligibility for Federal Reserve loans, but on December 4 he came out for a WFC-like corporation; he then made public his intention to ask Congress for a new government agency in his annual message.[42] Meanwhile, Meyer, Walter Wyatt, and their colleagues at the Federal Reserve drafted a bill calling for an agency larger than the old WFC and involving the country's entire financial structure. Senator Joseph T. Robinson volunteered Democratic votes if the president would accept Meyer's bill and appoint him to head the corporation.[43]

On December 8, when Hoover presented Congress with an eighteen-point program to combat the depression, he included a Reconstruction Finance Corporation, with a capital of $500 million and authority to borrow up to $3 billion more, either from the Treasury or from private sources, to be used to aid a variety of institutions, including banks "which cannot otherwise secure credit where such advances will protect the credit structure and stimulate employment."[44]

41. Bruère, COHC, p. 47; Reynolds, COHC, pp. 153–54; Nadler and Bogen, *Banking Crisis*, pp. 101–04.

42. *New York Times*, 15 Nov., 5, 6 Dec. 1931.

43. Meyer, "From Laissez-Faire to RFC," *Public Policy*, 1954, pp. 25–26; Meyer, COHC, pp. 612–27; Nash, "Hoover and Origins," pp. 464–65; Louis B. Wehle, *Hidden Threads of History: Wilson through Roosevelt* (New York: Macmillan, 1953), pp. 71–77.

Some congressmen, such as John Nance Garner, feared that the RFC would be an endless drain on the public treasury; Garner accepted the new agency only on condition that its life be limited to the period of crisis. Others, such as Senator Carter Glass, felt that the powers of the RFC would be more useful if placed in the Federal Reserve System; but Glass accepted the bill because his opposition might destroy confidence and his insistence on Federal Reserve control might "defeat its own ends" in his fight for general banking reform.[45]

After some squabbling, Congress substantially agreed to Hoover's plan. Meyer felt that the president had been unnecessarily afraid of Democratic opposition,[46] but the RFC passed the Senate on January 11 by a vote of 63 to 8, and the House on January 15 by 335 to 55; it was approved by both houses on January 22.[47] The final bill granted fewer powers than Hoover had first proposed, and in his opinion it came "six weeks later than was at all necessary in view of its manifest urgency." The president found security conditions on loans "unnecessarily stringent," and he objected to the failure to pass additional aid for farmers or to permit loans to closed banks. But in signing the law, he commended the patriotism of those who had passed it as "proof of their devotion to the welfare of their country irrespective of political affiliation."[48]

The Reconstruction Finance Corporation Act established a government agency with capital stock of $500 million to be subscribed by the United States Treasury (plus $3 billion by note and debenture issues). A board of seven members, including the secretary of the Treasury, managed the corporation, which would aid agriculture, commerce, and industry by loans to banks and other

---

44. Hoover, Memoirs, 3:98–100; Messages to Congress, 24 Dec. 1931, 4 Jan. 1932, Congressional Record 72 (1): 1262–63.

45. Timmons, Dawes, p. 313; Russell Leffingwell to Glass, 8 Jan.; Glass to Willis, 9 Jan.; Willis to Glass, 11 Jan. 1932–all in Glass Papers, University of Virginia, boxes 283, 314; Palmer, Carter Glass, pp. 213–14; statement by Eugene Meyer, 18 Dec. 1931, Congressional Record 72 (1): 1264–69.

46. Meyer, COHC, pp. 692–93.

47. Congressional Record 72 (1): 1583, 1657–1705, 2049–81, 2565–66; New York Times, 10–14, 16, 23 Jan. 1932. Most of the opposition came from Southerners and Midwesterners.

48. Hoover, Memoirs, 3:107–08; Myers and Newton, Hoover Administration, pp. 163–64; Joslin, Hoover Off the Record, pp. 164–65; Hoover, State Papers, 2:106–07.

agencies. Insofar as it dealt with banks, the RFC could assist solvent institutions or use up to $200 million for reorganization or liquidation of closed banks.[49] *Business Week* called it "the most powerful offensive force imagination has, so far, been able to command."[50]

The new agency began work immediately. Hoover appointed the first officers–Eugene Meyer as chairman of the board and Charles Gates Dawes as president–before the act was even signed. Dawes had served as vice-president under Calvin Coolidge; at the time of his appointment to the RFC he was ambassador to England. Ike Hoover, White House usher and gossip *extraordinaire*, wrote later that the RFC presidency had been created to shelve Dawes so that he "would no longer be a political menace," either by making indiscrete statements or by bidding for a return to elective office.[51] Dawes's appointment also created a convenient vacancy in London, to which Hoover appointed Secretary of the Treasury Mellon, thus leaving the Treasury post open for Ogden Mills. Meyer, on the other hand, thought of the RFC as his own project and agreed to head the agency in order to get it off to a quick and efficient start. As chief of both the RFC and the Federal Reserve Board, he could coordinate federal credit resources. But he was not overjoyed at having Dawes as a colleague, and Washington gossips would soon report them "at swords' points" in the RFC.[52]

Hoover felt that the rest of the board should be bipartisan. Eager to gratify several prominent Democrats, he appointed Harvey Couch from Senator Robinson's home state and Jesse Jones of John Nance Garner's Texas. Republican Gardiner Cowles, Sr., of Iowa,

---

49. U. S. Department of Commerce, "Outline of New Credit Agencies and of Credit Facilities Provided by Them," undated memo, Treasury Secretary's Correspondence, NA: RG 56, box 10.

50. "First Reconstruction Job Is Release of Lending Power," *Business Week*, 27 Jan. 1932, p. 5. Many contemporary publications thought of the RFC as a para-wartime operation; *New Republic*, 27 Jan. 1932, p. 291; *Literary Digest* 112 (13 Feb. 1932): 9. For a discussion of the World War I precedent and the war analogy in anti-Depression measures, see William E. Leuchtenburg, "The New Deal and the Analogue of War," in *Change and Continuity in Twentieth-Century America*, ed. John Braeman et al. (Columbus: Ohio State University Press, 1964), pp. 98–100; Albert U. Romasco, in *The Poverty of Abundance: Hoover, the Nation, the Depression* (New York: Oxford University Press, 1965), pp. 189–90, cited the RFC as "the first measure sponsored by the Hoover Administration frankly based on the analogy of war."

51. Hoover, *Forty-Two Years*, pp. 214–15.

52. Meyer, COHC, pp. 602–03, 617–28; Hamlin, Diary, 18 June 1932.

Democrat Wilson McCarthy of Utah, and Mills as *ex officio* director completed the board. Mills took Mellon's place even before the ambassadorship and cabinet shift were announced.[53]

Chairman Meyer quickly assembled a staff, calling in many former WFC employees to man the RFC's thirty-three field centers, and organized advisory boards of 363 bankers, farmers, and industrialists. Within a few days the RFC took over two floors of the old Department of Commerce building and set up branches wherever there was a Federal Reserve bank.[54]

On February 3, 1932, the RFC received and tentatively approved its first loan–$15 million to A. P. Giannini's huge Bank of America National Trust and Savings Association; the loan became final on February 15 when Giannini emerged the victor in a hotly contested proxy fight.[55] The RFC authorized its second bank loans on February 5: $200,000 to the Commercial National Bank and Trust Company of Lafayette, Louisiana, and a first installment on $6 million to the East Tennessee National Bank of Knoxville. Its first railroad loan went to the $3 billion, 28,631-mile transcontinental Missouri Pacific, controlled by Orris P. and Mantis J. Van Sweringen.[56] Within one month, the agency made almost a thousand loans, including $158 million to 858 banks and trust companies. By the end of its first four months, the RFC had approved $5 billion in grants to 4,000 banks, agricultural credit corporations, life insurance companies, and other financial institutions, contributing to a "groggy public confidence."[57] Only 46 banks failed in March, compared with 342 in January.

Critics, however, disagreed with this lending policy and philosophy. Certainly the RFC had departed from President Hoover's original intention of making loans to small institutions, and for this

53. Jones, *Fifty Billion Dollars*, pp. 512–14; Bascom N. Timmons, *Jesse H. Jones: The Man and the Statesman* (New York: Holt, 1956), pp. 164–65; Hoover, *Memoirs*, 3:108–09; Myers and Newton, *Hoover Administration*, p. 165.

54. Jones, *Fifty Billion Dollars*, pp. 514–16; Timmons, *Jones*, pp. 167–68; Nash, "Hoover and Origins," pp. 466–67.

55. Reconstruction Finance Corporation, Minutes, 2, 3, 4, 5, 15 Feb. 1932, NA: RG 234. Within its first five months of operation, the RFC loaned $64,488,644 to the Giannini bank, all of which was repaid by 18 June, 1933. Jones, *Fifty Billion Dollars*, pp. 19–20; Timmons, *Jones*, pp. 165–66.

56. Jones, *Fifty Billion Dollars*, pp. 518–19; Timmons, *Dawes*, pp. 314–15; Timmons, *Jones*, p. 167.

57. Hoover, *State Papers*, 2:203–06.

it was charged with "financial socialism" and a Hamiltonian idea that "salvation comes from the top."[58] Later critics decried the RFC's "trickle-down" policy of aiding banks and businesses rather than individuals in the war on the depression,[59] and board member Jesse Jones accused his colleagues of being divided on broad lending.[60] To President Hoover, on the other hand, nothing had ever been devised in our history "which has done more for those whom Mr. Coolidge has aptly called the common run of men and women." He felt that the only purpose in helping an insurance company, bank, or other financial institution was to protect its policyholders, depositors, borrowers, mortgagees, or employees—all of whom enjoyed a security they could not have had without the RFC.[61]

The RFC's directors did have a few bad moments. Eugene Meyer recalled a telephone summons from Senator Huey Long of Louisiana, demanding immediate assistance for the banks in his state. Meyer, at home nursing his neuritis, explained that such a step needed consent of the full board. Long then threatened to take the next train to New Orleans and close all the banks in Louisiana, Mississippi, and Arkansas. Meyer wished him a pleasant trip and hung up. The incident ended there.[62]

One RFC loan in particular invited criticism: an advance of $90 million to the Central Republic National Bank in Chicago, headed by Charles Dawes, just three weeks after Dawes resigned from the presidency of the RFC. Collapse of the Insull industries in April 1932 had wiped out the savings of thousands of Chicago investors and devalued countless bank loans. Suspicion and withdrawal of deposits followed. By June 24, bank runs had closed twenty-five suburban institutions and fifteen within the city. Only five large Loop banks remained open, and they suffered from vicious rumors of unsoundness; it took a dramatic speech by Melvin Traylor on the floor of the First National to avert total panic.[63] Dawes had re-

58. Coughlin, *Radio Discourses, 1931–1932*, pp. 149–50, quoted in Charles J. Tull, *Father Coughlin and the New Deal* (Syracuse, N. Y.: Syracuse University Press, 1965), p. 12.

59. David A. Shannon, *Between the Wars: America, 1919–1941* (Boston: Houghton Mifflin, 1965), pp. 135–36.

60. Jones, *Fifty Billion Dollars*, pp. 519–20.

61. Hoover, *State Papers*, 2:64; Myers and Newton, *Hoover Administration*, pp. 265–66.

62. Meyer, COHC, pp. 667–68.

63. Timmons, *Jones*, p. 169; Timmons, *Dawes*, pp. 316–17; F. Cyril James,

turned to Chicago to save Central Republic, a bank controlled by his family, but he concluded that it could not continue to withstand such pressures as losing $239 million in deposits in a single year. On Saturday, June 25, he decided that the Dawes bank could not afford to open for business on Monday morning. The next day he informed his colleagues and fellow bankers who launched a sixteen-hour rescue effort headed by Traylor of the First National Bank and Jesse Jones of the RFC. Dawes himself did not want the bank to continue, but President Hoover, notified of the Chicago crisis, issued an order: "Save that bank!" Joslin claimed that Hoover took personal charge of the situation, remaining in constant contact with Chicago until 3 a.m. on Monday, while Joslin announced to the press that the president was resting, a fib which caused him paroxysms of regret in his memoirs. "Never mind, Ted," Hoover consoled, "perhaps the press will never forgive you, but God will."[64]

Hoover had good reason for concern. If Central Republic closed, the four remaining Chicago institutions would have to suspend, leaving the city bankless. For this to happen in June 1932, while the Democratic national convention was meeting in Chicago, would have been a terrible blow to Hoover's chances for reelection.

Dawes rejected all preliminary plans which offered less than full payment of deposits. In conference with New York bankers and Federal Reserve authorities, Dawes was offered $50 million from the RFC but refused it; nor would he accept a package of $80 million from the RFC, $5 million from the Chicago banks, and $10 million from New York banks because it was impossible to reach all of the involved New York bankers on a Sunday for written confirmation of their pledges.[65] Finally, RFC examiners recommended a $90 million loan, if the Chicago banks would contribute $5 million. They agreed, and Central Republic opened on Monday morning less than an hour after the RFC board approved its loan application.[66] The

The Growth of Chicago Banks, Vol. 2: The Modern Age, 1897–1938 (New York: Harper, 1938), pp. 1030–37; Jones, Fifty Billion Dollars, pp. 72–74.

64. Hoover, Memoirs, 3:169–70; Timmons, Dawes, p. 319; Joslin, Hoover Off the Record, pp. 249–50.

65. Confidential memorandum of telephone conferences, 27 June 1932, dictated by W. Randolph Burgess for George Leslie Harrison, 28 June 1932, supplemented by same from Harrison Papers.

66. James, Chicago Banks, pp. 1030–40; Timmons, Dawes, pp. 317–21; Timmons, Jones, pp. 169–72; Hoover, Memoirs, 3:169–70.

Board had decided "that the closing of a bank as large as the Central Republic Bank and Trust Company would greatly aggravate the tense situation in Chicago and, because of the size and importance of the bank and the city, would cause repercussions which would be far reaching and further impair public confidence throughout the country."[67]

The Dawes loan became a political albatross around the neck of the incumbent administration. Although Democrat Traylor instigated the loan and Democrat Jones of the RFC approved it, a Republican administration had made a loan to a Republican bank headed by one of its own recent members; worse, Dawes had passed rapidly from dispenser of RFC funds to recipient of $90 million of that same money. Opponents questioned the collateral offered for the loan, and their criticism became more bitter as the bank defaulted on its interest payments and finally had to close.[68]

Under attack for the Dawes loans, the RFC came up for revision in the summer of 1932. Hoover had been disappointed in the limits placed on RFC powers in the original act; on May 31 he asked Congress to expand the authorization. Subsequently, Representative Henry T. Rainey introduced RFC amendments to a bill dealing with depression relief. When Speaker John Nance Garner insisted on adding provisions for full publicity of all RFC loans and direct lending to individuals and small businesses, however, the president chose to attack the attempt to make the RFC "the most gigantic banking and pawnbroking business in all history."[69] He even threatened to veto the relief bill if the two objectionable features were not removed in conference. On July 11, Hoover did refuse to sign the bill, charging that it was pork-barrel legislation; but primarily he objected to RFC loans "for any conceivable purpose on any considerable security for anybody who wants money." That power, the president said,

67. RFC, Minutes, 27 June 1932, NA: RG 234.
68. Five weeks after the loan was granted, Dawes submitted a plan for reorganization; a new bank, the City National Bank and Trust Company, replaced the old Central Republic, which went into receivership. The RFC received assessment payments from the Dawes family but had to prosecute 4,000 stockholders to collect their assessments to repay the loan. Eventually the RFC realized $94 million, the full principle plus 2 percent interest. Jones, *Fifty Billion Dollars*, pp. 79–81; Timmons, *Dawes*, pp. 321–23; Upham and Lamke, *Closed and Distressed Banks*, pp. 158–60.
69. *Time*, 18 July 1932, p. 8.

"would place the government in private business in such fashion as to violate the very principle of public relations on which we have built our nation, and render insecure its very foundation."[70]

Garner and Hoover differed over the RFC revisions because they held opposing views on the best means for overcoming the depression. Hoover and the conservative traditionalists believed that if government was to act at all, it had to operate indirectly through established institutions to reinvigorate the credit structure. Garner and the progressives desired direct action aimed at immediate sufferers and insisted on a democratic method, including information to the public on all government activities. Eugene Meyer regarded Garner's position as "Democratic sabotage," possibly inspired by the coming election.[71]

Under pressure, Congress eliminated direct loans from the final version of the bill but retained a clause calling for full publicity for all RFC loans. Senate leaders assured the president, however, that the provision would not be retroactive and that future monthly reports would go only to the Senate and certain selected government agencies, where they would be held in confidence. The final bill also placated the administration by reducing provisions for nonproductive public works. At the same time, the relief package contained three changes for the RFC: $300 million in temporary loans to states to finance relief, $1.5 billion in loans for self-liquidating public construction projects to aid employment, and broader authority for loans to agriculture.[72]

The same legislation removed Meyer as an *ex officio* member of the RFC Board. Despite rumors that he was not getting along with his colleagues at the RFC and had angered the administration by appointing too many Democrats to RFC posts, Meyer was in danger of physical breakdown by the summer of 1932 and needed release

70. Myers and Newton, *Hoover Administration*, pp. 221–23, 225, 226–29; Hoover, *State Papers*, 2:201, 228; Hoover, *Memoirs*, 3:109, 111; Jones, *Fifty Billion Dollars*, p. 520.

71. Meyer, COHC, pp. 676, 621–23. Fighting vigorously against the objectionable features of the relief bill, the president had Mills and Meyer organize a confidential letter from RFC members to be transmitted privately to "certain members of the Senate," urging the elimination of the publicity clause. Joslin, *Hoover Off the Record*, pp. 256–59.

72. Hoover, *State Papers*, 2:235; Myers and Newton, *Hoover Administration*, pp. 232–33.

from some of the pressure of his work. Consequently, Hoover wrote to Senator Peter Norbeck on July 8 asking for elimination of *ex officio* members of the RFC board. Meyer himself felt that he had put the legislation into operation and could now afford to relinquish control.[73]

In effect, the Emergency Relief and Construction Act failed to make significant changes in either the policy or the direction of the RFC regarding banks.

The Hoover administration had succeeded only slightly by departing from the voluntarism of 1931 and backing an RFC. The agency certainly loaned more freely than the NCC: during its first eight months, the board approved $1,410,026,518.02 in loans to 5,970 financial institutions, including 4,973 banks and trust companies. Of this amount, $44,178,509.00 went to reorganize or liquidate 443 closed banks; 95.2 percent of bank loans went into towns and cities with fewer than 200,000 inhabitants, primarily in the Midwest and South, where loans represented over 3 percent of total bank resources. At the same time, large city institutions called in their loans in an effort to make themselves more liquid, thus forcing weaker country banks to go to the RFC.[74] As later critics charged, however, the RFC acted as a sedative during a "period of lost opportunities"; it created false hopes of preventing bank failures and only postponed the inevitable crash.[75] Although Hoover extended the life of the agency by executive order in December 1932,[76] he rejected the principle of using the RFC to broaden lending policy. In effect, the same groups benefitted from RFC aid as from bank loans; Hoover's action only put the lending power in the hands of those who

73. Meyer, COHC, pp. 637–39, 641; Hamlin, Diary, 11, 13, 19 July, 21 Aug. 1932.
74. Statements of condition transmitted to President Hoover, 7 July, 20 Oct. 1932, Hoover Papers, Stanford, File 1643; Jones, *Fifty Billion Dollars*, p. 20; Atlee Pomerene, radio address, 10 Sept. 1932, typescript in White House Secretaries File—Lawrence Richey, AG5, Hoover Library, West Branch; Upham and Lamke, *Closed and Distressed Banks*, pp. 155–61; E. C. Smith, "A Study of Depression Emergency Relief," in *Studies in the Social Sciences* (Albany: Rensselaer Polytechnic Institute, 1933), pp. 22–23; *Congressional Record* 72 (2): 4421, 4422, 5414, 5654.
75. Nadler and Bogen, *Banking Crisis*, pp. 106–11; Ernest K. Lindley, *Half Way with Roosevelt* (New York: Viking, 1937), pp. 94–95.
76. Hoover-Atlee Pomerene correspondence, with Justice Department memoranda, 28 Nov. to 9 Dec. 1932, Hoover Papers, Stanford, File 1643; Hoover, *State Papers*, 2:531–32.

were willing to use stopgap lending a little more freely than the bankers.[77]

The Federal Reserve Board also experimented with more vigorous action in 1932. The Board remained largely passive after 1929, either because it was unwilling to move or because there was nothing it believed it could do to counteract the depression; consequently the System appeared impotent. When it changed policy in 1932, however, it failed to alter the fundamental attitude which had frustrated its earlier programs. Thus its efforts to free credit—by open-market purchases, changes in discount rates, direct loans to private enterprise, and establishment of Federal Reserve District Banking and Industrial Committees—proved only gestures at cooperation with the Hoover administration's feeble new activism.[78]

Two later economists have argued that the System's failure to take positive action probably rested on its assumption that it had no responsibility for banks which were not members of the System; these banks constituted the vast majority of failures during the 1920s and in 1930 accounted for 80 percent of suspended institutions. Where large-city member banks did fail, Federal Reserve officials blamed bad management.[79]

After the 1929 collapse the Federal Reserve Board favored a reversal of its previous credit-tightening position. It pursued a moderate open-market policy throughout 1930 and decreased the discount rate on negotiable paper until, by the summer of 1931, rates hit their lowest levels since 1760. The acceptance rate dropped from 5 1/8 percent in the autumn of 1929 to 1 7/8 percent by the end of 1930; in the same period, rates on commercial paper fell from 6¼ to 2 7/8 percent. New York had a 1½ percent discount rate in the summer of 1931.[80] The Board hoped to encourage member banks to expand loans out of their reserves, increased by open-market buying. Lowering the rate Federal Reserve banks charged for loans to mem-

77. J. Franklin Ebersole, "One Year of the Reconstruction Finance Corporation," *Quarterly Journal of Economics* 47 (May 1933): 464–92.

78. Herbert Feis, *1933: Characters in Crisis* (Boston: Little, Brown, 1966), p. 11; Douglass C. North, *Growth and Welfare in the American Past: A New Economic History* (Englewood Cliffs, N. J.: Prentice-Hall, 1966), pp. 169–71.

79. Friedman and Schwartz, *Monetary History*, pp. 357–59.

80. Federal Reserve Board, *Annual Report, 1930–1931*, pp. 4, 6; *Commercial and Financial Chronicle*, 9 May 1931, p. 3391.

bers should also have enticed banks to rediscount at the Reserve banks, thus increasing their reserves and enabling them to lend ten times as much money.[81] Neither operation worked, however. Members used the additional funds to increase their own liquidity by decreasing their indebtedness to the Federal Reserve; bankers chose to protect themselves rather than extend loans to business. The Reserve System did not provide leadership to convince them; as one critic charged, it believed that "the body economic will heal itself once 'normal' or 'desirable' liquidation has run its course."[82]

Meanwhile, another crisis had developed. On February 7, 1932, Secretary of the Treasury Ogden Mills informed President Hoover that the United States stood within two weeks of not being able to meet foreign withdrawals and earmarking, that unless something was done immediately the nation would have to leave the gold standard. In addition to outside drains, a great quantity of the country's gold was tied up in reserve accounts as backing for currency and deposits in commercial banks. Under the law, each Federal Reserve bank had to hold at least 40 percent of the security for Federal Reserve notes in gold; in addition, Federal Reserve bank deposits had to be covered by not less than 35 percent gold or other lawful money, with the remaining backing in gold, lawful money, or short-term commercial bills. Since most commercial banks did not have enough paper for coverage, they had to use more gold. The gold reserve rose in fact from 40 to 70 percent; even more was drained off by domestic hoarders and foreign withdrawals.

Senator Arthur Vandenberg had suggested a solution some time earlier: gold could be freed by substituting government securities for a portion of the metal thus encumbered. Vandenberg first suggested the idea to Hoover in July 1931 and repeated his proposal throughout the fall, despite bankers' objections and the administration's preoccupation with the NCC and RFC. He introduced bills into the Senate on December 9; in January 1932, Hoover sent for Vandenberg and urged him to push the bills.[83]

81. W. Randolph Burgess, *The Reserve Banks and the Money Market* (New York: Harper, 1936), p. 7.

82. James Harvey Rogers, "Federal Reserve Policy in World Monetary Chaos," undated memorandum, Rogers Papers, Yale University, box 85.

83. "Chronology of the Banking Bill," Scrapbook No. 3, Vandenberg Papers, Clements Library, University of Michigan.

On January 27, however, President Hoover called in Senator Carter Glass, a leading Democratic member of the Banking and Currency Committee, and asked him to introduce legislation for temporary expansion of eligibility under the Federal Reserve Act. The president hoped that government bonds could become security for currency. Glass refused to cooperate until, on February 9, Hoover called a breakfast meeting of Senate and administration leaders at the White House and there repeated Mills's statement that the United States would have to leave the gold standard within two weeks. Glass then agreed to offer the bill, and Representative Henry Steagall consented to sponsor a similar measure in the House. He and Glass also accepted the president's proposal that discussion of the bill "emphasize matters relating to liberalizing the discount privilege and credit expansion proposals in order to avoid disclosure of the gold situation which might create more alarm both at home and abroad during the interval before the law was passed."[84]

The Glass-Steagall Act passed both houses of Congress on February 26 by voice vote; President Hoover signed it the next day. The new law broadened the type of paper eligible for rediscount at Federal Reserve banks. It also permitted the substitution of government securities for commercial paper in backing Federal Reserve notes, a provision which encouraged the Federal Reserve banks to buy government securities through their open-market committee, thus increasing member banks' reserves; under the act these purchases would also no longer deplete the free gold supply.[85]

The Federal Reserve System immediately undertook massive open-market purchases which lasted through August 10, 1932, almost doubling its holdings. Reserve banks bought $1.1 billion of government securities, raising to $1,850,000,000 the System's total holdings.[86] This energetic buying in 1932 had the same objectives as

84. Hoover, Memoirs, 2:116–17; Myers and Newton, Hoover Administration, pp. 165, 171–72; New York Times, 11 Feb. 1932; Congressional Record 72 (1): 3734, 4321–22, 4331, 3801.
85. U. S., Statutes at Large, 47, Part 1, pp. 56–57; Hoover, State Papers, 2:128–29; Hoover, Memoirs, 3:117–18; New York Journal of Commerce, 26 Feb. 1932; Commercial and Financial Chronicle, 5 Mar. 1932, p. 1683; Ray Lyman Wilbur and Arthur Mastick Hyde, The Hoover Policies (New York: Scribner's, 1937), pp. 446–47; Walter Lippmann, Interpretations: 1931–1932, ed. Allan Nevins (New York: Macmillan, 1932), p. 325.
86. Federal Reserve Board, Annual Report, 1932, p. 11.

most modest purchases of 1930–to strengthen the liquidity of member banks, lessen their indebtedness to the Reserve banks, and allow members to reduce interest rates and expand loans. Open-market operations succeeded in all points but the last; outstanding bank credit did not increase, and business activity and prices of securities and commodities continued to decline. Once again the Federal Reserve had failed to convince the bankers to abandon their conservative stand on lending. Its action created excess reserves, but after two traumatic years bankers found it prudent to hold reserves substantially above the requirements of the law. Banks would not lend, nor would businesses borrow, while they remained uncertain about future conditions and even future policy of the Federal Reserve System itself. Consequently, the new effort was stillborn because the Federal Reserve could not convince member banks that it might be safe for them to lend.[87] By the end of the year, officers at the New York Federal Reserve Bank hoped that they might allow some of the System's holdings to "run off," but a joint meeting of the Open Market Committee and the Federal Reserve Board in January 1933 rejected any public announcement of such a change, probably because they feared inflation bills then pending in Congress.[88]

The Federal Reserve had no more success with a direct policy. As part of the Emergency Relief and Construction Act of July 1932, Congress authorized the Federal Reserve banks to make direct loans to private enterprise, an extension to the Reserve System of powers Speaker Garner had wanted for the RFC. Progressives believed that direct loans would offer more effective attacks on the depression. When Garner's efforts on behalf of the RFC failed, however, Charles Sumner Hamlin of the Federal Reserve Board suggested to Senator Glass that the Reserve System might take up direct lending; European central banks had that power. Hamlin even drafted the substitute amendment for Glass, a gesture which won him severe criticism from his colleagues on the Board, especially Meyer. At first the Reserve Board opposed the scheme, fearing runs on Federal Reserve

87. Hoover to Harrison, 26 Apr. 1932, and Harrison to Hoover, 3 May 1932, Harrison Papers, box 8; Friedman and Schwartz, *Monetary History*, pp. 347–49; memoranda of meetings, Board of Directors and Executive Committee, New York Federal Reserve Bank, 3, 13, 24 Oct., 7 Nov., 22, 29 Dec. 1932, Harrison Papers, binder 50, vol. 3:34–35, 38–57.

88. Hamlin, Diary, 4, 5, 20 Jan. 1933; Barger, *Management of Money*, pp. 100–108.

banks, but in a few days the Board and the Hoover administration reluctantly decided to endorse direct loans to individuals up to 1 percent of the capital and surplus of Federal Reserve banks.[89]

Making direct loans required a change in attitude, however. Although rumors circulated that Hoover and Mills would see to it that nothing was done under the new law, Hoover immediately asked the Federal Reserve Board to declare an emergency, thus legalizing direct loans. The Board took the president's request as an insulting usurpation of its prerogatives and told him so in a "curteous [sic] but positive" reply.[90] Meanwhile, the Federal Reserve bank in New York decided that commercial banks were meeting all legitimate demands for credit and that the Reserve banks probably should not approve loans which their member banks thought unsafe. Accordingly, it made a few loans as "a good grandstand play" and then decided to let "all real credit needs" be "cared for in the usual way."[91] Narrow interpretation thus defeated the intent of the direct loan amendment and ended hopes for a positive, aggressive Federal Reserve program to release credit. The Federal Reserve stipulated that borrowers must prove they could not receive credit elsewhere but also decided that borrowers did not deserve loans which they would not get elsewhere.

For much the same reasons, the administration failed in its efforts to work through the twelve Federal Reserve banks by establishing Banking and Industrial Committees to "promote recovery by normal capitalistic processes of reviving private capital investment through regular banking channels." In the spring of 1932 the Hoover administration persuaded the Federal Reserve to form groups of six bankers and six industrialists in each Reserve district to encourage credit expansion, stimulate business and construction, support the bond markets, and fight the depression.[92] But, as *Business Week* reported, the members remained "unduly cautious in increasing loans

89. Hamlin, Diary, 9, 12, 13, 14, 28 July 1932.

90. Ibid., 19, 22, 26, 29 July 1932; Hoover to Meyer, 23 July 1932, quoted in ibid., 29 July 1932.

91. Memoranda of meetings of Board of Directors and Executive Committee, New York Federal Reserve Bank, 25 July, 1, 4, 8 Aug., 6 Sept. 1932, Harrison Papers, binder 50, vol. 3:1–5, 9–11, 18–20.

92. Confidential History, National Conference of Banking and Industrial Committees, Ogden L. Mills Papers, box 59; Reynolds, COHC, pp. 156–61; Meyer, COHC, p. 689; "Congress, Hoover, Young's Group All Seek to Break Credit Dam," *Business Week*, 1 July 1932, pp. 5–6.

or adding to investment, over-emphasizing liquidity and retarding business recovery."[93] Therefore, government officials called a meeting of the twelve committees in Washington on August 26. There President Hoover asked for greater coordination of programs to distribute credit and spread employment; Mills proposed a central council with six working subcommittees to stimulate credit, employment, home improvement, and coordination with federal agencies, especially the RFC, Agricultural Credit Corporation, and Home Loan banks. But the administration stopped short of a fully activist program, warning that it was not setting up an "economic council to endeavor to direct the economic policies of the country."[94]

Hoover and Mills chose to work through the Federal Reserve organization but ignored the limits on its powers; in appealing to the Banking and Industrial committees, they repeated a request which had been refused by the same men half a dozen times in the past three years. At no time did the administration try to push the Board beyond its near-sightedness or woo the bankers from their self-protectionism.[95]

Some Americans recognized the need for more sweeping changes. Epidemic bank failures during the 1920s as well as the pre-1929 speculation convinced Senator Carter Glass and others that American banking needed structural reforms. In 1930, therefore, the House authorized hearings on branch banking, and the Senate instructed its Banking and Currency Committee to investigate the causes of the 1929 disaster, both with a view toward permanent legislation. Glass headed the Senate subcommittee which made a sweeping inquiry by questionnaire and hearings in 1931 and 1932, under the guidance of Professor H. Parker Willis of Columbia.[96]

93. "Private Initiative Takes over the Drive toward Recovery," *Business Week*, 3 Aug. 1932, pp. 3–4.

94. Myers and Newton, *Hoover Administration*, pp. 242–44; Hoover, "Address to the Conference of the Federal Reserve District Banking and Industrial Committees; Review of the Causes of Continued Depression and Suggestions for Remedial Aid," *State Papers*, 2:268–74; Hoover, *Memoirs*, 3:167; "Statement by Secretary Mills before the President's Conference of Banking and Industrial Committees," Mills Papers, box 138; "The Government Ties Business into the Recovery Program," *Business Week*, 7 Sept. 1932, pp. 5–6 "Hoover's Business Planning," *New Republic*, 7 Sept. 1932, pp. 85–86.

95. Hamlin, Diary, 6, 7 July, 1, 13 Sept., 3 Dec. 1932; Meyer, COHC, pp. 543–45.

Glass believed that long-range reform would eliminate the need for short-term rescue and therefore proposed four fundamental changes in American banking.[97] First, since Glass felt that Federal Reserve funds had been used unjustifiably to support speculation in the late 1920s, he asked for rigid restrictions on the use of such money for speculative loans. The Federal Reserve Board would have power to suspend System credit to any member bank which ignored official warnings against increasing collateral loans; it might also fix the percentage of bank loans to be made upon securities.[98] George Leslie Harrison felt that these provisions gave the Board too centralized a control over the System; instead he argued for continued autonomy of the Federal Reserve banks and their members. In particular, he felt that the Board could not regulate the *uses* of credit "once it is let loose."[99]

Second, Federal Reserve supervision of the entire banking system would reduce or eliminate unsound practices. Therefore, several men who testified on the bill suggested unification of banking through compulsory membership of all commercial banks in the Federal Reserve System. This proposal would challenge the rights of the states to control banking within their own borders, however, and senators with ties to local independent banks prevented unification being written into the bill. On the other hand, advocates of branch banking were most successful, obtaining a provision for national banks to establish statewide branches and even to cross fifty miles into an adjoining state if that territory fell within their "trade area." Comptroller of the Currency John W. Pole had been lobbying

96. Howard H. Preston, "The Banking Act of 1933," *American Economic Review* 23 (Dec. 1933): 587–90; Ray B. Westerfield, "The Banking Act of 1933," *Journal of Political Economy* 41 (Dec. 1933): 722; Moley, *First New Deal*, pp. 316–17; Timmons, *Jones*, p. 177; H. Parker Willis, "Banking Inquiry, 1931," Willis Papers, Columbia University; Peter Norbeck to Thomas J. Walsh, Walsh Papers, Library of Congress, Correspondence.

97. Willis to Glass, 8, 18 Feb., 21 Apr. 1932, Glass Papers, box 304; drafts of Glass bill, Willis Papers, 10 boxes.

98. H. Parker Willis and John M. Chapman, *The Banking Situation: American Post-War Problems and Developments* (New York: Columbia University Press, 1934), pp. 62–64, 70–71; Smith and Beasley, *Carter Glass*, pp. 304–06; Nadler and Bogen, *Banking Crisis*, pp. 52–56.

99. Harrison to Senate Banking and Currency Committee, comments on S. 4115, 6, 7 Apr. 1932, Federal Reserve Board files; commentary, unsigned (probably C. S. Hamlin) Adolph Miller Papers, Federal Reserve Board, Washington, D. C., box 1.

for trade-area branch banks since 1929. Representatives from the Midwest and South, however, preferred to protect the independent unit bank. One of its most vigorous defenders was Senator Peter Norbeck, a member of the Glass subcommittee and chairman of the full committee.[100]

Third, Glass believed that at least part of the securities speculation of the late 1920s had resulted from an irregular liaison between some 750 commercial banks and their securities companies, established to evade federal restrictions on banks dealing in stocks. He decided that federal charter and inspection of the affiliates would not be sufficient and instead chose to work for complete separation of the securities affiliates from their parent institutions.[101]

Finally, the Glass bill sought to protect depositors by establishing a federal corporation to liquidate deposits in closed banks. Agitation for some form of guarantee of bank assets had heightened with increasing suspensions during the 1920s; men such as Jesse Jones, John Nance Garner, and Henry B. Steagall offered a variety of guarantee plans, some going so far as to put the federal government behind all deposits. Glass, Hoover, and Mills resisted government guarantee, however, preferring a new agency to buy up holdings of banks as soon as they closed in order to let receivers make quick payments to creditors.[102]

The Glass bill also contained provisions regulating reserve backing on savings deposits and interest rates, as well as revising power relationships within the Federal Reserve System by placing control of foreign banking and open-market operations under the Board in Washington.[103]

100. Willis and Chapman, *Banking Situation*, pp. 78–82; Smith and Beasley, *Carter Glass*, p. 306; Gilbert C. Fite, *Peter Norbeck: Prairie Statesman* (Columbia: University of Missouri Press, 1948), p. 171; Hamlin, Diary, 22 Nov., 6 Dec. 1932.

101. Chester Morrill to Glass, 6 Apr. 1932, and Samuel Untermyer to Glass, 31 May 1932, Glass Papers, boxes 305, 46; Willis and Chapman, *Banking Situation*, pp. 67–70; Smith and Beasley, *Carter Glass*, pp. 306–07; Palmer, *Carter Glass*, pp. 212, 221.

102. Willis and Chapman, *Banking Situation*, pp. 64–67; Moley, *First New Deal*, p. 318; Timmons, *Jones*, pp. 177–78; George W. Norris to Glass, 13 May 1932, Glass Papers, box 252; Arthur A. Ballentine to John E. Otterson, 14 Sept. 1932, Treasury Secretary's Correspondence, NA: RG 56, box 14; Hamlin, Diary, 18 Nov. 1932.

103. Willis and Chapman, *Banking Situation*, pp. 71–77, 82–83.

Not everyone agreed with Glass that these permanent reforms offered the best chance of avoiding another 1929. Willis recorded the "ill-concealed hostility of the White House, of the Federal Reserve Board, of the Treasury Department, and of the Comptroller of the Currency toward anything in the way of banking changes." The Comptroller even attacked the bill in the press. Early in 1932 the Hoover administration still preferred to support emergency measures, especially the Reconstruction Finance Corporation and the Glass-Steagall Act of 1932. Officials of the Federal Reserve System refused to see any immediate gains from the Glass reforms, arguing that they could not be put into effect soon enough to stop bank failures. Bankers, too, lobbied against the measure, even persuading President Hoover to demand revision "by properly qualified experts," men who in fact opposed the bill. Associations of bankers, individuals, and chambers of commerce passed resolutions against the Glass bill, particularly its sections dealing with branch banking and separation of affiliates.

Even when Glass modified some of these provisions to pacify critics, he could not secure passage of the bill. First introduced into the Senate on January 22, 1932, it was returned to committee for revision five days later. Again reported on March 16, it went back to committee once more. Glass presented the bill for a third time on April 9, and on April 27 it received a place on the calendar, only to lose its privileged position on June 16. The Glass bill then remained in suspension until after the 1932 national elections.[104]

The Hoover administration conspicuously withheld its support from the Glass reform proposals throughout 1932. Hoover believed that banking and business could revive without fundamental changes if they merely received temporary supports from agencies such as the RFC or loans through the Federal Reserve banks. Thus the president held to a sustaining action, hoping to tide over the banks until they could work out their own survival.

104. Willis and Chapman, *Banking Situation*, pp. 84–85; Myers and Newton, *Hoover Administration*, pp. 166–67; Smith and Beasley, *Carter Glass*, pp. 52–56; Hoover, *Memoirs*, 3:123; Hamlin, Diary, 15, 17 June 1932; *Congressional Record* 72 (1): 2403, 6329, 8350.

CHAPTER III

Election and Interregnum

THE HOOVER administration faced the ultimate test of its policies, including those on banking, in 1932 when the president stood for reelection. That campaign would bring out vital depression issues, and on November 8, Hoover would learn whether the voters agreed with his efforts to solve the economic crisis or hoped for greater success from another approach.

At the same time, the president had to govern a nation suffering from severe banking problems. If the election returns proved favorable, he could continue those operations which the electorate had endorsed. But if he was defeated, Hoover would still have to finish out his term in office—without any popular support for his plans.

After two and a half years of battling the depression, Hoover had to fight for reelection during the summer and fall of 1932. The president felt obligated to run again—both to seek vindication for his policies and, if possible, to win four more years in which to continue the struggle for recovery.

Prospects looked bleak. Hoover himself recalled later, "General Prosperity had been a great ally in the election of 1928 and General Depression was a major enemy in 1932."[1] Coolidge Prosperity virtually insured a Republican victory in 1928. Four years later, however, thirteen million Americans had no jobs, industrial production had dropped by more than half; uncounted thousands lived in "Hooverville" shacks; and neither local nor national government seemed capable of providing adequate relief. Thus, Hoover's depression made it practically impossible for a Republican—especially the incumbent—to win in 1932.

The Republicans had little choice but to back Hoover, however. Repudiation of him could not free the party from the onus of the depression, since many hind-sighted analysts now blamed the severe decline on exactly those policies which had given the Republicans victory throughout the 1920s. The party had to stand on its record and name Hoover to head its ticket; Vice-President Charles Curtis would retain second place.

The choice of Hoover's running mate raised the only real question for the national convention. Many delegates hoped to recapture something of the positive aura of the Coolidge days by naming former Vice-President Charles G. Dawes to share the ticket with Hoover. Dawes renounced the nomination out of hand, since he had even left his RFC post to go home and save his family's bank. Hoover personally favored the vigorous and liberal Theodore Roosevelt, Jr., whose name might help to counter that of another Roosevelt on the Democratic slate. A conservative convention feared young Roosevelt's progressivism, however, preferring the safe and colorless incumbent.[2]

The Democratic party suffered no such limitations. A Republican depression would work to the Democrats' benefit. Progressive Democrats, who went to the convention determined to select a liberal nominee, united behind Franklin Delano Roosevelt, governor of New York, whose record on unemployment relief and industrial welfare made him an attractive alternative to Hoover.[3] Al Smith, the 1928 nominee, believed that he deserved the 1932 bid, however. Although he could not get the spot himself due to the overwhelming rancor of 1928, he might deadlock the convention and force the selection of a weaker compromise candidate. Another front runner, John Nance Garner, prevented his impasse when he turned over the crucial California delegation to Roosevelt. All but Smith's diehards swung behind the candidate, and the Democrats decided on a

1. Hoover, Memoirs, 3:218.
2. Hamlin, Diary, 18 June 1932.
3. William E. Leuchtenburg, Franklin D. Roosevelt and the New Deal: 1932–1940 (New York: Harper and Row, 1963), pp. 3–4; Rexford Tugwell, F. D. R.: Architect of an Era (New York: Macmillan, 1967), p. 70.

Roosevelt-Garner ticket. In Franklin Roosevelt they had a man who pledged a "new deal for the American people." Whatever that new deal might be, it held out a promise to the "forgotten man" seemingly neglected by the Hoover administration.[4]

Neither convention gave its candidate a definitive platform, particularly on depression and recovery issues. Both formulated conservative documents; each reiterated standard economic positions; neither offered a keynote for the campaign.

From the beginning of the 1932 contest, the candidates themselves became an essential campaign issue. Hoover had worked desperately hard at combatting the depression, yet his weak policies and lack of political personality made him appear exactly what Roosevelt called him: "a solemn defeatist, with little hope and with no consciousness of people as human beings or of their needs." Garner agreed that the president would do himself little good; "Hoover is making speeches and that's enough for us," he said.[5] In contrast, although Roosevelt said little in his speeches, he offered an infectious warmth, charm, and confidence; *he* would not overlook the "forgotten man."

Hoover entered the campaign hamstrung. His entire approach to recovery depended upon confidence, and he believed that any bad news or pessimistic revelation would precipitate a further slide in the economy, more bank runs, a worsening of the depression. Hoover later admitted that the choice in 1932 had been a hard one, but the potential economic losses outweighed any political gains.[6] He could not afford discussion of some issues. If he wished to prove, for example, that he should not be blamed for the orgy of speculation before 1929 and had, in fact, opposed that policy, he would have had to indict the Federal Reserve Board for its deliberate inflationary policies on behalf of Europe from 1925 to 1928.[7] Therefore, he waged a cam-

4. Samuel I. Rosenman, ed., *The Public Papers and Addresses of Franklin D. Roosevelt*, 1:647–59; Elliott Roosevelt, ed., *F. D. R.: His Personal Letters, 1928–1945* (New York: Duell, Sloan and Pearce, 1950), 1:248–51; Leuchtenburg, *Roosevelt and New Deal*, pp. 7–8.

5. Frances Perkins, *The Roosevelt I Knew* (New York: Viking, 1946), p. 115; Marquis James, *Mr. Garner of Texas* (Indianapolis: Bobbs-Merrill, 1939), p. 130.

6. White, "Herbert Hoover–The Last of the Old Presidents or the First of the New?" *Saturday Evening Post* 205 (4 Mar. 1933): 6–7, 53–56.

7. Hoover, *Memoirs*, 3:249–50, 252–53.

paign of vague defenses interspersed with loud praises of the American Spirit and hoped feebly for the best.

Hoover's administration had not been wholly inactive. It had established the Reconstruction Finance Corporation, Federal Land Banks, Federal Home Loan Banks, and nonproductive public works. Moreover, Hoover had secured legal authorization for Federal Reserve loans to small businesses and liberalization of Federal Reserve credit expansion. In an economy drive, he had reduced expenditures by $300 million and increased federal revenues by $1 billion; and he had supported direct relief by appropriations of wheat and cotton to the Red Cross.[8] Conservative administration of the new agencies, however, together with fiscal policies working against the restoration of ease in money and credit markets, revealed a confused and inadequate grasp of the needs of the situation.

Nevertheless, the administration believed that its efforts had been rewarded in the summer of 1932, when the economic indices turned upward. Foreign runs on the dollar subsided in June. The bank failure epidemic and hoarding panic seemed over as a result of RFC loans. Industrial production improved. Commodity prices rose actively, as did the stock markets. Believing that the depression had hit bottom,[9] Hoover expected this upswing to "carry complete public conviction as to the rightness of our policies"; it held his best hope of victory in November. But the average man needed personal experience of recovery to accept it fully, and the president estimated that it would have taken another six months for the improvement to diffuse throughout the nation at a level where it would influence the ordinary citizen—and his vote.[10] Hoover felt that it was unfortunate and unjust that he did not have six months before election day to let

---

8. Ibid., 161–63; Myers and Newton, *Hoover Administration*, p. 236; Harold Wolfe, *Herbert Hoover: Public Servant and Leader of the Loyal Opposition* (New York: Exposition, 1956), pp. 310–11; Ogden Mills, speech before American Bankers Association, Los Angeles, 4 Oct. 1932, *New York Times*, 5 Oct. 1932.

9. Myers and Newton, *Hoover Administration*, pp. 236–37, 270–72; Eugene Meyer, COHC, p. 619; Hoover, *State Papers*, 2:364, 383, 449; Ogden L. Mills, "Recovery or Bust," speech before Indianapolis Chamber of Commerce, 25 Oct. 1934, Mills Papers, box 140; Hamlin, Diary, 5 July 1932; Hoover, speeches at Detroit and St. Paul, 22 Oct., 5 Nov. 1932; "Banking Situation Improves by Dint of Long, Hard Work," *Business Week*, 16 Sept. 1931, p. 5; Sullivan, *Prelude to Panic*, pp. 6–12, 79; Nadler and Bogen, *Banking Crisis*, pp. 128–31.

10. Hoover, *Memoirs*, 3:267–69.

the workings of the economy convince the "forgotten man" that he had not been forgotten, although there is no reason to believe that his expectation was soundly based.

Roosevelt made the most of the situation, charging that the Hoover administration could not handle the depression which it had helped to cause. He indicted the administration's credit measures, for example, accusing Hoover of imposing excessive burdens of taxation at the same time that he spent too much and created a deficit which impaired the entire credit structure.[11] The Democratic standard-bearer passed over the administration's efforts to strengthen the financial structure. When he did discuss the new agencies, such as the RFC, the Federal Land Banks, and the Home Loan Banks, he charged that Hoover had failed to use his new powers for adequate relief;[12] the "forgotten man," Roosevelt implied, deserved better.

No single issue dominated the 1932 campaign, but the Republicans hoped to focus attention on banking and currency. Although Hoover did not endorse any of the current proposals for reform, such as the Glass bill, he did call for regulation of investment banking, particularly of the securities affiliates of commercial banks; and he told voters that the Democratic Congress had thwarted his desires to provide relief for depositors in closed banks by temporary use of federal credit to distribute frozen assets.[13] The president and other Republican spokesmen repeatedly attacked inflation and exhibited the administration's accomplishments on behalf of better banking and finance: the RFC, the moratorium on international payments, the Glass-Steagall Act of 1932, and the new Federal Reserve policies.

The Democrats, on the other hand, chose to pay banking and currency less attention. Their platform made only vague and timid references to the need for banking reform; it differed little from Republican positions on speculation and sympathy for depositors in suspended banks. Roosevelt took no part in this position paper ex-

11. FDR, address on the federal budget, Pittsburgh, Pa., 19 Oct. 1932, *Public Papers*, 1:795–811.
12. FDR, speech at Springfield, Ill., 21 Oct. 1932, in Rosenman, *Public Papers*, 2:812–19; Jones, *Fifty Billion Dollars*, p. 259; Moley, *First New Deal*, p. 132.
13. Hoover, speech at Indianapolis, 28 Oct. 1932, *State Papers*, 2:389–407; Roy D. Peel and Thomas C. Donnelly, *The 1932 Campaign: An Analysis* (New York: Farrar and Rinehart, 1935), pp. 131–32, 139–40.

cept to quash a plank demanding guarantee of deposits. Moreover, his acceptance speech and subsequent addresses "slithered"—as one of his own supporters phrased it—on economic affairs.[14] The nominee's specific demands, aired at Columbus, Ohio, on August 20, called for more rigid supervision of national banks, complete separation of investment and commercial banking, and restrictions on the use of both Federal Reserve and commercial bank credit for speculation.[15] He did not elaborate on these points and confined the rest of his campaign remarks to occasional negative references to Hoover's economic policies. Raymond Moley claimed that he and Roosevelt's other advisers "regarded any talk about the banks as politically dangerous and against the public interest," apparently agreeing with Hoover that it would only disturb confidence and deepen the depression.[16] Roosevelt avoided taking a position even in private letters to constituents; he refused to define what the New Deal might mean for banking,[17] declaring only that "special interests" should not be permitted to control American economic life.[18]

Roosevelt said even less about money. The Democratic platform pledged "a sound currency to be preserved at all hazards," but it did not promise to retain the gold standard, and the convention included a fair representation of inflationists. Roosevelt himself had had close contacts with a group of economists from Cornell University who advocated the commodity dollar,[19] and a young Brains Truster warned President Hoover early in the campaign that his opponent planned to tinker with the currency if elected. Hoover, therefore, accused the Democrats of planning to introduce fiat money.[20] Roosevelt waited until the end of the campaign to answer these charges and then scoffed, "The President is seeing visions of

14. Feis, *1933*, p. 8; Walter Lippmann, *New York Herald Tribune*, 28 June, 1 July 1932.
15. Rosenman, *Public Papers*, 1:669–84; Franklin D. Roosevelt, *Looking Forward* (London: Heinemann, 1933), pp. 227–28.
16. Moley, *First New Deal*, p. 131.
17. Seymour E. Allen to FDR, 15 July 1932; FDR to Allen, 30 July 1932; Allen to FDR, 5 Aug. 1932; FDR to Allen, 10 Oct. 1932; Allen to FDR, 14 Oct. 1932; FDR to Allen, 26 Oct. 1932–all in Franklin Delano Roosevelt Library (hereafter cited as FDRL), President's Personal File (hereafter cited as PPF) 67.
18. Rexford Guy Tugwell, *The Brains Trust* (New York: Viking, 1968), pp. 124–25.
19. Lindley, *Roosevelt Revolution*, pp. 19, 23–24.
20. Hoover, *Memoirs*, 3:279; Hoover, *State Papers*, 2:416–17; Sullivan, *Prelude to Panic*, pp. 19–22.

rubber dollars." He endorsed the platform statement and committed himself to the gold clause in government bonds, but he preferred to leave that area of debate to sound-money Democrats, such as Carter Glass.[21]

Hoover's defenders, on the other hand, praised the president for his fiscal courage. Both the president and his secretary of the Treasury, Ogden Mills, repeatedly claimed that the administration had rescued the nation from a grave crisis; they implied that the peril had something to do with gold. Mills cited administration successes with the RFC, broadened reserve and discount facilities for the Federal Reserve System, and mobilization of other credit agencies, all of which reinforced America's position when the wave of bank failures and gold disasters swept westward out of Europe.[22] Hoover also spoke of these pressures on the economy in his Des Moines address on October 4; he affirmed that the United States had stood within two weeks of leaving the gold standard in February 1932. At that time, the president said, he had rejected the advice of bitter-end liquidationists as well as those who counselled the use of the printing press for currency or bonds. Rather, he determined to "render the credit of the United States Government impregnable"and then lend that sound credit "to aid private institutions to protect the debtor and the savings of our people." Therefore, he had decided on the Federal Reserve changes Mills had already outlined and "won his great battle to protect our people at home."[23]

Senator Glass counterattacked for the Democrats; he denied that there had ever been a gold crisis. If the president and his advisers had ever worried about the gold standard, Glass said, they had withheld that information from him, from other key members of Congress on whom cooperation depended, and from the banks and private investors who bought Treasury notes because of their faith in gold. The senator claimed that his fellow Democrats had resisted administration efforts to use the Reserve amendments to introduce wholesale inflation; thus it was the Democrats, not the

21. New York Times, 5 Nov. 1932; Frank Freidel, Franklin D. Roosevelt: The Triumph (Boston: Little, Brown, 1956), pp. 350–51.

22. Mills, speeches at Detroit and Baltimore, 23 Sept., 19 Oct. 1932, Mills Papers, box 138.

23. Hoover, State Papers, 2:293–318; Hoover, Memoirs, 3:119; Wilbur and Hyde, Hoover Policies, pp. 407–08; Joslin, Hoover Off the Record, pp. 304–07; Hamlin, Diary, 14 Oct., 26 Nov. 1932, 24 Mar. 1933.

Republicans, who represented the true sound-money position.[24]

Hoover's men leaped to the rebuttal. Senator James Watson publicly reminded Glass that they had both attended a confidential White House conference in February 1932 at which the president outlined the gold situation and asked for immediate legislation to allow the Federal Reserve "to prevent imminent jeopardy to the gold standard of the United States."[25] Secretary Mills broadcast a review of the causes of the depression, Hoover's proposals for banking and credit revival, Democratic obstruction in the House, and Glass's own role in the gold crisis legislation.[26] (In April 1933, Glass apologized for his role in the campaign statements on this issue, claiming that he had been misled by Roosevelt.) On election day, however, the voters had to decide which version to accept.

The great gold panic debate was typical of the 1932 presidential contest: vocal arguments about closed issues and little clear indication of what either party intended for the 1933–1937 term. The Republicans stood on a three-year record of coping with the depression; it seemed likely that Hoover would continue with the same policies if reelected. The Democrats, on the other hand, promised a vaguely defined "new deal" to be worked out by the highly personable Roosevelt. Here, too, the electorate could choose.

On November 8, the voters rejected Hoover overwhelmingly. In the worst Republican defeat since 1912, Hoover carried only 15,750,000 votes to Roosevelt's 22,800,000 and received a mere 59 electoral votes to 472 for his opponent. Prosperity had put Hoover in the White House in 1928 and depression evicted him in 1932, leaving the mansion for Franklin Roosevelt.

In the last days of the campaign, President Hoover had to withdraw his attention from the coming election and the usual tasks of governing the nation to focus on an extraordinary banking development—the closing of the Nevada banks.

Nevada's peculiar banking arrangement centered around a single individual, George Wingfield, who controlled virtually all

24. Glass, draft of statement to E. L. James (managing editor, *New York Times*), n.d., Glass Papers, University of Virginia, box 4; Palmer, *Carter Glass*, pp. 215–17; *Washington Post*, 2 Nov. 1932; *New York Times*, 2 Nov. 1932.

25. Hoover, *Memoirs*, 3:284–85; *New York Times*, 2 Nov. 1932.

26. Mills, radio address, 1 Nov. 1932, Mills Papers, box 177; *New York Times*, 2 Nov. 1932.

of the state's banks and involved himself deeply in its economy. Born in Arkansas and raised as a cowboy in Oregon, Wingfield had come to Nevada as a prospector but turned to gambling, which earned him over $100,000 per year. By the age of twenty-seven, he was worth $2 million and had used the profits from his gambling enterprises to acquire choice properties around the rich silver and gold mines at Tonopah and Goldfield. In 1906, he joined a prosperous Winnemucca banker, George S. Nixon, in a partnership to take the largest share of profits from those mines. Wingfield oversaw the partners' mining interests, and Nixon (also a United States senator) concentrated on banking, taking over institutions in Tonopah, Carson City, Reno, and Winnemucca. For the first time, Nevada miners and businessmen could do their banking within the state; they no longer had to seek financing in San Francisco. Nixon's death in 1912 left Wingfield in charge of a network of twelve banks in nine towns as well as large holdings in hotels, cattle ranches, and other properties. Although he refused appointment to fill out Nixon's term in the Senate, Wingfield served as Republican national committeeman while one of his lawyers held the same post for the Democrats. Some observers claimed that he ran Nevada's bipartisan political machine, that his office in the Reno National Bank Building was the real capital of the state.[27]

Wingfield's banks handled most of the financing for Nevada's industry, perhaps 80 to 85 percent of loans outstanding, primarily in livestock. During the agricultural depression of the 1920s, he extended many of these loans without additional security. State banking authorities overlooked regulations on the investment of savings deposit funds and ignored provisions in the state's Banking Act of 1911 which forbade loans secured by chattel property. After 1929, when depression hit the rest of the country and Nevada suffered severe droughts, livestock prices plummeted and the ranchers could no longer meet even their interest payments. Wingfield's banks were obliged to foreclose on 150 ranches that owned 70 percent of the cattle and sheep in Nevada, nearly 800,000 head. The banks often received only twenty-five cents in the depressed markets

27. Gilman M. Ostrander, *Nevada: The Great Rotten Borough, 1859–1964* (New York: Knopf, 1966), pp. 134, 138–42; Richard G. Lillard, *Desert Challenge: An Interpretation of Nevada* (New York: Knopf, 1949), pp. 31–34, 246–47.

for sheep on which they had loaned up to eight dollars per head.[28]

By 1932, Wingfield needed help. Since his banks held more than 80 percent of the banking resources of the state, as well as funds of counties, school districts, municipalities, and the university, and his personal and political friends occupied many of the state's highest offices, Wingfield's trouble was also Nevada's. A small state —its population numbered 91,000 in the early 1930s—Nevada was too closely tied to the economy that Wingfield had been sustaining to find other local resources to bring to his aid now. State officials, however, joined their pleas to his efforts to find new funds. He tried to convince A. P. Giannini of the Bank of America in California to extend his huge banking complex into Nevada.[29] When that effort failed, both banker and state applied to the RFC for loans. The agency authorized three emergency relief loans for Nevada, totaling $54,967,[30] but the RFC Board refused to advance $2 million to Wingfield. One government official later recalled that no one had known enough about the Nevada situation to take responsibility for a loan.[31] Therefore, Nevada's Governor Fred B. Balzar flew to Washington on October 30 to lay the banks' case clearly before Hoover and the director of the RFC, and persuaded the RFC Board to investigate his state's banks.

Meanwhile, the Wingfield banks lacked sufficient funds to meet depositors' withdrawals. The state superintendent of banking had not properly evaluated their free assets and had permitted them to remain open while depositors drained off available cash. Wingfield and his officials told other bankers, the state bank examiner, the state attorney general, and the lieutenant governor that their situation was perilous; they asked for a suspension of banking and business in Nevada until they could reorganize the banks and locate additional funds, perhaps from the RFC. The governor agreed from Washington and telegraphed orders to issue the necessary proclama-

28. *Reno Evening Gazette*, 1 Nov. 1932; report of investigation by Nevada legislature, ibid., 13 Mar. 1933; F. W. Barsalou, "The Concentration of Banking Power in Nevada: An Historical Analysis," *Business History Review* 29 (Dec. 1955), 350–62; Marquis James and Bessie Rowland James, *Biography of a Bank: The Story of Bank of America N.T. and S.A.* (New York: Harper, 1954), pp. 362–63.
29. James and James, *Biography of a Bank*, pp. 362–63.
30. *New York Times*, 1, 21 Oct., 3 Nov. 1932.
31. Eugene Meyer, COHC, pp. 674–75.

tion. On the evening of October 31, therefore, the lieutenant governor of Nevada declared a twelve-day bank and business "holiday" whereby financial institutions could remain closed if they chose. Simultaneously, George Wingfield announced the reorganization of his banks.[32]

Residents of the Silver State reacted calmly to their banking moratorium. Fifteen of the state's twenty-six banks closed the first day, including the twelve Wingfield institutions; several banks used the holiday only temporarily and opened again after an hour; a few limited withdrawals. At the end of two weeks, however, only thirteen banks—Wingfield's and one small state institution—had not reopened. Groups of businessmen, apparently unhampered despite the suspension, publicly commended Wingfield for his "heroic efforts" in sustaining the state's industries and businesses before the holiday. One newspaper called the moratorium another of those "ups and downs" to which citizens of the mining and livestock states had become accustomed. The legislature saw no reason for emergency measures; tax relief, for example, would be unsound and unnecessary, they thought, since more than half of the next tax installment would come from railroads and utilities which could obtain funds through their New York offices, and thousands of smaller taxpayers could fulfill their obligations without drawing on bank deposits.[33] Even frozen school and county funds excited little furor; officials expected that $350,000 in school funds would become available in time to meet December and January payrolls for 650 teachers in thirteen counties; county clerks would get the money from the reopened banks or apply for it to the bonding companies.[34] The suspension did displace politics "as a street corner conversational subject," but local pundits believed that it had come too late to have any real effect on the election.[35] Nevadans even accepted a two-week extension of the holiday when Governor Balzar decided that the banks needed more time to arrange their reopening.

Wingfield and his associates began work on reorganization as soon as the moratorium was declared. Two RFC examiners arrived

32. *Reno Evening Gazette*, 1 Nov. 1932; *New York Times*, 2 Nov. 1932.
33. *Reno Evening Gazette*, 10 Nov. 1932.
34. Ibid., 24, 25, 28 Nov. 1932.
35. *Reno Evening Gazette*, 5, 9 Nov. 1932; *New York Times*, 9 Nov. 1932; Ostrander, *Nevada*, pp. 150–55.

on November 2, as promised, to investigate the banks' position for a loan and to help in finding a solution; they remained in close consultation with the banking group and state officials until they had evolved a potential reopening plan. First, they sought refinancing of the bad livestock loans. Since the Regional Agricultural Credit Corporation, an affiliate of the RFC, was scheduled to open an office in Reno very soon, the two federal examiners recommended that part or all of the loans to livestock men be transferred to the new agency. Individual borrowers could obtain funds from the credit corporation which they would use to pay off their notes to the Wingfield banks, which in turn could reduce their debts and have some "free assets" on which to negotiate further loans.[36]

The rest of the reorganization plan called for unification of the twelve Wingfield banks into a single institution with new capital. A parent bank in Reno would have branches in those towns currently serviced by Wingfield banks. Of course, Nevada's banking laws would have to be revised to permit branch banking. But first, Wingfield had to refinance his operation. He and the RFC men met with officials of Standard Oil, Southern Pacific and Western Pacific Railroad, Sierra Pacific Power Company, and other concerns; none could or would supply the additional money. Under another proposal, current depositors would take two-thirds of the stock in the new parent bank, the rest to be held by others who would advance capital for its operation. The usually conservative *Reno Evening Gazette* editorialized in favor of this depositor ownership, which worked out successfully in the reorganization of the one state bank outside the Wingfield group that had remained closed.[37] Committees of depositors in each closed bank had to vote on participation in this plan; depositors were also asked to vote waivers of their claims against the banks, because at the time of the moratorium it appeared that they would lose $3.1 million, one-fifth of the combined total deposits. Wingfield, his associates, and the RFC examiners submitted their arguments to the depositors' committees, but in each case they had to reveal that probably only a portion of deposits (ranging from 45 to 60 percent at the Reno National Bank up to 90 or 95 percent at Riverside) would probably be made available under the

36. *Reno Evening Gazette*, 8, 10 Nov. 1932.
37. Ibid., 19, 22, 25 Nov. 1932.

new system. The Virginia City Bank received the gloomiest report; of $196,901.51 in assets, $87,894.03 had been lost irrevocably, and only $42,341.21 in good assets remained free for distribution.[38] Not surprisingly, depositors in the more stable banks protested merger of their assets with those of less liquid banks and voted to be omitted from the branch bank plan; others asked for a postponement until they could commission an independent appraisal of the assets. To give them time, Governor Balzar again extended the Nevada banking holiday, now until December 18; unlike the two earlier proclamations, this moratorium applied only to banks, not to businesses or debt payments. Depositors' committees resisted the idea of capital contribution, but Wingfield was able to secure the necessary waivers from two-thirds of his creditors.[39]

Still in need of capital, Wingfield turned to the RFC. The reorganization plan, as originally conceived, seemed to bypass the RFC, since that agency was then empowered only to make loans; it would not yet subscribe to capital stock. Wingfield officials admitted that their preholiday request for $2 million from the RFC could not have saved them. By December, however, they had exhausted all other sources—the depositors, California investors, Nevada industry —and approached the RFC again. This time, Wingfield offered a plan for merger of his twelve banks into a single chain under a parent bank in Reno, all financed through a new large mortgage company. On February 4, 1933, the RFC announced that it would advance $1.5 million to the mortgage company.[40] Four months later, plans had been completed for the Bank of Nevada, to be formed by merger of Wingfield's banks, with supportive loans from the Regional Agricultural Credit Corporation, the RFC, and California corporations.[41]

Nevada's moratorium had very little effect upon the presidential election or—in the short run—the American banking system. It occurred too close to the election and in too circumscribed an area to influence the outcome. Moreover, the state had a very small population; its banks had almost no ties beyond Nevada; and the cause of failure, overcommitment to bad livestock loans, was limited to a

38. Ibid., 19 Nov. 1932.
39. Ibid., 19, 26, 27, 29, 30 Nov. 1932; *New York Times*, 26, 27 Nov. 1932.
40. *Reno Evening Gazette*, 24 Dec. 1932, 4, 5 Feb. 1933; *Commercial and Financial Chronicle*, 11 Feb. 1933, pp. 950–51; *New York Times*, 5 Feb. 1933.
41. *New York Times*, 4 June 1933.

single group of banks. Thus, Nevada's banking crisis produced few immediate reverberations outside the state. As one Federal Reserve official said, "Nevada is a minor state in a financial way."[42]

The Wingfield episode did hold some significant lessons for the handling of a banking crisis, however. A state's governmental administration had become closely tied with its financial institutions, and when those banks were imperiled, the state did all in its power to save them. In one sense, at least, the interests of Nevada and those of George Wingfield were the same. Despite its willingness to help, however, Nevada had no means whereby it might rescue those banks; accordingly, it went to larger agencies to find the necessary funds— to the federal government. But national authorities could not agree to sustain the Wingfield banks within a reasonable period of time.

For the first time, therefore, a state had to resort to total suspension of its financial operations because a sizable portion of its banking facilities was imperiled. The Nevada holiday suggested that other states, perhaps the entire nation, might have to face such a moratorium unless they halted bank failures.

The 1932 election left Herbert Hoover in the uncomfortable position of defeated incumbent. Although the voters had repudiated him, he faced another four months of the obligations and responsibilities of the presidency, with small hope of success.

Hoover would have been spared some of the painful and frustrating interregnum had the twentieth amendment been ratified in time. On March 3, 1932, Congress sent to the states Senator George Norris's revision of the Constitution to eliminate the lame duck session, substituting an earlier meeting of the newly-elected Congress on January 3 and advancing inauguration day from March 4 to January 20. But the required thirty-six states did not ratify this amendment until February 6, 1933, leaving Hoover in office for four months after his defeat. Franklin Roosevelt had favored the change since 1923.[43]

A bolder plan might also have shortened the interregnum: Hoover could have turned over the White House to Roosevelt at

42. Meyer, COHC, pp. 671–72.
43. FDR to *New York World*, 15 Feb. 1923; Frank Freidel, *Franklin D. Roosevelt: The Ordeal* (Boston: Little, Brown, 1954), p. 161.

once. If the secretary of state would resign, Hoover could name Roosevelt to that office; then Hoover and Vice-President Curtis could resign and Roosevelt would succeed to the presidency. This proposal could hardly be taken seriously, however, since Hoover would not have considered handing the country over to his late opponent a moment sooner than he had to by law. Moreover, the president-elect had not worked out his program or selected his cabinet, and he had no wish to cope with "the unmanageable collection of lame ducks"; therefore, he too probably would have rejected the scheme had it been offered.[44]

During the four-month interregnum, the country endured severe economic decline. Despite a worldwide recovery in the summer, the United States suffered radical drops in employment from the latter part of October through early March. Fifteen million persons had no jobs; many others were working at reduced wages. At least three million crowded the relief rolls; and in countless places welfare facilities had broken down entirely. The money value of American exports in the winter of 1932 hit its lowest level in thirty years. Prices of farm products fell off ruinously, as did the commodities and stock markets. Although bank opening had surpassed closings during the summer, in November the situation reversed and failures exceeded openings by $30.8 million; losses doubled in December and quadrupled in January. Foreign governments, especially France, and private citizens withdrew and hoarded gold, thus draining the stock of money and bank reserves.[45]

For each of these difficulties, Hoover blamed fear—fear of the incoming administration. The president reasoned that the positive influence of the Republican administration had ended with the election and that the New Deal dominated the country after November 8; thus he concluded that Franklin Roosevelt, rather than himself, bore primary responsibility for the nation during the interregnum. Rather illogically, Hoover argued that the same voters who had elected his opponent now so feared the same man's unannounced intentions that they devastated the economy for their own protection. (As early as September, Boston bankers had advised customers

44. *Washington Evening Star*, 9 Nov. 1932; Joslin, *Hoover Off the Record*, pp. 330–31; Lindley, *Roosevelt Revolution*, p. 43.
45. Meyer, COHC, pp. 669–70; Feis, *1933*, p. 10; Sullivan, *Prelude to Panic*, pp. 24, 35, 67.

to prepare for a collapse of security values if Roosevelt was elected.) Hoover concluded that Roosevelt's election was wrecking the nation's finances.[46]

Hoover particularly charged that Roosevelt, in giving no indication of his intentions for the currency, masked a plan to devalue the dollar and leave the gold standard. In Hoover's opinion, his successor was too accessible to the advocates of "reflation" and "commodity dollars";[47] and even if the president-elect himself was not one of these inflationists, he was culpable in refusing to repudiate their proposals, even when members of Congress claimed his endorsement of their inflation bills.[48] Roosevelt also remained silent when administration spokesmen and newspaper editors appealed to him for a statement on currency.[49] Hoover and his partisans felt that Roosevelt's refusal to speak out against devaluation meant that he favored it. They further believed that the business world shared their opinion and therefore reduced production, adding to unemployment; depositors, too, feared monetary instability, they believed, and for that reason converted bank deposits into gold, while bankers sought to strengthen reserves by calling in loans and refusing new credits.[50]

Roosevelt himself did nothing to counter Hoover's impres-

46. Ogden L. Mills, "Recovery or Bust," speech before Indianapolis Chamber of Commerce, 25 Oct. 1934, Mills Papers, box 140; Joslin, *Hoover Off the Record*, pp. 350–53; Myers and Newton, *Hoover Administration*, p. 275; Sullivan, *Prelude to Panic*, p. 23; Hamlin, Diary, 23 Sept. 1932.

47. The Committee for the Nation to Rebuild Prices and Purchasing Power, George F. Warren of Cornell University, James Harvey Rogers and Irving Fisher of Yale, and Henry A. Wallace worried Hoover by their closeness to Roosevelt as much as by their advocacy of inflation. Fisher to FDR, 25 Feb., 3 Mar. 1933, Fisher Papers, Yale University, box 14; E. A. Rumely to Louis Howe, with interim report of Committee for the Nation, 1 Mar. 1933, FDRL:Official File (hereafter cited as OF) 230, box 1; Rogers to Herbert Feis, 28 Feb. 1933, Rogers Papers, Yale University, box 20.

48. *Washington Herald*, 30 Jan. 1933; Meyer, COHC, pp. 672–73; Smith and Beasley, *Carter Glass*, p. 327.

49. *New York Times*, 23, 24 Jan., 1 Feb. 1933; Hoover, *Memoirs*, 3:199–201; John H. Williams (Department of Economics, Harvard University), manuscript essay on inflation, Mills Papers, box 69. For a documentary history of Roosevelt and gold, see Jordan A. Schwartz, *1933: Roosevelt's Decision; The United States Leaves the Gold Standard* (New York: Chelsea House, 1969).

50. "The True Causes of the Banking Panic of 1933," Hoover Papers, West Branch, Post-Presidential Papers, 1933–1964, AG6; Hoover, *Memoirs*, 3:201–02; Myers and Newton, *Hoover Administration*, pp. 348–50; Joslin, *Hoover Off the Record*, pp. 350–53; Sullivan, *Prelude to Panic*, pp. 23, 45, 69–77, 81–82; Moley, *After Seven Years*, p. 38; Moley and Rosen, *First New Deal*, pp. 134–35; Ballantine, "When All the Banks Closed," pp. 134–35; George Leslie Harrison, memoranda, 10 Oct. 1932, 9, 10, 16 Feb. 1933, Harrison Papers, binder 46.

sion. Like Abraham Lincoln, he saw no reason to underwrite the programs of the defeated incumbent or to dissipate his own mandate by forecasting his reactions to events still four months in the future. Therefore, he reserved himself for March 4, remained a private citizen, and left the governance of the nation to Hoover.[51] As he said on the question of international debts, it was "not his baby."[52]

Hoover's tenacious belief that Roosevelt was responsible however, prevented him from either taking an active role during the interregnum or questioning his own policies in their effect on public confidence. Hoover knew that the voters had rejected him and felt that all energy now belonged to his more popular successor; therefore, he never considered vigorous action on his own to counteract the economic slide. Moreover, he did not ask whether the reaction of fear might really be directed at his own feeble policies and thus did nothing to alter them. Thus, between November 9, 1932, and March 4, 1933, the United States drifted without direction from the incumbent administration.

Bipartisan cooperation offered little hope, too. Immediately after the election, Hoover appealed for "unity of national action" to promote recovery and prevent further deterioration; he particularly asked Republicans to cooperate with the new administration.[53] At the same time, the president and his key advisers believed that there was little the Republicans could do beyond the routine affairs of government during the interregnum. Secretary of the Treasury Mills stated privately that the Democrats could not "avoid the responsibility of leadership between now and March 4," since the country had voted a lack of confidence in the Hoover regime and Democrats dominated the lame-duck Congress ("if you include Progressive Republicans who went Democratic"). If bipartisan action was to be taken on such issues as the economy, taxes, budget balancing, debts, and banking legislation, the Democrats should initiate it, and quickly, lest they face a much worse situation in March.[54] This attitude on

51. Denis W. Brogan, *The Era of Franklin D. Roosevelt: A Chronicle of the New Deal and Global War* (New Haven, Conn.: Yale University Press, 1950), pp. 40–41; Walter Lippmann, *Interpretations: 1933–1935* (New York: Macmillan, 1936), pp. 1–2; Lindley, *Roosevelt Revolution*, pp. 43–47; E. Francis Brown, "America Meets the Emergency," *Current History* 38 (May 1933): 201–11.

52. *New York Times*, 23, 24 Nov. 1932.

53. Hoover, *State Papers*, 1:480–81; Myers and Newton, *Hoover Administration*, p. 276.

the part of the Hoover men is hardly surprising, given the bitterness of the recent campaign and the president's complaints that the Democrats had obstructed legislation in Congress so that the recovery of the summer came too late to affect the election results. Leading Democrats, on the other hand, believed they would be criticized either way, for following Hoover and not offering their own program or for sabotaging Hoover.[55] But the president felt obliged to ask for cooperation on war debts, international currency stabilization, budget balancing, banking reform, and reorganization of the bankruptcy laws. "I do not expect Congress to do much," he told a confidant, "but I can complete my part."[56]

Hoover's best hope for cooperation rested on his plea to balance the federal budget. Both parties had spoken loudly during the campaign about reducing expenditures and putting the budget into balance. The president wished, therefore, to convince Congress to vote cuts in expenditures and a general manufacturer's sales tax of 2½ percent; he told Senate Democratic leader Joseph T. Robinson and Speaker John Nance Garner that Roosevelt could come into office with a disagreeable job out of the way if the Democrats would pass his recommendations. Garner and Robinson agreed. The following day, however, Roosevelt told newsmen that he was "amazed" and "horrified" at the general sales tax, and a week later he informed Garner that he could not accept the proposal. Garner, acutely embarrassed, had to return to the president and withdraw his support. "Governor Roosevelt is opposed to what we have planned, and it is a waste of time to try any legislation to which he will not agree," Garner said.[57] The budget remained unbalanced, to Hoover's dismay.

The president also worried about an increasingly critical banking situation. Despite the Reconstruction Finance Corporation

54. Mills to Harrison, memoranda of telephone conversations, 9, 10, 11 Nov. 1932, Harrison Papers, binder 46.

55. Bascom N. Timmons, *Garner of Texas: A Personal History* (New York: Harper, 1948), p. 139; Jordan A. Schwartz, "John Nance Garner and the Sales Tax Rebellion of 1932," *Journal of Southern History* 30 (May 1964): 162–80.

56. Joslin, *Hoover Off the Record*, pp. 330–31; Myers and Newton, *Hoover Administration*, p. 303; Daniel P. Showan, "The Hoover-Roosevelt Relationship during the Interregnum," *Lock-Haven* (Pa.) *Bulletin* 1 (1961): 34.

57. Timmons, *Garner of Texas*, pp. 171–72; Myers and Newton, *Hoover Administration*, pp. 302–14; Hoover, *Memoirs*, 3:192–93; Showan, "Hoover-Roosevelt," pp. 34–35.

and Federal Reserve measures, banking had not revived; conditions were so bad that the Treasury could not place a large refunding loan. In addition, the Nevada moratorium offered poignant testimony on how far suspensions might extend.[58]

Thwarted in each of its own efforts, the Hoover administration now looked to the Congress—to the Glass banking reform bill—for relief. Annual reports by the secretary of the Treasury and the Comptroller of the Currency, as well as the president's message to Congress, made it clear that the administration now favored prompt action on reform.[59] Hoover and his advisers had attempted to save the banks, independently of a permanent bank reform bill; now, their own failures convinced them that they must support more extreme action or face a banking disaster.

Financiers, too, had come to accept the bill's general purposes, but they were not enthusiastic and still hoped that individual features could be altered. The American Bankers Association sent a memorial to Congress endorsing the main objectives of the Glass bill but still objecting to provisions which would give the Federal Reserve control over the kinds of loans commercial banks could make, and which would separate commercial and investment banking.[60] Thomas W. Lamont of the House of Morgan came out for "sensible provisions" for regional branch banking and compulsory membership in the Federal Reserve System for all commercial banks.[61] The United States Chamber of Commerce also recommended that federal banking laws be changed, now endorsing Federal Reserve control by law over member banks' lending for speculation, regulation of securities issues, and removal of bank officers for continued unsound practices; on the other hand, it still opposed deposit guarantee and separation of affiliates.[62]

The ill-fated Glass bill came before the Senate for the fourth

58. Hamlin, Diary, 18, 16, 28 Nov., 9 Dec. 1932; Willis and Chapman, Banking Situation, pp. 94–98.
59. Hoover, State Papers, 2:500–501; Myers and Newton, Hoover Administration, pp. 315–16; Hoover, Memoirs, 3:124–25; "Bank Reform," Business Week, 21 Dec. 1932, pp. 3–4.
60. "Bank Reform," Business Week, 4 Jan. 1933, pp. 3–4; 'To Make Banking Safe for Depositors," Literary Digest 114 (24 Dec. 1932): 3–4.
61. "Strong Medicine for Bank Failures," Literary Digest 114 (10 Dec. 1932): 7.
62. New York Times, 10 Dec. 1932; Commercial and Financial Chronicle, 7 Jan. 1933, pp. 52–53.

time on January 5, 1933. The measure had been under consideration since 1931. In its latest form the legislation called for nationwide branch banking, divorce of security affiliates from national banks within five years, Federal Reserve controls over speculative credit, Federal Reserve removal of officers and directors of member banks who persisted in unsound practices, and establishment of a liquidating corporation to protect bank deposits. Immediately, Senator Huey Long of Louisiana launched a filibuster which delayed all other Senate business for ten days. Long particularly objected to the branch banking features of the bill, believing them at threat to unit banks, such as abounded in his home area. His obstruction ended only after Senate leaders threatened to invoke cloture; but Long obtained a concession that the bill be amended to limit branching of national banks to states which permitted their own banks to branch. On January 25, the Senate passed the revised bill by a vote of 54 to 9.[63]

A companion bill in the House had little chance of acceptance without approval by the president-elect. Hoover had consulted Glass and the Democratic leaders of both houses on December 7; they agreed to prompt passage of the Glass bill and obtained Roosevelt's support the next day. A few days later, however, Roosevelt told Garner that he could not endorse the measure, that it would waste the time of the lame-duck Congress.[64] Roosevelt believed the Glass proposals did not go far enough; he wanted protection of investors against fictitious or bad securities, segregation of savings from commercial deposits, revision of the liquidating corporation clause to permit immediate reopening of failed banks, and branch banking limited to no more than a countrywide basis.[65]

Observers questioned whether the House would agree to con-

63. "Carter Glass Urges the Need for Banking Reform," *Review of Reviews* 88 (Jan. 1933): 20–22; "Glass Bill Cracked," *Business Week*, 1 Feb. 1933, p. 14; *New York Times*, 6, 8, 10–13, 17–26 Jan. 1933; Smith and Beasley, *Carter Glass*, pp. 346–47; *Congressional Record*, 72d Cong., 2d Sess., pp. 1573–74, 1624–36, 1835–51, 2005, 2007, 2144–45, 2208, 2264–66, 2272–83, 2293–94, 2392–98, 2508, 2517; 73d Cong., 1st Sess., pp. 56–59, 66, 182, 191.

64. Hoover, *Memoirs*, 3:125; Timmons, *Jones*, p. 178; Myers and Newton, *Hoover Administration*, p. 317.

65. Willis, memorandum of conference with FDR, Rexford Guy Tugwell, H. Parker Willis, and James Harvey Rogers, 17 Nov. 1932; and Willis to Glass, 19 Nov. 1932, both in Glass Papers, box 274; Rogers to Tugwell, 19 Nov. 1932, Rogers Papers, box 19; Tugwell, Diary (expanded form), FDRL: Group 80, 17 Nov. 1932; Tugwell, "Transition: Hoover to Roosevelt, 1932–1933," *Centennial Review* 9 (Spring 1965): 170–71.

sider the bill at all without Roosevelt's acceptance. When it did, debate bogged down over the guarantee of bank deposits. Despite Glass's meetings with House leaders, Hoover's conferences with leading Democrats, and even a formal appeal from the president to the Congress on February 20, the congressional session ended with the Glass bill buried in the House.[66]

The Hoover administration came late to the support of essential banking reform. As a matter of conviction, the president and his advisers clung to the idea that the banking system remained fundamentally sound and could cure itself. Therefore, they had chosen short-term assistance, such as the National Credit Corporation, the RFC, and Federal Reserve open-market purchases to bail out the banks. When these measures failed to expand credit or revive business, Hoover was forced into broader plans. Yet he waited so long to espouse consequential change that the opportunities for passing an effective law had narrowed hopelessly. In the closing days of his term, Herbert Hoover faced a daily worsening of the banking crisis, armed only with the weapons which had failed him in the past.

Meanwhile, the banking system faced abnormal strains. The Nevada moratorium in November had not excited a general alarm because it appeared to be local in origins and effect. By December, however, increasing numbers of rural banks faced devastating runs. The RFC stepped in to help institutions in Wisconsin, Pennsylvania, Minnesota, and Tennessee. In January 1933, the administration claimed that its aid had narrowly avoided panics in Cleveland, Chattanooga, Little Rock, Mobile, St. Louis, and Memphis.[67] Each of these eruptions instilled greater caution in the banking community, until, by the beginning of February, quick mobilization of reserves and the intercity transfer of adequate protective funds had become nearly impossible.

66. George W. Norris to Glass, 20 Feb. 1933, Glass Papers, box 305; G. M. McWilliams to Glass, 22 Feb. 1933; J. E. Ridder to Glass, 2 Mar. 1933; Lessing J. Rosenwald to Glass, 3 Mar. 1933—all in Glass Papers, box 271; Timmons, *Jones*, pp. 178, 183–84; Smith and Beasley, *Carter Glass*, pp. 327–29, 339–40; Hoover, *Memoirs*, 3:213, 215; Hoover, *State Papers*, 2:597–99; Myers and Newton, *Hoover Administration*, pp. 320–21; *New York Times*, 19, 21, 25, 27, 28 Jan., 1, 20, 21, 24, 28 Feb. 1933.

67. "The True Causes of the Banking Panic of 1933," unsigned memorandum, Hoover Papers, West Branch, Iowa, AG6.

On February 2, the crisis reached New Orleans. Because a huge insurance group there had collapsed in January despite RFC aid, Representative Hamilton Fish of New York asked the House to investigate all companies which had failed subsequent to RFC support. The congressman demanded full publicity of the "rotten mess" and called for the resignation of Rudolf Hecht, president of the Hibernia Bank and Trust Company in New Orleans. Fish charged that Hecht had known the insurance company was in danger but had used his position on the RFC advisory committee to obtain approval of a $4 million loan to the group, part of which was used to pay off loans from Hibernia. New Orleans newspapers did not carry these accusations, knowing that the story would prompt runs on Hibernia, the city's third largest bank. Northern papers publicized the charges, however, and Hibernia suffered heavy withdrawals from out-of-town correspondent banks. Word filtered into the New Orleans financial district, and local depositors also began to remove their money. By Friday evening, February 3, Hibernia could not meet another day's withdrawals.

Louisiana Senator Huey Long and Governor Oscar K. Allen came to Hibernia's defense. Long had saved the Louisiana banks twice before when the bankers feared a panic; in one case he persuaded secure banks to lend money to those in danger, and in the other he got the National Credit Corporation to help.[68] But this time, Long was so involved with a Senate investigation of his political organization that he did not learn of the New Orleans bank difficulties until Friday evening. Immediately he summoned the leading bankers and the governor and proposed that they obtain $20 million in cash for Hibernia from the RFC and the Federal Reserve System. Since the transfer could not be effected until Monday, February 6, however, he had to find some way to tide the bank over Saturday's banking hours. He determined to find some pretext on which Governor Allen could proclaim a legal holiday, so that the New Orleans banks could remain closed. But neither the assembled bankers nor the city librarian—roused from bed to conduct the research—could find a significant historical event on a February 4 to justify the hol-

68. Huey P. Long, *Every Man a King* (New Orleans: National Book, 1933), pp. 242–44; T. Harry Williams, *Huey Long* (New York: Knopf, 1969), pp. 543–45; B. Deutsch, "Paradox in Pajamas," *Saturday Evening Post*, 5 Oct. 1935, p. 38.

iday; the best they could come up with was that the United States had severed diplomatic relations with Germany on February 3, 1917. Long arbitrarily decided that so momentous a decision should have taken two days instead of one. Therefore, on February 4, 1933, Louisiana celebrated the sixteenth anniversary of America's break with Germany, to the amazement of the local German consul. When a newspaper printed an early edition revealing the true cause of the "holiday," Long ordered the militia to take it over. Few in New Orleans or elsewhere realized that the holiday had anything to do with the banks.

On Sunday, officials at Hibernia announced loans of $20 million from the RFC and $4 million from other banks; the panic was over. Hibernia opened early on Monday morning. Huey Long, one of its first customers, deposited twelve thousand dollars and declared, "I can't think of a safer place to put the money than right here."[69]

The same day, an Associated Press survey showed twelve states revising their banking laws to protect depositors. Some states offered to act as repositories for funds. Others authorized emergency powers for their governors or banking commissioners.[70] Federal relief no longer seemed sufficient.

69. New York Times, 5, 6, 7, 12 Feb. 1933; Time, 13 Feb. 1933, p. 41; Congressional Record, 72d Cong., 2d Sess., pp. 4658–75; Williams, Huey Long, pp. 614–17.

70. Legislatures had changes in the banking statutes under consideration in Massachusetts, Ohio, Illinois, Minnesota, Wisconsin, Iowa, Nebraska, Missouri, Oklahoma, Kansas, Washington, and New York. New York Times, 6 Feb. 1933.

CHAPTER IV

Michigan

SHORTLY after midnight on Tuesday, February 14, 1933, Governor William A. Comstock closed the banks of Michigan for eight days—tacit admission of the collapse of that state's banking structure and prelude to the national banking disaster three weeks thereafter. Years later writers would label this emergency a "time bomb," "an infection of panic spreading across the country," and the end of "an era in which 'Detroit the Dynamic' overreached itself."[1] To Charles and Mary Beard, "the news from Michigan jangled the American System from center to periphery."[2]

Banking had lagged twenty-five years behind the phenomenal growth of population and industry in the Detroit area. From 285,704 people in 1900, Detroit expanded to 1,568,602 in 1930, with similar booms in Grand Rapids, Lansing, Flint, Dearborn, Highland Park, and Royal Oak. Manufacturing accelerated in the 1920s, although most of Michigan remained a one-industry region, prosperous solely because of motor vehicles and their parts. Detroit depended on the national economy since it consumed less of its own products than any other city in the country.[3]

Until the late 1920s the city also remained chained to outside sources for commercial banking facilities. In June 1927, however, a group of bankers obtained a state charter for the Guardian Detroit Bank complex—a bank, an investment affiliate, and a trust company. Stock owners held an equal number of shares in the Guardian Detroit Bank and the Guardian Detroit Company, and one-fifth as many shares in the Guardian Trust Company (organized in 1925).[4] Motor company personnel sat on the boards of all three institutions, and Guardian quickly became known as an automobile bank.

Once formed, Guardian grew rapidly. Early in the summer of 1929 its directors increased the original $7.5 million capital by $3,694,500 and established the Guardian Detroit Group, Inc., which, at the same time, began to acquire shares in banking institutions throughout the area in order to form a statewide association of strong banks. Guardian's officers reasoned that part of the banking business which flowed to New York and Chicago could be handled at home. Earlier institutions had not been large enough to handle the volume of industrial Detroit's financing, but state law permitted holding companies, which could become extensive enough to manage the necessary credit.[5] Therefore, the Guardian Detroit Group and another holding company, the Union Commerce Corporation of Detroit, acquired all or substantially all of the capital stock (except shares which directors had to hold to qualify for board memberships) of twenty-three banks and trust companies. The two merged in December 1929, organizing the new Guardian Detroit Union Group, Inc., which took over eight more institutions. Subsidiaries usually joined Guardian through exchanges of stock. Committees from each bank examined assets and fixed a rate of exchange based on book value and earning power. When 75 percent of stockholders had accepted the arrangement and deposited their shares, the transaction

1. Barnard, *Independent Man*, p. 213; Schlesinger, *Crisis of the Old Order*, p. 476; Keith Sward, *The Legend of Henry Ford* (New York: Holt, Rinehart and Winston, 1948), p. 252.

2. Charles A. Beard and Mary R. Beard, *America in Midpassage* (New York: Macmillan, 1939), p. 155.

3. According to the United States *Census of Manufactures* for 1927, 56 percent of Detroit's total product represented the automobile industry. The *Census of Population* for 1930 showed a 64.2 percent increase in the value of Detroit's manufactures from 1919 to 1929. E. A. Goldenweiser, in his *American Monetary Policy* (New York: McGraw Hill, 1951), p. 137, stressed that the 1920s boom was not general but localized in geography and manufacturing.

4. This view of the structure and history of the Guardian Group is based primarily on testimony of its officers and directors, particularly president R. O. Lord, before the Senate Committee on Banking and Currency, *Hearings: Stock Exchange Practices*, 73d Cong., 1st Sess., 1933, Part 9: Guardian Detroit Union Group, pp. 4203–4403 (hereafter cited as SEP).

5. George Walter Woodward, *The Detroit Money Market* (Ann Arbor: Bureau of Business Research, University of Michigan, 1932), p. 245.

was complete.[6] The parent corporation could act as clearinghouse for information on policies and practices of its units, making the standards of the best available to all; the group also supervised building construction, coordinated business development, bought quantities of standard equipment and supplies, provided an independent examining force to supplement local audits, and offered investment counsel and statistical data which small institutions could not afford by themselves.

The Detroit Bankers Company, Guardian's larger rival, developed in much the same way. It was founded in January 1930 around the nucleus of the First National Bank of Detroit, an institution with 194 branches and 76 directors, the third largest separate bank outside of New York City.[7] Ultimately the Detroit Bankers Company held 40 banks.[8]

A tight association controlled each group. When the Detroit Bankers Company was organized, twelve men each contributed $1,000 for 10 shares of stock; these 120 shares constituted all the *voting* stock in the corporation, while the public bought 2.5 million shares of *nonvoting* stock at $20 per share. Twelve men thus managed Detroit's five leading banks and thirty-five others, holding exclusive power in the election and removal of directors for five years. Guardian claimed to be less arbitrary, allegedly retaining local control by member banks. In practice, however, local boards proved eager to please the group directors and cooperated in both personnel and policy "suggestions."[9]

Henry Ford dominated Guardian, although he avoided publicizing the connection. An unfriendly biographer called him the "last person whom the average American would have expected to find doing business in 1929 on Griswold Street, the Wall Street of Detroit."[10] Ford and his company had always opposed banks on principle. In May 1930, the Fords issued a statement that they were "not buying bank stock anywhere," just four days after they bought

6. SEP, pp. 4208–22.
7. Ferdinand Pecora, *Wall Street under Oath: The Story of Our Modern Money Changers* (New York: Simon and Schuster, 1939), pp. 234–37.
8. SEP, facing p. 5084.
9. Ibid., pp. 4213–14, 4227–29, 5077, 5089, 5129–31; Pecora, *Wall Street*, p. 239; Pecora, COHC, pp. 863–75.
10. Sward, *Legend*, p. 242.

into the National City Bank of New York.[11] Perhaps they made convenient distinctions between Henry Ford, the Ford Motor Company, and Henry's son Edsel. The younger Ford and his brother-in-law, Ernest C. Kanzler, chief of Ford's Universal Credit Corporation, were among the cofounders of the Guardian Group. Edsel held three directorships in the Group; Kanzler headed the parent board of directors; and Henry Ford himself owned 1,188 shares of Guardian stock which he transferred to Edsel as a gift.[12]

In addition to these great concentrations of control, both groups used certain banking procedures not illegal in themselves but extremely harmful to stability. Officers joined in the stock-buying mania of the 1920s, frequently with funds borrowed from their own banks, often on inadequate collateral or on pledge of their Guardian stock. Laws prohibited banks from lending against their own stocks, but the holding company made technical distinctions which "sufficed to satisfy the easy standards that prevailed."

When the 1929 crash struck, returns on these loans diminished and the Guardian stock, which had sold as high as $350, dropped to $74 in 1930, $30 in 1931, $10 in 1932, and finally to nothing.[13] Unit banks also felt the pinch of depression. Real estate loans had been hard to collect as early as 1926; after 1929, when automobile sales dropped and many Detroit workers lost their jobs, they could not meet mortgage payments and the banks' holdings became frozen. It did little good to prosecute defaulting debtors, since the banks could find no market for the confiscated properties. By February 1933, an estimated 72 percent of the assets of the Union Guardian Trust Company were thus immobilized.[14]

Group banking also created false pictures of the units while it drained their resources. Since the holding company had no independent income, it met annual expenses of operations and interest on its loans with dividends from member banks, milking the units "against every dictate of banking prudence and caution." The Group

---

11. *Detroit Free Press*, 14 May 1930; *New York Journal of Commerce*, 10 May 1930.

12. SEP, p. 4661.

13. Pecora, *Wall Street*, pp. 241–42, 245–46; SEP, p. 4607; *Detroit News*, 3 Jan. 1933, 1 Mar. 1934.

14. SEP, pp. 4803–06; *New York Times*, 16 Feb. 1933.

pressed its units especially hard for dividends in 1931 and 1932; in one case the Union Guardian Trust Company had to go out of the state to negotiate emergency loans from the Continental Illinois Bank of Chicago and the Bankers Trust Company of New York to maintain liquidity. (Edsel Ford's coendorsement of its note brought to $8.5 million the bank's debt to the Fords.) To meet interest payments on these and other loans, the trust company drew on other units through the Group. In the first quarter of 1932, for example, the Guardian National Bank of Commerce paid a $200,000 dividend, although it lost approximately $1.2 million that same year. Another unit paid out 24.7 percent of its capital for the 1931 dividend.[15] Examiners thought these payments excessive, unwarranted, and probably illegal in the face of "serious conditions"; they also criticized real estate loans which composed too great a portion of the holdings of many banks. Actual losses and "doubtful items" on ledgers far exceeded listed losses; in one case *questionable* loans alone ($18,692,876.22) surpassed the entire capital funds of the bank ($17,945,433.93).[16] Occasionally unit banks used technicalities to mask their true conditions: a critic accused Guardian's members of "barefaced juggling and shifting about of funds from bank to bank, on the eve of an expected examination, so that banks really heavily in debt could make fictitious show of being wholly out of debt." One bank would borrow from another; the lender would then deposit a like amount in the debtor bank; and the bill payable would be balanced on the borrower's accounts.[17]

The Detroit Bankers Company employed the same manipulations even more spectacularly than Guardian. Promising its stockholders a 17 percent return, it paid 17 percent throughout 1930 and 1931, despite depression and contracting values, by increasing demands on its units. In the years 1925–1929, before it joined the group, the First National Bank averaged $975,000 in dividends per year; as a group member it paid out $1,137,000 in 1930, $4,650,000

15. SEP, pp. 4252, 4313, 4677–85; Pecora, *Wall Street*, pp. 247–48.
16. SEP, pp. 4506–17, 4619–20. This evidence rested on examinations of the Guardian National Bank of Commerce in May and November 1932.
17. Pecora, *Wall Street*, p. 243. For sample balance sheets see Howard Ralph Neville, *The Detroit Banking Collapse of 1933* (East Lansing: Bureau of Business and Economic Research, Michigan State University, 1960), p. 34.

in 1931, and $2,800,000 in 1932, when, in the opinion of the chief national bank examiner, "the First National Bank of Detroit was not rotten—it was putrid."[18]

Detroit's banks also sought sustaining loans to survive the depression. The National Credit Corporation and its Michigan Association offered little help, and borrowers hesitated to pay the 5 percent interest asked by the Reconstruction Finance Corporation. When other sources dried up, however, the banks were forced to turn to the RFC. In June 1932, the Union Guardian Trust Company, fearing overwhelming withdrawals, asked the RFC for $28 million to liquidate its entire deposit liability. As a temporary stopgap the RFC loaned $8,733,000 and strongly recommended that Union Guardian reorganize its credit structure. The trust company borrowed another $3.5 million from the Fords later in the year and again approached the RFC but did not change its policies.[19]

With such loans the Detroit banks lasted through 1932 and felt confident about 1933. Even difficulties in Nevada, Maryland, Ohio, Pennsylvania, and Louisiana caused no alarm in Michigan. Despite unkind words about "banksters" from Father Coughlin, the "radio priest," and the Detroit Times's suspicions about certain tax arrangements within Guardian,[20] the opening of the new year carried no fear of a banking crisis.

Unknown to the public, however, the asset position of the Guardian Group had deteriorated dangerously. By January 15, 1933, the Guardian National Bank of Commerce and the Union Guardian Trust Company, two of its largest members, had reached the point where board chairman Kanzler said, "We have to get considerably more money, or the whole group is going to collapse." During the preceding year, the RFC had urged the trust company to correct the causes of its problems. Now its officers hoped to get the support of

18. SEP, pp. 5057–5850 passim; Pecora, COHC, pp. 863–75; John T. Flynn, "Michigan Magic," Harper's Magazine 168 (Dec. 1932): 1–11.

19. SEP, pp. 5561–71, 4738, 4809–15; Jones, Fifty Billion Dollars, pp. 58–59; Timmons, Jones, pp. 179–80; Upham and Lamke, Closed and Distressed Banks, pp. 151–55.

20. Albert E. Date to William Woodin, 6 Apr. 1933, U. S., Department of the Treasury, Office of the Comptroller of the Currency, Banking Emergency Records, General Correspondence, NA: RG 101, box 4.

chief national bank examiner Alfred P. Leyburn on an application for a new RFC loan to the entire group. As inducement, they promised that Henry Ford would not remove his $7.5 million in deposits; thus their $14 million deficit would stand at a mere $6.5 million. Edsel Ford later testified that he had agreed to the freezing of deposits.[21]

Nine days later, at the annual stockholders' meeting, Kanzler claimed that the Guardian banks enjoyed greater liquidity than any group in the entire state and that only one unit had lost ground during the year. His report dealt only with the members, however; nowhere did he admit that the holding company had operated at a loss in 1932. (Kanzler later reasoned that such information was irrelevant and misleading.[22]) He left for Washington the next day to offer the RFC a plan which included subordination of the Ford deposits and certain group-owned assets; Union Guardian Trust would use the proceeds from the loan to pay all deposits in full.[23]

The RFC sent John Keown McKee, its chief examiner in charge of bank reorganization, to Detroit to "sift" the bank's portfolio for "good collateral." McKee knew before leaving Washington that examiners had rated the unit "embarrassing," and he concluded that the 1932 loans were as much as the collateral could sustain. Yet the RFC had already agreed to another loan of $37,720,000 if the Group could raise $3,457,000 elsewhere.[24] Therefore, McKee went to Detroit less to examine collateral than to try to find sufficient backing to support the loan. He took with him the Guardian officers' statement of their requirements and collateral to serve as a "factual basis" for his calculations. McKee estimated that the net face value and real estate equities submitted actually were worth about $88 million carrying (face) value; their liquidating value (the amount at which they would probably sell) was about $20 million; and their loan value (the amount which might be borrowed against them) was approximately $17 million.[25]

On January 27 in conference with Kanzler, Lord, Longley, and Leyburn, McKee learned that the officers wanted to keep Union

21. SEP, pp. 4517, 4638–39, 4687, 4692.
22. Ibid., pp. 4543–53.
23. Ibid.
24. Jones, *Fifty Billion Dollars*, p. 59; SEP, pp. 4724, 4552–55.
25. SEP, pp. 4724–38, 4755.

Guardian Trust open because of its size and earning power. They proposed a chainlike arrangement whereby the trust company would buy up undesirable assets from other shaky banks in the organization and then discharge its full liability with RFC money. McKee felt that this unit could not carry such a burden; instead he suggested a new mortgage loan company to take over assets of units whose mortgage loans exceeded 50 percent of their portfolios. These banks could subscribe to the $5 million capital of the new company. Both Guardian officers and RFC officials agreed to the plan, and a dozen examiners began the night-and-day job of evaluating collateral in time for formal submission of the application on February 6. On a total $64,870,000 face value of assets, the RFC agreed to lend $37,762,000, the full liquidating value. McKee felt that the evaluation had been as liberal as anywhere else in the country.[26]

At the February 6 meeting of the board of directors of the RFC, McKee stated flatly that the Union Guardian Trust Company was insolvent. It had deposit liabilities of $20.5 million and free assets with a face value of $12 million (of which only $7,940,000 was available to pledge for a loan). Without aid, the trust company would close, bringing down the entire Guardian Group and probably all of Michigan; a loan of $65 million could save it. McKee then presented the mortgage company scheme: new cash capital of $5 million would purchase assets from the units, which would be pledged to the RFC for a loan of $47 million. Since the RFC had already agreed to another loan of $18 million, Guardian's problems would be solved. For the total $65 million loan, however, the collateral which Guardian offered would support only $35 million, according to McKee. Leyburn corroborated McKee's report, particularly the sensitive relationship between the unit banks, the group, the state, and possibly the entire nation. Representatives of the Guardian Group agreed, admitted the inadequacy of their assets, and now doubted whether they could even deliver the Ford subordination. Kanzler said that he personally doubted the justice of asking further sacrifices of large depositors (read Ford) who had been so generous in the past three years.[27]

26. SEP, pp. 4723–26, 4740–42.
27. Reconstruction Finance Corporation, Minutes, 6 Feb. 1933, NA: RG 234; SEP, pp. 4727–29, 4561–63.

This loan application put the RFC in an awkward position. Federal law prohibited any but fully secured loans. Moreover, the RFC still reeled from an attack in a magazine article by John T. Flynn, who hinted that earlier Michigan loans had been obtained through the "influence" of Secretary of Commerce Roy D. Chapin, a former executive of the Hudson Motor Company.[28] "Why," thought the RFC directors, "should we bail out Mr. Ford?"[29] One disgruntled Michigan banker later charged that Secretary of the Treasury Mills and RFC board member Jesse Jones were biased against the Michigan banks because of their own Wall Street affiliations, and insinuated that Wall Street was plotting to take over Michigan banking.[30] At least so far as Jones is concerned the accusation seems unwarranted, since at the time of his appointment to the RFC Jones noted strongly "that most of our country lies west of the Hudson River, and none of it east of the Atlantic Ocean."[31]

These objections notwithstanding, the RFC board agreed tentatively to the mortgage company plan, but stipulated that the Guardian Group must raise $5 million for the new institution and find enough local cash or subordination of deposits to bring its liabilities down to where its assets would support the RFC loan.[32]

New attacks handicapped the Detroit bankers as they searched for funds. Father Coughlin renewed his damnations of bankers and bank reform proposals, slurring the distinction between international investment bankers and local commercial bankers, and charging that Detroit's financial leaders had deliberately brought on a money panic.[33] Jesse Jones noted the effect: "As regularly as Monday morning business hours followed these Sunday afternoon orations," he said, "the Michigan bankers noticed an increasing amount of withdrawals by small depositors."[34]

28. Flynn, "Michigan Magic," pp. 1–11.
29. SEP, p. 4627.
30. Orla Benedict Taylor, "The Detroit Banking Tragedy of 1933," typescript essay, in Taylor Papers, Michigan Historical Collections, University of Michigan, p. 17.
31. Jones, *Fifty Billion Dollars*, pp. 512–14.
32. RFC, Minutes, 6 Feb. 1933, NA: RG 234.
33 Charles E. Coughlin, *Driving out the Money Changers* (Detroit: Shrine of the Little Flower, 1933), pp. 5–13, 23–32, 48, 70; Donald W. Sweeney to Wilson W. Mills, 31 Jan. 1933, quoted in SEP, pp. 5551–52.
34. Jones, *Fifty Billion Dollars*, p. 59.

At the same time, millionaire industrialist Henry Ford and millionaire Senator James Couzens resurrected a long-standing feud which now involved the bankers. Ford and Couzens had begun their association a generation earlier when Couzens invested his life savings in the infant Ford Motor Company and became its general manager. They also went into the banking business together; Couzens boasted of running their Highland Park State Bank "from across the street, in my office of the Ford plant." By 1912, however, they had drifted apart and finally split because of Ford's World War I pacifism. Ford bought out Couzens's interest in the company for $29,308,857.80 and became sole owner. Couzens turned to politics and entered the United States Senate in 1922, where he remained for fourteen years. The two former partners quarrelled periodically, usually over political issues such as Ford's offer to take over the government's Muscle Shoals project in the 1920s.[35] When they met again in 1933, each believed that the other should have the Detroit banks.

Couzens did not know that Guardian intended to apply for an RFC loan. The Group's representatives had not requested his support and asked RFC officials not to tell him of their problems. After the Flynn article, perhaps they feared that his endorsement might do more political harm than good; or possibly they knew the senator would deliver a stern lecture on sound banking.[36] Couzens had probably heard about the application as a member of the Senate Banking and Currency Committee (the RFC usually consulted members whose home constituencies had appealed for funds) and he may have felt neglected, receiving such news at secondhand.[37] Jesse Jones and Harvey Couch of the RFC also mentioned the Detroit banking situation during conversations about railroad

35. James Couzens, testimony before grand jury investigation held before Judge Harry B. Keidan, 22 Aug. 1933, reported in Detroit newspapers, 22, 23 Aug. 1933. (The original transcript of these hearings was destroyed by fire; newspaper coverage was complete, however.) Arthur J. Lacy, oral history interview, in Lacy Papers, Michigan Historical Collections, University of Michigan, pp. 24–27; Allan Nevins and Frank Ernest Hill, *Ford: Decline and Rebirth, 1933–1962* (New York: Scribner's, 1962), p. 13; Barnard, *Independent Man*, pp. 3–8, 78–80, 97–98, 158–87; Malcolm W. Bingay, *Detroit Is My Own Home Town* (Indianapolis: Bobbs-Merrill, 1946), pp. 126–28.

36. Wilson W. Mills, interview with Harry Barnard, 1941, cited in Barnard, *Independent Man*, p. 222; SEP, pp. 4876–77.

37. Nevins and Hill, *Ford*, p. 13.

loans on February 3 and 4; both men told Couzens that the RFC could not legally authorize the necessary loan. The senator agreed and told Jones that "he was not in favor of trying to save any banks that were not sound and solvent."[38] Finally, on February 8 and 9, two Guardian men explained to Couzens that they had asked no government official to participate in their loan request because they feared charges of political influence; Couzens told them they had behaved properly, but did not encourage their hopes for actually receiving the loan.[39] Since Couzens was the senior senator from Michigan and a severe critic of earlier RFC loans, especially the Dawes fiasco, his opposition could be crucial to Guardian's chances.

All efforts now shifted to convincing Henry Ford to freeze his deposits. The RFC would not lend on inadequate security, nor would Governor Comstock deposit state funds in banks which could not grant "any surety or bond that was worth anything."[40] Only Ford's agreement to leave his deposits untouched could influence other large depositors to do the same and insure sufficient reserves to meet demands of smaller depositors. On February 10, when Edsel Ford told Treasury and RFC officials that he could not make a commitment for his father, Charles Miller of the RFC suggested that President Hoover might call the elder Ford to urge cooperation.[41]

The president had already begun to fight for Detroit. At a White House meeting on Thursday, February 9, Hoover reviewed the banking situation with Ogden Mills, Arthur Ballantine, Roy Chapin, Charles Miller, and Michigan Senators Couzens and Arthur Vandenberg. "All present agreed that the trust company would have to be supported by voluntary contributions to merit RFC aid," according to Vandenberg.[42] Neither senator objected when Miller made a strong case against an immediate loan; Couzens particularly believed such a grant illegal and promised to "denounce from the housetops" any loan made without absolute security. As an alterna-

38. John Carson to James Couzens, 6 Sept. 1933; Couzens to Carson, 7 Sept. 1933; Carson to Couzens, 15 Sept. 1933–all in Couzens Papers, Library of Congress, box 99; Couzens, testimony before Keidan grand jury, *Detroit News*, 17 Aug. 1933; Couzens, notebook, 7 Feb. 1933, cited in Barnard, *Independent Man*, p. 222; Jones, *Fifty Billion Dollars*, pp. 60–61.
39. SEP, pp. 4876–77; Barnard, *Independent Man*, p. 224.
40. *Detroit News*, 7 Feb. 1934.
41. SEP, pp. 4694, 4627.
42. *Detroit News*, 25 Aug. 1933.

tive, Hoover had obtained agreement from Henry Ford not to touch his $7.5 million and from the General Motors and Chrysler companies to deposit $1 million each in the bank to back an RFC loan. When Hoover asked Couzens for another $1 million, however, the senator "professed to be astonished and indignant."[43] Couzens claimed that the Guardian Group was Henry Ford's responsibility and did not feel that either he or the federal government should advance money to support Ford. He added that Ford was bluffing and would come to the rescue eventually.[44] Arthur Krock of the *New York Times* recalled that he, too, had suggested a pool to Senator Couzens and was refused for the same reasons Hoover stated. "Mr. Ford tells me that if you will put up ten million dollars, he will, to save the situation in Detroit," Krock said. Couzens countered, "He is just showing off. I could put it up easily, but he wouldn't if I did, because he is a miser."[45] Unable to understand this lack of cooperation, Hoover decided to switch operations to Detroit. Ballantine and Chapin would leave the next day to "take the situation up with the officers of the bank there, and be in communication with the RFC officials here, and see whether a practicable plan could not be devised and put into effect."[46] They would have forty-five hours—from bank closing at noon on Saturday, February 11, until reopening at 9 a.m. on Tuesday, February 14, after the Lincoln's birthday holiday—to do what no one else had been able to do.

In Detroit the two federal officers found a situation which chief examiner Leyburn called "a hell of a mess."[47] As soon as the banks closed on Saturday, they began two-and-a-half days of conferences with Kanzler, Longley, Lord, and Bodman of the Guardian Group, and McKee of the RFC. After spending all of Saturday looking fruitlessly for money, Ballantine and Chapin concluded that the mortgage company plan offered the only possible solution and that

43. Hoover, *Memoirs*, 3:206–07; Jones, *Fifty Billion Dollars*, pp. 59–60; Hoover to Harry S. Toy, quoted in *Detroit News*, 23 Aug. 1933; John Carson to Harry Barnard, 25 Oct. 1941, cited in Barnard, *Independent Man*, p. 224; *Detroit News*, 20 June 1933.

44. President Hoover made a memorandum of these comments at the conclusion of the meeting; Roy Chapin repeated the "log" entry in another memorandum relative to the grand jury investigation, 2 Oct. 1933, Chapin Papers, Michigan Historical Collections, University of Michigan, v. 98.

45. Krock, COHC, pp. 15–16.

46. SEP, p. 5793.

47. *Detroit Free Press*, 16 Aug. 1933.

Henry Ford held the key to its success. The RFC agreed; although it would not make an immediate loan, it urged John McKee to co-operate in the mortgage company scheme so long as there was any hope of securing the necessary funds in Detroit. At this point, the RFC was considering a $37,720,000 loan secured by $62,253,000 (face value) collateral, which included a loan of $15 million on $31 million already approved. On February 11, Jesse Jones moved that the board make the full loan, but his motion was voted down; the board decided to wait.[48] At a breakfast meeting in Washington, Walter P. Chrysler of Chrysler Motors and Alfred P. Sloan, Jr., of General Motors renewed their million-dollar pledges to President Hoover because they believed that suspension of Union Guardian might precipitate a general panic.[49]

New York and Chicago bankers joined the conference on Sunday.[50] None of the participants recalled who had invited the outsiders; McKee assumed that "someone" had telephoned Chicago and New York on Saturday. At least one banker was present at the request of the government; Ogden Mills later revealed that he had asked George W. Davison of New York's Central Hanover Bank and Trust Company to go to Detroit.[51]

Sunday's conversations remained focused on the subordination of deposits. General Motors, Chrysler, and Hudson Stores agreed to cooperate, on condition that Ford also freeze his holdings, but Ford made it clear that he would not come into the pool.[52] Even if the others had been willing to act without Ford, their deposits would not have made up the $6.5 million needed in addition to his $7.5 million. From Detroit, Ballantine reported to a special RFC meeting that

48. RFC, Minutes, 11 Feb. 1933, NA: RG 234; SEP, pp. 5793–95, 4732–35.

49. SEP, p. 4729; Jones, *Fifty Billion Dollars*, p. 61; Timmons, *Jones*, pp. 181–82; Taylor, "Detroit Tragedy," p. 22.

50. The new arrivals included Melvin A. Traylor, chairman of the First National Bank of Chicago, and his executive vice-president, Edward Eagle Brown; Abner J. Stillwell, vice-president of the Continental Illinois National Bank and Trust Company; E. A. Potter, Jr., vice-president of the Guaranty Trust Company of New York; S. Sloan Colt, president of the Bankers Trust Company of New York; George W. Davidson, chairman of the Central Hanover Bank and Trust Company of New York; Donaldson Brown, vice-president and chairman of the finance committee of General Motors; B. E. Hutchinson of the Chrysler Corporation, and later Mr. Chrysler himself on his return from Washington. SEP, pp. 4732–35; Jones, *Fifty Billion Dollars*, p. 63.

51. Ogden L. Mills to W. G. Zeamer of *Detroit Times*, 26 June 1933, in Mills Papers, box 42.

52. SEP, pp. 5795, 4735–37.

the Guardian Group had obtained pledges of only $825,000, with no hope of raising more than $1 million. Consequently, the RFC again postponed action "until the Guardian Group had further opportunity to raise the necessary amount."[53]

Until February 11, no one informed any member of the Detroit Bankers Company of Guardian's perilous condition. On that day, Leyburn and the Guardian officers told Wilson W. Mills, president of the First National Bank, that Union Guardian would probably fail and take the Guardian National Bank of Commerce down with it. Mills expected runs on his bank following these suspensions. He therefore asked McKee to approve an RFC loan of $100 million (the bank had ample assets) to bring his institution to better than 40 percent liquidity. RFC examiners, finding the collateral satisfactory, foresaw no difficulty and recommended a loan; but the RFC board refused the application without explanation.

An already bleak Monday morning dimmed perceptibly when the *Detroit News* carried an interview with Senator Couzens repeating his earlier criticisms of RFC loans. As a progressive he had favored a more direct loan policy and now felt that the federal government must either support the debt structure for all the citizens or stop the rescue of any of them. Couzens added that he saw no reason to rescue unsound banks.[54] The senator had said the same thing earlier to government officials, but publication at this moment was especially damaging. At least one person agreed with Couzens, however. Told of the statement, Henry Ford commented, "For once in his life, Jim Couzens is right."[55]

Hoover in desperation urged the RFC to act. Calling in chairman Atlee Pomerene, he begged for immediate announcement of *some* plan. Compared with the probable effects of a banking collapse in Detroit, the president felt that the sums involved in emergency loans were insignificant.[56] Before leaving for New York to make his Lincoln Day address, Hoover telephoned Henry Ford again, this time to arrange an appointment for Ballantine and Chapin to make a last plea for subordination. Ford agreed to see them, but nothing more.

53. RFC, Minutes, 12 Feb. 1933, NA: RG 234.
54. *Detroit News*, 13 Feb. 1933.
55. Jones, *Fifty Billion Dollars*, pp. 63–64; Timmons, *Jones*, p. 182.
56. Sullivan, *Prelude to Panic*, p. 86.

At Ford's Dearborn offices, Chapin and Ballantine first encountered Edsel Ford. He was polite but warned at the outset that he could not agree to anything they had to propose. Young Ford could not understand the legal restrictions on loans; why could the RFC not advance that particular sum when it had loaned much larger amounts, he argued.

The government men had even less success with his father. Henry Ford told them that he was aware of the plan to save the trust company and would be glad to discuss the situation, although he would not cooperate. If he had ever given the impression that he would freeze his deposits, Ford said, "he had not fully understood it," and in any case, "he had changed his mind."

As Ballantine painted a grim picture of the cumulative effect of a Union Guardian Trust collapse, Ford became very interested in the First National. Not only would he not aid Guardian's trust company, he now promised that if it failed he would immediately withdraw his full deposit from the First, probably bringing that bank down as well; Ford authorized Ballantine to report his position to the RFC and remained adamant even when Ballantine dwelt on the inevitable sufferings of three million persons, paralysis of the state's business, and the ultimate extension of the banking crisis to other states. How, asked Ford, could the government allow such a disaster to occur for the sake of a few millions? He refused to accept Ballantine's reasoning that the government was impotent until Ford agreed to the subordination, without which there could be no rescue plan. The manufacturer felt that neither Ballantine nor Chapin understood the situation; he charged that the "plan came from sources which they did not know about," that it was part of the same conspiracy which had led to a strike at the Briggs plant, that his competitors or "people back of them" wanted to destroy his business. Rather, the country needed "a general cleaning up process," and "he did not care how soon it came about." He "still felt young," Ford said, and could begin again if purchase contracts for automobiles fell off. As he showed his guests out, he offered his only terms: fully backed endorsed notes for his trust deposits.

Back at Guardian headquarters, Chapin and Ballantine reported the Ford interview to the local and visiting bankers. Melvin Traylor, suggested they tell Ford that many banks might have to go on a clearinghouse certificate basis which would stifle the automobile business. When Ballantine telephoned this information, he also volunteered the thought that the Ford Motor Company might suffer from adverse public opinion if Ford did not ally himself with rescue efforts. Again, Ford refused. That decision, said Ballantine, "appeared to entirely end the hope of any support for the plan to save the trust company by Mr. Ford."[57]

If the Ford interview had no positive results in saving the Union Guardian Trust Company, it did add another negative dimension. Ford's threat to withdraw his full deposit from the First National endangered a second major bank and with it the second great banking group in Detroit. With over $20 million in the combined Ford accounts, Ford was the First's largest depositor.[58] Consequently, Wilson W. Mills renewed his efforts for an RFC loan, again unsuccessfully. He also wasted his luncheon meeting trying to convince Ford to leave his money where it was.[59] In 1907, Ford had told Couzens, "I am going to built a vault and take our money out of the banks and put it in the vault, so that we can pay our men in cash."[60] Twenty-six years had not changed his mind on liquidity.

When word reached Washington of Ford's final refusal to freeze his Guardian deposit and his threat against the First, alternatives narrowed. A loan was impossible without him, and both Detroit bankers and government officials had to face the probability of the banks' closing. A joint RFC-Federal Reserve Board meeting considered contingency programs. Most of the Federal Reserve Board favored a one-week moratorium on all banking in the state of Michigan, but Acting Comptroller of the Currency F. Gloyd Awalt vigorously opposed a banking holiday on the ground that it "could not be localized, but that it would extend to other states, and that it would mean a general crash." Instead, Awalt, supported by Adolph Miller of the Federal Reserve Board, proposed that the Michigan

---

57. Arthur A. Ballantine and Roy D. Chapin, "Statement of interview with Mr. Henry Ford," 13 Feb. 1933, Comptroller's files, NA: RG 101, box 6; SEP, pp. 4694–95, 5795–97; Ballantine, "When All the Banks Closed," p. 136.

58. Memorandum, Joseph M. Dodge Papers, banking box 1, Burton Historical Collection, Detroit Public Library.

59. Jones, *Fifty Billion Dollars*, pp. 62–63; Timmons, *Jones*, pp. 182–83.

60. Couzens, interview with Judge J. H. Neil, 27 July 1926, cited in Barnard, *Independent Man*, p. 81.

banks convert to a clearinghouse certificate basis. Rather than do business in cash, they could issue negotiable scrip, backed by the assets in their banks; this "money" would substitute for cash in meeting withdrawals and clearing checks. But from Detroit, Ballantine reported that there was not enough time left to put the plan into effect.[61]

In one last desperate attempt to win Ford, at eight o'clock on Monday evening, February 13, RFC officials convinced Couzens to send a telephone message to his old partner via Longley of the Guardian. Reversing position, Couzens now offered to put up half of the collateral to cover an RFC loan to the trust company if Ford would advance the other half. Ford said no.[62]

At ten o'clock that night, the Detroit bankers decided that they must now consult the governor to "consider the possibility" of a statewide banking holiday "for a sufficient length of time to enable them to formulate and complete the details of some reorganization plan." Informed of this move, the RFC suspended all earlier approvals of loans to Guardian.[63] Now the issue rested completely with Detroit. If the banks were not to be gutted by runs, they would have to remain closed on Tuesday morning. No one questioned their solvency, but they obviously lacked enough liquid assets to meet the heavy withdrawals which would come as soon as they opened. Moreover, if the banks did conduct business on Tuesday, that very act might favor their larger and more diligent creditors over smaller depositors and prevent rebuilding the banks.[64]

Governor William A. Comstock and his adviser, Arthur Lacy, arrived in Detroit in the midst of these deliberations. As the bankers reviewed their situation, they made it clear that they wanted the governor to close all Michigan banks to give them an opportunity to work out a plan for reopening Detroit, thus relieving pressure on outside instituitons. In addition, they desired the legislature, then in session at Lansing, to give them the protection of state law.[65] Kanz-

---

61. RFC, Minutes, 13 Feb. 1933, 11 a.m., NA: RG 234; Hamlin, Diary, 13 Feb. 1933; SEP, pp. 5799, 5834–44.

62. Couzens testimony before Keidan grand jury, 17 Aug. 1933, confirmed by Longley, 15 Sept. 1933, *Detroit Free Press*, 18 Aug., 16 Sept. 1933.

63. RFC, Minutes, 13 Feb. 1933, 6:15 p.m., NA: RG 234.

64. SEP, pp. 5800–5801.

65. Ibid., pp. 5798–99, 4628–30, 5656.

ler, Ballantine, McKee, Leyburn, and Chapin unanimously urged the governor to make the proclamation, and State Banking Commissioner Rudolph E. Reichert approved the holiday idea by telephone. It was, he said, "the only thing to do under the circumstances."[66]

The governor, understandably, was hesitant to accept responsibility for so extreme an action; he had to be convinced that he possessed authority to keep the banks closed. In particular, he asked for a formal application from the United States Treasury Department and the Federal Reserve banks. Eugene M. Stevens, Federal Reserve agent for the Seventh District, told Comstock that he had no power to make such a request on behalf of the Reserve but "would offer no objection." John McKee made the same point for the RFC, saying that Comstock "would have to sign the proclamation on his own responsibility."[67] Since the appeal had to come from someone, John C. Hicks, president of the Michigan Bankers' Association, and Robert O. Lord, president of the Detroit Clearing House Association, drafted a letter which they handed to the governor. In view of the "acute financial emergency," they asked for a "public holiday to be observed by Banks, Trust Companies, and other financial institutions" for eight days beginning February 14; the letter specified that they took this step only after consultation with national and state banking authorities, representatives of the United States Treasury Department, the State Banking Department, the Federal Reserve Bank, the Reconstruction Finance Corporation, and the United States secretary of commerce.[68] Still uncertain, Comstock and Lacy left the meeting shortly after midnight to take a walk and discuss the situation. Lacy recalled later that they "dropped into a hot dog stand for a hot dog." Comstock asked advice and Lacy "told him that everybody at the meeting was agreed that a bank holiday was imperative and that if we didn't have one it would cause a nation-wide banking collapse."[69] Lacy recalled that Comstock had asked his advice and he had said, "Bill, I think it is the only thing you can do" in light of the unanimous requests. Lacy later qualified

66. Testimony before Keidan grand jury, *Detroit News*, 15, 16 June 1933.
67. SEP, pp. 5815, 4738–39.
68. Hicks and Lord to Comstock, 14 Feb. 1933, in RFC Files, NA: RG 234, box 3, part 3.
69. Lacy testimony before Keidan grand jury, 19 Aug. 1933, *Detroit Times*, 29 Aug. 1933.

his advice, however, claiming that he favored a holiday only because he assumed that it would be temporary. Otherwise, he would have kept the banks open and "when Mr. Ford came for his deposits, I wouldn't have given him a nickel," on the grounds that his withdrawal would give him preference by taking out money that should be available to other depositors as well."[70] Returning to the anxious bankers, Comstock agreed to close the banks.

Thus at 1:32 on Tuesday morning, February 14, Governor Comstock signed a proclamation calling for a banking holiday in the state of Michigan from that day through Tuesday, February 21. His statement accompanying the decree repeated the arguments of the Hicks-Lord letter. By this action the governor closed 550 national and state banks, representing $1.5 billion belonging to 900,000 depositors.[71]

Not everyone welcomed the moratorium solution. President Hoover had gone to bed on February 13 thinking that his telephone call to get "Ford back on the track" had saved Detroit. Apologists for Hoover later claimed that Comstock issued his proclamation without consultation with either the White House or the Treasury, "cutting the ground from under the Washington rescue plans." But since federal officials were with the governor when he signed the decree, and since neither Washington nor Detroit had any program to offer at that late date, these criticisms seem weak. Nor did Hoover's secretary have much evidence for his claim that "the governor of that state lost his head; if he had not become panicky, that catastrophe would have been avoided."[72] On the other hand, Governor Comstock was vulnerable in one area. Technically, his proclamation was illegal, since he sealed not only state-chartered institutions over which he had authority but national banks as well. The latter institutions came under the jurisdiction of the federal Comptroller of the Currency; only he could order them closed. In the Michigan situation, however, Acting Comptroller Awalt chose to take no action, allowing the governor's decree to cover all banks within the state.

70. Lacy Papers, pp. 43–47.
71. *Detroit Free Press*, 14 Feb. 1933; *Detroit News*, 14 Feb. 1933; *Detroit Times*, 14 Feb. 1933; *New York Times*, 14, 15 Feb. 1933; *Commercial and Financial Chronicle* 136 (18 Feb. 1933): 149–50.
72. Jones, *Fifty Billion Dollars*, p. 65; Sullivan, *Prelude to Panic*, p. 86; Joslin, *Hoover Off the Record*, p. 363.

The Michigan closing shocked the nation and probably contributed materially to the national banking collapse three weeks later. A moratorium in itself might not have had that result; the action of February 14 left options open. If the bankers and federal agents could find a plan to reorganize and reopen the Detroit banks, the same program might be applied elsewhere, thus avoiding a nationwide collapse. If not, the financial consequences of the Michigan denouement, plus the blow to public morale, could bring the whole country down.

While public officials issued encouraging statements,[73] the state legislature met at Lansing to legitimate the holiday. They commended Governor Comstock for "courageous statesmanship" in avoiding "one of the greatest financial crashes in the history of the country." Although the legislators did not pass a general law authorizing such emergency declarations until April 7, they did act against time (it usually took twelve days to pass a bill) to legalize the holiday retroactively on February 20, one day before it expired.[74]

Meanwhile, as a first step to free funds, the Detroit Clearing House ordered the release of 5 percent of depositors' net balances as of February 11; all banks and branches would make change, and safe deposit departments would maintain regular hours. Armored trucks sped currency from New York and Chicago; $40 million arrived by midnight on the fourteenth. In cooperation, the public utilities commissioner asked for extensions on current bills, and life insurance companies arranged to accept checks as conditional payment of premiums.[75]

As soon as he heard of the holiday, President Hoover met with Treasury Secretary Mills, Federal Reserve Governor Meyer, and Governor Harrison of the New York Federal Reserve Bank.[76]

73. *New York Times*, 15 Feb. 1933.

74. *Detroit Free Press*, 15 Feb. 1933; Michigan Statutes Annotated, Act 47, vol. 17 (1933): 59; James B. Alley to Stanley Reed , 21 Feb. 1933, RFC Files, NA: RG 234, box 3, part 3; *New York Times*, 18, 21 Feb. 1933; *Commercial and Financial Chronicle* 126 (18 Feb. 1933): 1150. A full chronology of emergency banking measures after 14 Feb. 1933 may be found in D. Maitland Irwin Papers, Michigan Historical Collections, University of Michigan.

75. *New York Times*, 15 Feb. 1933.

76. Secretary of State Henry Stimson recorded that the president claimed he had "saved weak spots, such as Memphis, St. Louis, Kansas City, and New Orleans. But," said Stimson, "now it had come in Detroit, and the Lord only knows how far it will go." Diary, Stimson Papers, Yale University, 15 Feb. 1933. How

To save Michigan, Hoover proposed to issue scrip; each bank could offer its depositors certificates in proportion to its good assets. But the Federal Reserve banks wanted nothing to do with such a plan. Both Meyer and Harrison protested that it would bring the bad odor of Detroit onto the Federal Reserve System; Meyer called the scheme "just a bunch of nonsense."

Instead, Meyer and Harrison urged the "New York Plan" in which banks could reopen immediately on the basis of their liquid assets, with each depositor receiving a prorated share. Slow assets could be held for eventual liquidation and distribution when market conditions improved.[77] But Senator Joseph T. Robinson, Democratic floor leader, warned the president that discussion of such a bill in Congress might excite a nationwide panic. Moreover, enabling legislation could not pass both federal and state legislatures before the Michigan holiday expired, and the bill could become a vehicle for "all kinds of bad amendments."[78]

To get around the legislative impasse, Senator Couzens introduced a joint resolution in Congress on February 21, empowering the Comptroller of the Currency to extend to national banks any privileges granted to state banks by their respective state legislatures. If Michigan, or any other state, could enact laws providing for segregation of fluid and frozen assets, national banks could legally participate. Thus, any plan that could be worked out would apply to all banks in the state. President Hoover signed the Couzens resolution of February 25.[79]

Meanwhile, Michigan authorities were still trying to free money. The governor, attorney general, and banking commissioner petitioned the president for release of the 12 percent reserves deposited by Michigan state and national banks in Federal Reserve banks. "Release of these funds," they said, "will immediately result in opening of banks and will save the business institutions and the public of Michigan from tremendous loss and inconvenience." The United States attorney general, however, told Hoover that such pay-

---

far was indicated by reports from Cleveland; officials there informed the Federal Reserve Board, the White House, and the RFC that they might not survive the week. Sullivan, *Prelude to Panic*, p. 90.

77. Meyer, COHC, pp. 678–80; Colt and Keith, *28 Days*, pp. 10–11.
78. Stimson, Diary, 15, 17 Feb. 1933; *New York Times*, 16 Feb. 1933.
79. *New York Times*, 16–26 Feb. 1933.

ment would give Michigan undue access to funds which should be equally available to all banks. The plan died there. And a later request for release of these funds did not even reach the attorney general.[80]

The Michigan banks might still reopen by the end of the holiday, however. Some experts, such as George W. Davison of the New York Clearing House, continued to urge scrip[81] but most preferred cash arrangements. Large depositors, such as Sloan and Chrysler, insisted that more money be made available for the benefit of industry.[82]

At a meeting at the Detroit Club on the evening of February 14, Detroit bankers began to consider a new bank to take over the usable assets of the decaying institutions, rather than reopen the old banks. When John McKee of the RFC proposed this replacement as the only workable solution, Kanzler and Longley of Guardian denied the necessity of superseding the established banks. Sloan and Chrysler of the motor companies, however, were clearly interested;[83] so were the New York banks. In addition to Sloan, Chrysler, Kanzler, and Longley, those present included several Chrysler vice-presidents, other Guardian officers, and some Ford employees, in addition to Mayor Frank Murphy of Detroit, who had called the meeting, and his corporation counsel and police commissioner. No representative of the First National Bank was invited.

Two days later, national bank examiner Leyburn suggested for the first time that the First National was not solvent (which he later defined as absolutely liquid). Davison then visited the governing committee of the First National Bank and suggested that they, too, take their liquid assets and open a new bank to make gradual payments to the old depositors. Later, when the directors approached Davison for fuller discussion, they found him with the Chrysler and General Motors officers and attorneys, and concluded that it would be useless to talk further. Believing that they were in

80. William A. Comstock, Patrick O'Brien, and Rudolph Reichert to Hoover, 26 Feb. 1933, Comptroller's Files, NA: RG 101, box 6; William D. Mitchell to Hoover, 28 Feb. 1933, Secretary's Correspondence, NA (Suitland); H. E. Hackney to Arthur A. Ballantine, 17 Mar. 1933, Comptroller's Files, NA: RG 101, box 6.
81. Sullivan, *Prelude to Panic*, p. 90; Colt and Keith, *28 Days*, pp. 13–15.
82. *New York Times*, 17 Feb. 1933.
83. Taylor, "Detroit Tragedy," pp. 34–35.

danger of being taken over by New York, the bank's officers rejected the whole proposal as "unthinkable."[84]

First National hoped to work out its survival independently. At the board meeting of February 19, chairman Wilson Mills and Comptroller Awalt outlined the alternatives: the bank could obtain a state charter and do business under the lesser restrictions of the state banking law, or consolidate with other banks into one or two new institutions, or seek huge loans and establish a new national bank to liquidate the old institution. The board decided on the last course and tried for a loan under the Glass-Steagall Act of February 1932. Because not all of its eligible paper had yet been exhausted and it could not get another bank to cosign the loan, First National's application failed. The officers then decided that they could reopen on a 50 percent basis at the end of the holiday with loans from the Federal Reserve Bank at Chicago, the RFC, and correspondent banks in New York. Directors at the Chicago Reserve Bank were anxious to do everything possible to help in the emergency but questioned whether they could get a valid lien on collateral offered by First National for the advance. Moreover, they were not confident that the bank would reopen; now they challenged more than its liquidity, wondering if it was solvent. They feared a dangerous precedent in lending money to a bank in such an uncertain condition.[85]

John McKee examined the First National and the Guardian National Bank of Commerce for the RFC when both banks proposed to open on a 50 percent basis, contingent upon RFC loans. Reporting to the RFC board, he stated flatly that insolvency had caused the holiday. The banks were now asking the RFC to commit itself to $140 million in advances because, he said, it would be "ruinous to the larger banks to reopen without preparation for meeting a severe run from depositors of all character." First National would require $100 million and Guardian National $40 million in addition to their acceptable assets and other funds to be borrowed elsewhere—First would have to raise $34 million itself and Guardian $7 million—in

84. Ibid., pp. 37–39; *New York Times*, 17–19 Feb. 1933; *Detroit Free Press*, 8 Sept. 1933; *Business Week*, 1 Mar. 1933, p. 6.

85. Federal Reserve Board, Minutes, 18 Feb. 1933; chronology of the banking crisis, First National Bank, meeting of the board, 19 Feb. 1933, 2:30 p.m., Taylor Papers; corroborated by memoranda, 19 Feb. 1933, 10:30 a.m., 2:30 p.m., Dodge Papers, box 1; SEP, pp. 5816–19.

order to pay out 50 percent of deposits. McKee recommended that if the loans were made they be "in such amounts that the relief to the creditors of both banks should be in equal percentages."[86]

Once again, the RFC would lend money only if the Detroit banks could find other funds locally or from correspondent banks. The First already had $20 million in loans from New York banks; but New York's refusal to renew these loans ended hope of RFC aid. At the same time the RFC board finally cancelled its pledge on the Wolverine Mortgage Company and concluded that Guardian, too, could not raise the required capital.[87] Senator Couzens also continued to oppose a loan which would favor city over country banks.

On Tuesday, February 21, Governor Comstock issued another proclamation technically ending the holiday on the morning of February 23, but in fact continuing the moratorium. Individuals could withdraw a portion of their accounts, computed in relation to the banks' holdings in cash, reserves, and government securities, but they could only make withdrawals for necessary living expenses. New deposits would be accepted but must be held separately in trust accounts.[88] In practice the holiday was extended indefinitely. While newspapers carried encouraging stories, such as Henry Ford's pledge to "take his chances" along with smaller depositors,[89] Roy Chapin wrote Senator Couzens predicting a "riotous Detroit and a prostrate Michigan" by the beginning of the next week unless something was done.[90]

For a while, it seemed that something would be done. On February 26, newspapers printed a joint letter from Henry and Edsel Ford, in facsimile for heightened effect. It proposed two new banks: the People's National Bank, to replace the First National, and the Manufacturers National Bank, to supplant the Guardian Nation-

86. SEP, pp. 4742–54, 5902–07; RFC, Minutes, 21 Feb. 1933; memorandum, John R. McKee, 22 Feb. 1933, Comptroller's Files, NA: RG 101, box 6; *New York Times*, 22 Feb. 1933.

87. Taylor, "Detroit Tragedy," pp. 49–51; Sullivan, *Prelude to Panic*, pp. 96–97.

88. *Detroit Free Press*, 22 Feb. 1933; *New York Times*, 22 Feb. 1933; Federal Reserve Board, Minutes, 23 Feb. 1933.

89. *New York Times*, 24 Feb. 1933; *Commercial and Financial Chronicle* 136 (25 Feb. 1933): 1242–43, 1308–09.

90. Chapin to Couzens, 25 Feb. 1933, quoted in Barnard, *Independent Man*, p. 240.

al Bank of Commerce. The Fords offered to provide $8,225,000 in new capital and specified that they eventually wanted the two new banks united "into one institution founded on what we think sound banking should be."[91] These two banks would take over the assets and indebtedness of the established banks, add the new capital plus an RFC loan, and open for business to pay out thirty cents on the dollar to the old depositors; as slow assets became liquid, creditors would receive more money. Under pressure from federal authorities, the Detroit bankers accepted Ford's proposition; the People's National and the Manufacturers National were scheduled to open on February 27 and March 2 respectively.

But even as Dearborn street banners proclaimed "Bank with Hank,"[92] the bankers suddenly reversed themselves. The Ford loan offer had been contingent upon the RFC loan, which failed because the New York banks would not renew their loans to the First. In addition, speculation that Ford would "start over with a new personnel" soured officers and directors on the proposal. Rumors also circulated of a revolt of the large stockholders at a joint meeting with the First National's board on February 27. Consequently, on February 28, Wilson Mills telephoned Edsel Ford and withdrew his bank's agreement.[93]

On March 1, Senator Couzens returned to Detroit at the request of Henry Ford, E. D. Stair of the *Detroit Free Press,* and Wilson Mills to see if he personally could restore the banks to a working basis.[94] For three days he looked for a plan to present to the state legislature, but the bankers could not unite on a program until it was too late for the legislators to act. Couzens's other suggestion, an

---

91. *Detroit Times,* 27 Feb. 1933; *Detroit News,* 27 Feb. 1933; *Detroit Free Press,* 27 Feb. 1933; *New York Times,* 27, 28 Feb. 1933; Taylor, "Detroit Tragedy," pp. 54–55; William Adams Simonds, *Henry Ford: His Life, His Work, His Genius* (Indianapolis: Bobbs-Merrill, 1943), pp. 234–35; Myers and Newton, *Hoover Administration,* p. 355.
92. *Literary Digest,* 11 Mar. 1933, p. 10.
93. RFC, Minutes, 1 Mar. 1933, NA: RG 234; Wilson W. Mills to John McKee, 28 Feb. 1933, quoted in RFC, Minutes, 1 Mar. 1933, NA: RG 234; copy in Comptroller's files, NA: RG 101, box 6; Taylor, "Detroit Tragedy," pp. 54–55; memorandum, Taylor Papers; *Business Week,* 5 Apr. 1933, p. 5; Barnard, *Independent Man,* pp. 243–44; Sward, *Legend,* pp. 252–53; Myers and Newton, *Hoover Administration,* pp. 357–58.
94. Couzens notebook, 28 Feb. 1933; E. D. Stair to Couzens, 28 Feb. 1933, quoted in Barnard, *Independent Man,* p. 244.

RFC loan to the First to cover a 5 percent distribution of deposits, did not get past the RFC board.[95] The senator left Michigan for President Roosevelt's inauguration before he learned that his proposals had aborted. He assumed that the two old banks would continue, that the bankers were grateful to him, that the RFC would make the necessary loan, and that confidence would be restored in a few days.[96] He was to be disappointed, and so was the nation. Michigan was no different on March 4 than it had been on February 11, except that now the world knew of its weaknesses and its failures.

95. *Detroit Times*, 1, 2 Mar. 1933; *New York Times*, 2, 3 Mar. 1933; Taylor, "Detroit Tragedy," pp. 56–57; RFC, Minutes, 2, 3 Mar. 1933, NA: RG 234.

96. *Detroit Free Press*, 3 Mar. 1933; Couzens to C. L. Cardwell, 4 Mar. 1933, Couzens Papers, box 95.

CHAPTER V

Investigation

ON THE HEELS of the Michigan banking moratorium, precisely when they most needed moral support, America's commercial bankers endured nine days of shatteringly bad publicity. Revelations before the Senate Banking and Currency Committee about business practices within the National City Bank of New York profoundly shocked the "moral sense of the nation."[1] Although the bankers were guilty of most of the charges, the timing of these "confessions" in the last days of February 1933 focused public reproach on them when they were most vulnerable to popular reactions. With Michigan down and other states such as Maryland slipping, any further loss of confidence could mean fatal runs.

Until the Depression, bankers had commanded great admiration. None doubted the methods or integrity of men who served their clients and themselves so well. The stock market crash of 1929 and lengthening depression eroded that image, however, until by 1931 the inexplicable helplessness of bankers and businessmen stood in sharp contrast to their image during the 1920s. Failure of the National Credit Corporation destroyed the last remnants of the self-help illusion. If the perpetrators of prosperity could not or would not save themselves, how could they engineer general recovery? How could they face down crises like Michigan? Clearly the stock of the banker had dipped as low as the securities he occasionally peddled. As early as 1932 a columnist had written the obituary of the doctrine that "money is itself omnipotent, so great a power that those who control the world's wealth can do almost anything."[2]

Stock dealings which had made bankers rich and respected in the era of affluence now glared as scarlet sins in the age of depression. Disillusionment with speculators and securities merchants carried over from investment bankers to commercial bankers; the two were often the same, and an embittered public did not care to make fine distinctions. Thus, during those nine days when the Senate committee turned its investigation of stock exchange practices to the National City Bank, the commercial bankers suffered great damage at the worst possible time.

President Hoover, opponent of stock speculation in the 1920s, believed that after 1929 "continuous uses of the New York and other stock exchanges" contributed to public fear. He tried to persuade officials at the New York Stock Exchange "to restrain the use of the Exchange for manipulation, destructive speculation and distribution of doubtful securities."[3] Hoover believed the stock market should regulate itself, and that if any government action was warranted prime responsibility fell on Franklin D. Roosevelt, then governor of New York, in whose jurisdiction the New York Exchange conducted its business.[4] Each time Hoover asked the Exchange's directors to reform themselves, they agreed but did nothing. Frustrated, he threatened congressional investigation and federal control if the Exchange did not clean house. Neither the exchanges nor the investment houses were then subject to federal supervision, except for the Federal Reserve's limited authority over those banks which belonged to the System.

The president finally made good his threats. On February 26, 1932, he asked Senator Peter Norbeck, chairman of the Senate Banking and Currency Committee, and its leading Republican member, Frederick Walcott, for an investigation and legislation regarding stock exchange practices. Hoover later recalled that he had been "extremely loath to take this step, as we had enough burdens to carry, without all the discouraging filth such exposure entailed. But the

1. "Banksters Must Go," *Colliers* 91 (Apr. 1933): 50.
2. Anne O'Hare McCormick, "Main Street Reappraises Wall Street," *New York Times*, 28 Feb. 1932.
3. Hoover, *Memoirs*, 3:125; Myers and Newton, *Hoover Administration*, p. 51.
4. Hoover, *Memoirs*, 3:126.

truth could be brought out only under the compulsion which a Senate committee could exert."[5] Senator Walcott offered another reason for the investigation; he told Hoover that "certain New York groups," ostensibly led by prominent Democrats, were planning a series of bear raids and short sales in the spring of 1932 to depress security values and hinder Hoover's chances for reelection the following November. But both political parties wished an investigation and the Senate voted to initiate hearings.[6]

Delays followed Senate authorization of the hearings, however; opponents tried first to kill and then to postpone an investigation. Although New York bankers memorialized Hoover on the "virtues of the Exchange," the president believed that manipulation of stocks undermined public confidence and therefore pressed the committee to begin.[7] The senators agreed on April 8, while Chairman Norbeck was out of town and apparently ignorant of their action.[8] According to the acting chairman, Senator Smith Brookhart, the committee hoped to forestall a great bear raid, rumored for April 9, which would drive the United States off the gold standard.[9] Norbeck rushed back to take personal charge, believing that enemies of the investigation had engineered a brief whitewashing expedition to end the hearings quickly. He wondered if even the Hoover administration didn't prefer a few nominal disclosures and a routine report, fearing that deeper revelations might postpone recovery.[10] Certainly the president understood the risks in such an inquiry. He must weigh the consequences of unpleasant exposures, perhaps even another stock market collapse or bank runs, against a chance to reform abuses he *knew* undercut his whole battle against the depression. Hoover gambled.

5. Ibid., 126–27; Myers and Newton, *Hoover Administration*, pp. 175–76; Vincent P. Carosso, *Investment Banking in America: A History* (Cambridge: Harvard University Press, 1970), pp. 322–23.

6. Ferdinand Pecora, COHC, pp. 661–62. Financier George Barr Baker gave the president the same news. *New York Herald Tribune*, 9 Apr. 1932.

7. Hoover, *Memoirs*, 3:127–29; Myers and Newton, *Hoover Administration*, pp. 189, 192–93; Richard Whitney to Ogden Mills, 26 Aug., 2 Sept. 1932, Mills Papers, Library of Congress, box 1.

8. Peter Norbeck to J. D. Coon, 11 Apr. 1932, Norbeck Papers, University of South Dakota.

9. *New York Times*, 9 Apr. 1932.

10. Norbeck felt that Brookhart was being used. Norbeck to James E. Stewart, 25 Mar. 1932; and Norbeck to J. D. Coon, 11 Apr. 1932, Norbeck Papers; Fite, *Norbeck*, p. 174.

Hearings began on April 11, lasted until June 23, suspended during the presidential campaign, and resumed early in 1933. During this first phase, stories of "pools" in stocks and bonds, artificially high securities prices, raids, and price manipulations hit the investment bankers. Commercial bankers remained relatively untouched until 1933, when attention shifted to those whom Charles and Mary Beard have called the "legitimate members of the banking fraternity."[11]

When hearings resumed in January 1933, the subcommittee had a new counsel. On January 22, Senator Norbeck offered the post to Ferdinand Pecora of New York.[12] Pecora, a self-made man, was the eldest son of Sicilian immigrants. He had left college in order to contribute to the support of his family and completed his education by working as a law clerk by day while he attended New York University Law School in the evenings. A Republican until 1912, the young Pecora joined the Bull Moose effort in that year but subsequently became a member of the Democratic party. His work in local politics was rewarded in 1918 when he became an assistant district attorney for New York County; four years later, he rose to chief assistant district attorney, a post he retained until 1930, when he went into private practice.

At the time Norbeck approached him, Pecora had only a vague impression of the committee's work from newspaper accounts and actually thought that the hearing had been concluded. Norbeck explained to him that only five or six weeks remained before the end of the congressional session and that the committee had to complete its examination of witnesses, digest the collected evidence, and prepare a report offering recommendations to the Congress. After discussing the appointment with his family and law partner, Pecora agreed to assist the committee in the final weeks of the stock market investigation.[13]

Neither the committee nor its new counsel intended any re-

11. Beard and Beard, *America in Midpassage*, p. 161; Hoover, *Memoirs*, 3:129.

12. Pecora, COHC, p. 655; David Saul Levin, "Regulating the Securities Industry: The Evolution of a Government Policy" (doctoral dissertation, Columbia University, 1969), p. 196; Norbeck to O. I. Brownlee, 23 Aug. 1934, Norbeck Papers.

13. Pecora, COHC, pp. 654–58.

vamping of the investigation in its last few days; yet Pecora's arrival in Washington signalled an entirely new, expanded, and more sensational approach to the hearings. The original enabling resolution directed the committee to look into "matters connected with the issuance and sale of securities," but until now they had concentrated almost exclusively on bear raids and short sales. Pecora told a surprised Norbeck that the authorization included "any process or method by which securities were issued or manufactured or offered to the public, whether on the over-the-counter market, whether by door-to-door sale, or on the Exchange markets." Norbeck was amazed that no member of the committee had discovered the broad power, and thought it might be applied to a study of high-pressure salesmanship before 1929. Perhaps a conclusive argument for Norbeck, in addition to his hatred of Wall Street, was his realization that, had he broadened the investigation earlier, he might not have had to campaign so hard for reelection in 1932, and the rest of the Republican ticket might not have lost in South Dakota. Ironically, Norbeck who had headed the committee which drafted the original bill, had specifically eliminated a preamble which limited investigation to short selling. Thus the language was purposely broad.[14] Yet in 1933, according to Pecora, Norbeck seemed amazed at the wider implications of that language.

Pecora began his job immediately, assembling a staff and cementing relations with the subcommittee. Old friends, new volunteers, and committee regulars worked sixteen to eighteen hours per day, probing into hitherto uninvestigated fields. Particularly in the early cases, counsel had to develop raw testimony on the stand from witnesses encountered for the first time. Some faded, but Pecora bloomed.[15] By mid-February he was presenting his first testimony to the subcommittee members. He rapidly formed a special attachment for Senators Duncan Fletcher, Peter Norbeck, James Couzens, and Edward Costigan, all of whom supported him as he pushed the inquiry. Some showed less enthusiasm, either for the investigation or for Pecora's methods, notably Senator Carter Glass during the later hearings on J. P. Morgan and Company. On the whole, how-

14. *Congressional Record*, 72d Cong., 1st Sess., 3 Mar. 1932, p. 5182. Interpreted by Fite, *Norbeck*, p. 172.
15. Pecora, COHC, pp. 664–67, 858–59.

ever, Pecora felt that "the committee as a unit, and the individuals on it, were in favor of pursuing the investigation along the lines that had been planned." He was particularly impressed that this support was bipartisan.[16] (In fact, he so appreciated the senators that he later dedicated *Wall Street under Oath*, his account of the hearings, to the four committee members who had died before the time of its publication.[17]) As the sessions took on something of Pecora's intensity, the chairmen—Norbeck and later Fletcher—cooperated fully with his methods, accepting, for example, his arguments against permiting news filming in the hearing room.[18]

The direction of the stock exchange hearings shifted perceptibly with Pecora's first "case," the bankrupt Insull empire. Here a holding company rather than a brokerage house was on trial and the mess splattered onto a few commercial bankers. Former Vice-President Charles G. Dawes, then head of the Central Republic Bank of Chicago, testified that he had made monumental loans to various Insull companies before he himself was compelled to go to the Reconstruction Finance Corporation for $90 million to save Central Republic. After Dawes admitted that almost 90 percent of his bank's deposits were distributed in loans to Insull companies, and that Illinois law limited loans which a bank could make to a single borrower to not more than 10 percent of total assets, he could hardly find an answer for Pecora's question: "Mr. Dawes, would you say that making these loans to the Insull companies, if they didn't constitute a violation of the letter of the laws of the State of Illinois, that they violated the spirit of those laws?"[19] On such evidence William E. Leuchtenburg labelled the Pecora investigation "one of a series of spectacular episodes that destroyed the financier as a folk hero."[20] Worse was to follow.

New York's huge National City Bank, chosen for its prominence, offered the next target.[21] With so little time, Pecora's staff

16. Ibid., pp. 662, 728–32.
17. Ibid., pp. 728–29.
18. The committee made only two exceptions, with J. P. Morgan and Edsel Ford. Ibid., pp. 713–17.
19. SEP, pp. 1397–1458; Pecora, COHC, pp. 688–97.
20. Leuchtenburg, *Roosevelt and New Deal*, p. 20.
21. *Business Week*, 8 Feb. 1933, p. 18.

felt they could get an accurate general picture "by inquiring into the activities of a selected few, those whose activities embraced larger areas of finance."[22] In this case, "larger areas of finance" meant that National City was a commercial bank with an investment banking "partner." Moreover, its size and wide reputation guaranteed maximum exposure. Although Pecora claimed that his choice of firms was nonpartisan, he cited contradictory evidence: the investigators selected the "Republican house" of Dillon, Read but neglected Lehman Brothers and Brown Brothers, associated with Democrats Herbert Lehman and W. Averell Harriman respectively.

Since the National City investigation led to changes in plans for concluding and summarizing the hearings, Pecora had only four days to sift reams of material for his case. Over a weekend in the New York law offices of Sherman and Sterling, counsel for the National City Bank, he read the bank's minute books for 1924 to 1929— "literally, stacks of books about a yard from the floor, big volumes." Pecora had agreed to examine the records personally and on the premises, although he felt "somewhat appalled" at the task. As he worked, the senior partner who had supplied the books sometimes maneuvered to read over his shoulder, but in Pecora's words, "on those occasions I professed to be a little bit weary, and I closed the book and relaxed for a few minutes. And he would walk away."[23] Information in these books gave Pecora a great advantage in cross-examining officers of the bank. His intimate knowledge disarmed several who did not know that he had seen the records.[24]

The United States Treasury also contributed evidence, though reluctantly. Pecora asked Secretary Ogden L. Mills for reports filed by national bank examiners after audits of the National City Bank. Mills consulted Undersecretary Arthur A. Ballantine, and they agreed to produce the records, but only after Pecora threatened to go to the Supreme Court for a ruling on whether the Treasury had to open its files to congressional committees. He had scarcely hinted that the newspapers might also be interested when Mills and Ballantine graciously offered full cooperation.[25]

22. Pecora, COHC, pp. 760–62.
23. Ibid., pp. 669–72.
24. Ibid., p. 672.
25. Ibid, pp. 831–34; Pecora to Norbeck, 1 Feb. 1933, Norbeck Papers.

With these compressed preparations, Pecora went into the hearings on February 21, calling as his first witness Charles E. Mitchell, the imposing chairman of the boards of both the National City Bank and the National City Company. Mitchell, born in Chelsea, near Boston, and educated at Amherst College, had served as assistant to the president of the Trust Company of America during the 1907 panic, and after five years in his own investment house, had joined the National City Company as its president in 1916. The company had been established in 1911 as an investment twin for James Stillman's National City Bank. When Stillman died and his son left the bank as a result of a scandalous divorce suit, Mitchell succeeded to the presidency of the bank, as well.[26]

As head of the bank and the company, Mitchell held a formidable position, both in Wall Street and among his own employees. Edmund Wilson recounted one story of a young bank clerk who interrupted an inspection tour to request a word in private with Mitchell: "The young man politely pressed him to step aside out of earshot of the others present. Still scowling, Mitchell complied. Said the young man 'Your trousers are unbuttoned, sir!' " He was fired on the spot, leading Wilson to comment, "In those days the trousers of Charles E. Mitchell could no more be unbuttoned than Louis XIV's grammar could be at fault. He was the banker of bankers, the salesman of salesmen, the genius of the New Economic Era."[27]

Now Mitchell returned to Washington to testify before the Senate Banking and Currency Committee, as he had in 1932. Tall, dignified, gray-haired, the prototypical banker-promoter, he apparently expected to meet briefly with the senators, offer his evidence, and resume his own work; he arrived with a retinue of bank officials and employees carrying stacks of records. For the next week, however, Mitchell, Hugh Baker, Gordon Rentschler, and their colleagues faced an efficient and remarkably well-prepared interrogator who elicited some very embarrassing information.

26. Allen, *Lords of Creation*, pp. 304–05, 311; [Clinton W. Gilbert], *The Mirrors of Wall Street* (New York: Putnam's, 1933), pp. 155–56; SEP, p. 1967; George Whitney, COHC, pp. 44–48.

27. Edmund Wilson, "Sunshine Charley," in *Travels in Two Democracies* (New York: Harcourt, Brace, 1936), pp. 52–62.

Pecora first attacked National City's structure, which consisted of a commercial bank, a securities company, and a trust institution. In 1911, to get around a federal law which prohibited a national bank from dealing in investment securities, stocks, and bonds, the bank had established a related company (in which it held all voting stock) to engage in those operations. Probing the records of the National City organization, Pecora had unearthed a copy of the opinion submitted by Solicitor General Frederick W. Lehman to Attorney General Charles W. Wickersham on November 6, 1911, holding that under federal law banks might take stocks of another corporation as collateral for loans or in payment of previously-incurred debts but could not deal in stocks or buy and hold the capital stock of another bank. From this Lehman concluded "that both the bank and the company, whether considered as affiliated or as unrelated, are in violation of the law."[28] Justice Department files held no record of action by the Taft or Wilson administrations, nor was there any evidence that the bank had been informed that its affiliate was illegal.[29] The National City Company was chartered by New York State in 1911 and operated for over twenty years without challenge. Commercial and investment banking were virtually the same at National City, as at Chase and many other of the nation's largest banks.

Senator Glass had revealed the same information to the Senate on May 9, 1932, without naming the parties; he implied that the Taft and Wilson administrations had deliberately suppressed the opinion. Attorney General William D. Mitchell, who supplied Glass with the opinion, objected to this conclusion, and in several exchanges of correspondence Glass apologized.[30]

Since 1911, the National City Bank had completely controlled its affiliate. Under the original terms of incorporation, the bank owned all stock in the company, the two properties being printed on opposite sides of the same certificates. Three trustees voted this stock on behalf of the stockholders of the bank; they were chosen by the bank's board of directors (acting as individuals rather than in formal capacity as a board), and they served the company

28. SEP, p. 2028, full text quoted on pp. 2030–42.
29. Pecora, COHC, pp. 673–76, 829–31.
30. *Congressional Record*, 72d Cong., 2d Sess., pp. 9899–9904; Mitchell-Glass letters, May 1932, Glass Papers.

only while they were also officers or directors of the bank. In his cross-questioning, Pecora attempted to establish that the trustees were not accountable to the bank's stockholders, but Mitchell argued that they were chosen by the directors and were answerable to the shareholders at annual meetings which considered operations of both institutions.[31] For day-to-day operations a team of vice-presidents had charge of securities buying and selling under Mitchell's general supervision.

A board of directors which met weekly governed the National City Company. Apparently neither the board nor its executive committee kept minutes, since no one testifying in 1933 could recall any records. Because the executive committee consisted of most of the board members, it ceased to function separately in 1926, on the premise that one meeting would be more efficient than two. Mitchell actually directed the company, but he could not spend the entire day in the company's offices since he also had duties at the bank. Therefore, operations devolved onto company President Hugh Baker, and management was vested in seven or eight vice-presidents who met informally every day to decide on the nature and kind of securities for purchase and resale to the public. These vice-presidents operated in an officers' council like a general partnership; no stock issue was taken on except by unanimous approval of the officers. Once made, these decisions stood, even when officers of the company—in their private capacities, Mitchell stressed—were parties to the transactions.[32]

Mitchell compared the actual work of the company to manufacturing. He contended that its executives devoted most of their time to the development of long-term credits suitable for public investment rather than to the sale of a ready-made product. Baker embellished the argument. Any well-organized bank advises its depositors concerning investment, he said. Research by a securities affiliate would put the bank in a better position to determine the true value of stock and bond issues for those clients. Baker refused to give in to Pecora's contention that the affiliate might be tempted to steer depositors toward securities it was sponsoring. He simply

31. SEP, pp. 1762–66, 1780–83, 1893, 2030–42.
32. Ibid., pp. 1765–69, 1776–77, 1783.

concluded that the interwoven affiliate was "good banking practice."[33] In the same vein, when Senator Couzens asked whether the company might have sold some securities which it possibly did not want for itself, Mitchell replied that one might wish to have certain types of holdings for himself but would willingly approve the sale of other securities to those who desired a different kind of portfolio.[34]

As originally organized and operated, the National City Company confined itself to fixed-maturity securities, namely bonds, notes, debentures, and acceptances, rather than common stocks. It took up stocks in 1927 with two issues, added half a dozen the next year, and presented only two or three to the public in 1929, although its own portfolio increased.[35] When the company's offerings expanded, its sales methods also broadened to create new demands, and Charles Mitchell was just the man to handle that transition.

Hardly the quintessential conservative banker, Mitchell led the National City Company into "creative" marketing. At the Senate hearings, he repeatedly refused to distinguish between salesman and financier, claiming that securities sales were only one phase of the company's business, that it was in fact a manufacturer of credits rather than a hawker of stocks and bonds. He did, however, accept as a compliment Senator Couzen's statement that he was a better salesman than financier.[36]

In the 1920s finance rested on sales promotion, particularly at National City, where only a technicality separated commercial from investment banking. If Mitchell lacked the training and personality of a stereotype banker, he had a supreme talent for marketing. Consequently, he hired staffs of bright young college graduates — "self-starters" he called them — to knock on doors, make telephone calls, and sell. Bruce Barton, the man who billed Jesus Christ as an A-1 salesman, might have recruited Mitchell as the thirteenth disciple, the perfect "financier" of that era. In a 1923 story about marketing success, Barton described Mitchell's training program for his salesmen. If a promising young fellow was having difficulty, Mitchell would take him to the pinnacle of the Bankers' Club, from

33. Ibid., pp. 1775–76, 1942–43.
34. Ibid., pp. 1777–78.
35. Ibid., pp. 1808–10, 1838–40.
36. Ibid., pp. 1774–75.

whose windows he would show him the kingdoms and canyons of New York. "Look down there," Mitchell would say. "There are six million people with incomes that aggregate thousands of millions of dollars. They are just waiting for someone to come and tell them what to do with their savings. Take a good look, eat a good lunch, and then go down there and tell them."[37]

With 350 of these young men, Mitchell built up a finely articulated network comprising 11,386 miles of private wires, sixty-nine district offices in fifty-eight cities, sales representatives in the bank's twenty-six branches, and smaller dealers including investment departments of other banks. Sales contests with cash prizes kept the "self-starters" very competitive in marketing Brazilian bonds, Lautaro Nitrate stock, and Oliver Farm Equipment Company issues. A cooperative home office compiled lists of prospective clients from automobile registrations and tax lists, over 169,000 names in 1927 and 1928 alone. Sales increased accordingly. After several years of stability, transactions spurted in 1925, hit a high of $2 billion in 1927 or 1928 (Mitchell could not recall which of the boom years was the better) and declined to only about $1 million by 1932.[38]

Some were critical of Mitchell's methods and accomplishments. Indicting him as a would-be "master of money" (as John D. Rockefeller was the master of oil), Clinton W. Gilbert likened Mitchell to a turn-of-the-century actor who had all the elements of his art but could not create the necessary total illusion because he was too perfect at each of the separate tricks. The actor's favorite role, Gilbert noted, was "Lear—the Mad King."[39]

To complete its round of operations, in the spring of 1929 National City Bank merged with the Farmers Loan and Trust Company, because, said Mitchell, "the particular advantage, over and above the trust business which they had, which was large, was the fact that it was the oldest trust organization in the State of New York and the men connected with it had had unusual and long experience in trust work."[40] In this neat organizational package, National City

37. Bruce Barton, "Is There Anything Here that Other Men Couldn't Do?" *American Magazine* 95 (Feb. 1923): 16–17, 128.

38. SEP, pp. 2010, 1766, 1863–65; Werner, *Privileged Characters*, pp. 477–78; Pecora, *Wall Street*, pp. 70–83.

39. [Gilbert], *Mirrors of Wall Street*, pp. 158–60.

40. SEP, pp. 1764–65.

Bank handled commercial banking, the City Farmers Loan and Trust Company supervised all trust business, and the National City Company dealt in investments—all quite legally, and all supposedly for the greater service of their clients.

Mitchell refused to be complacent, however, about the organization of his companies, particularly the investment affiliate. Invited by Senator Fletcher to offer criticisms and suggestions for improvements, Mitchell came out firmly for regulatory legislation. He felt that the investment affiliate was an established and accepted institution handling "something over" 50 percent of the total volume of long-term credit business, and that its elimination would retard recovery. The affiliate must stay, but it must be controlled by the government just as banks were supervised; he could not offer a concrete proposal, however, for the form of this regulation.[41]

If the great bankers might accept federal supervision, they did not go so far as to support full publicity for their operations. When asked whether clients should know the "spread" between purchase and offering prices for securities presented by investment houses, Mitchell stated that the public was in no position to judge the value of a stock based on such information and that such publicity could be misleading. He did point out, however, that the National City Company was then offering more complete prospectuses on the condition of the companies it financed than at any time in its history. Mitchell believed that the spread of price depended upon the officer who negotiated a particular issue, and sidestepped Pecora's hint that spread might rest on public "gullibility." Potential investors would be able to see their own interest when offered a good thing. In 1929, Mitchell had sent his field agents a dispatch entitled "Loaves from Crumbs," showing clients the advantage of buying National City Bank stock with cash balances in their National City Company accounts, or even of buying at least one share by making up whatever cash might be lacking.[42]

One of the "victims" of these practices appeared before the Senate committee, a pathetic, crushed, bilked, and broken man. Edgar D. Brown of Pottsville, Pennsylvania, a retired theatrical owner-manager-producer with assets of $125,000 in 1928, had sunk

41. Ibid., pp. 2026–27.
42. Ibid., pp. 1801–09, 1767–68, 2017–19, 2020, 2172–82.

by 1933 to the position of clerk for the Pottsville poor board, living on only his salary, and totally confused about what had happened to him.

In 1928 Brown had decided to go to California for his health (he was deaf and tubercular) and sold his theaters for $100,000. Before he departed, he found an advertisement in an unspecified national magazine which might have been drafted specifically for him. Appealing to persons about to take a long trip, it suggested that they might want to contact the National City Company for investment advice while they were out of touch with their local bankers. Brown replied to the invitation (in 1933 he thought that he had addressed his letter to the National City Bank). One Fred Rummel had answered as representative of the National City Company, to discuss Brown's investment situation. In addition to $100,000 soon to come due from the sale of his chain of theaters, Brown held another $25,000 in United States and Italian government bonds. He asked for advice on how to handle this money.

After discussing the matter with his company, Rummel recommended that Brown convert all his assets into cash and purchase other bonds. Brown could not remember in 1933 whether specific issues were mentioned, but he thought one proposal was the Peruvian bonds which had been the subject of testimony the day before. Brown was certain, however, that Rummel had urged him to replace his holdings, saying that they were entirely wrong for him. Moreover, Rummel advised Brown to borrow even more money to buy bonds, and National City Bank granted him a $75,000 loan. As the securities man said, if Brown borrowed money at 5 or 5½ percent and invested it in bonds with a par value of 7½ percent which were then selling below par, he could pay off all his loans when the bonds returned to par, as expected, and make a nice profit on other people's money. Part of the $100,000 was invested in the same way as the borrowed funds. Expansion seemed limitless. Brown could buy Greek government 6 percent bonds and have them sent to a Reading bank which would lend him two or three times their value, which he could then invest in more bonds, and so on, to another issue and another bank. Brown desired fixed interest and income security, and therefore limited his account to bonds rather than stocks; otherwise, he left transactions entirely to Rummel's judgment. Figures which Brown submitted to Pecora showed that he had invested between $200,000 and $250,000 in the twelve months between December 14, 1927, and December 5, 1928, but the purchases and sales were so complex that Brown himself had no idea what was happening. At least five banks advanced him money, and he had never been inside four of them.

Despite expectations, the value of Mr. Brown's bonds declined, and in answer to his complaints, Rummel said that it was his own fault for insisting on bonds at a time when the stock market was booming. Consequently, Brown authorized the purchase of stocks, although again he did not specify which issues to buy. A dejected Brown testified flatly that Rummel had bought him "a lot of stock."

Because he questioned an irregularity in the purchase of some Andes Copper stock early in 1929, Brown made an unannounced visit to the National City Company offices in New York. He recalled later that he suspected he was being "taken" and wished to inform the officers of the company. Conferring with W. H. Beebe, Brown complained that his original sum of money—as nearly as he could determine—had shrunk despite a rising market and the tremendous volume of his trading. (Brown admitted to Pecora that he could not be sure of his financial condition in 1929, although he made an effort to get his several bank accounts balanced.) When Brown confessed his fears that violent trading and a market reaction might wipe him out, leaving him without income, Beebe promised to make recommendations to the Philadelphia office, and Brown left, apparently satisfied. On his return to Pottsville, he heard from Rummel again, who now advised that he exchange his present holdings for a portfolio of National City Bank and a few other sure items. Then he should sit still and wait.

In August 1929, Brown moved to Los Angeles. Since he was out of their territory, the Eastern banks followed their usual practice and asked that his loans be moved. Consequently, a Mr. Anderson of the Los Angeles office of the National City Bank arranged a $105,000 loan for Brown from the Farmers and Merchants Bank: $95,000 would be used to reduce his $100,000 Eastern loans, and $10,000 would be kept on hand in the bank.

A month later, when he noticed stock prices declining, Brown decided to sell out. Salesmen at the Los Angeles office warned that he would be foolish to sell, especially since National City Bank stock was then quoted in the vicinity of $500. The next day Brown received an unsolicited telegram from Rummel (with whom he had had no contact in four months and who apparently had not known where he was), telling him that National City Bank was now $525 and urging him to sit tight. Brown claimed that he continued to direct the company to sell him out, but each time learned that his holdings had risen several points. Inexplicably, on October 29, without any specific order from Brown, the company liquidated his holdings on the false information that the Farmer's Bank was calling his loan; they told Brown that he must either get out or be sold out by the bank. Hopelessly confused, he learned that National City Bank stock closed at $460 on the 28th (the *Wall Street Journal* quotes $360 for the 29th), yet the company itself bought Brown's stock for $320. He still did not understand in 1933. Brown felt that he "had been very badly used, and protested."

Writing and telegraphing to Beebe, Brown explained that he was forty years old, tubercular, deaf, and ruined. Dismissing Anderson as innocent but rattleheaded, he asked for a loan of enough money to buy 1,000 shares of Anaconda Copper stock; Brown would put up $25,000 and the bank could lend him the difference. Beebe replied that Anaconda was an attractive security, but it was not National City's policy to make loans where the borrower would use the funds to make security purchases, except where those holdings would have sufficient earning power to pay off the loan promptly, allowing the purchaser to lock his security in a safe-deposit box. He was impervious to Brown's argument that his financial condition was identical to 1928 when he had obtained his first loan.[43]

When Brown appeared before the Senate Banking and Currency Committee in 1933 his unfortunate story found a sympathetic audience. No agent or official of the National City complex refuted Brown's claims. Nor did any other clients appear to tell how their investments had made them wealthy. In fact, by the end of February 1933, the poor board clerk enjoyed more sympathy than the titanic Mitchell, although both men had attempted the same thing:

---

43. Ibid., pp. 2170–82; Werner, *Privileged Characters*, pp. 479–82; Beard, *America in Midpassage*, pp. 172–78.

quick riches. If the public had trouble following the intricacies of structure involved in the investment affiliate, or if newspaper readers showed impatience with details of stock transactions, they could more readily identify with Mr. Brown who had lost so much and still had no real comprehension of what had happened to him. His very confusion sharpened the poignancy of his downfall.

Hundreds of these Edgar Browns had bought heavily in Cuban sugar loans and foreign government bonds. Investment outside of the United States had spurted in the 1920s, and as long as profits continued few complained. Declining values embittered the speculators, however, and put them in a mood to be shocked by reports of National City's questionable dealings in these areas. National City Bank had established a branch office in Havana in 1915 and advanced large loans to Cuban sugar millionaires during the 1915–1921 sugar boom. The bank carried these loans after the boom broke, but in 1926 national bank examiners criticized the liability, and the bank's officers felt that they must liquidate the bad loans, although they could not openly admit the loss of several million dollars per year. In a triple operation on February 15, 1927, the bank resolved its problems by issuing more stock and shifting the Cuban debt from the bank to a new corporation (and ultimately to the National City Company). Pecora accused National City of "bailing out" a bad loan, but Mitchell defended the operation as replacing a short-term risk with a sound long-term investment. The bank's officers never troubled to inform the stockholders of this maneuver, perhaps because a new sugar boom improved the outlook.[44]

They repeated the sin of omission in other transactions. In 1927, the National City Company took $5 million worth of Peruvian bonds, syndicated through J. and W. Seligman and Company as part of the "Tobacco Loan" issue. The bonds were offered to the public at 96½, with a spread of 5.03 points; by February 1933 the bonds were selling at 7, and President Hugh Baker stated that National City Company was not buying Peruvian bonds at that time. These losses might have been dismissed as an unfortunate consequence of the worldwide depression, but Pecora revealed that the company should

44. SEP, pp. 1788–99, 1827–38; Pecora, *Wall Street*, pp. 121–23; Pecora, COHC, pp. 680–82; Werner, *Privileged Characters*, pp. 466–69.

not have become involved in the first place. National City agents on the scene had warned before each bond flotation (two in 1927 and one in 1928) that Peru was a bad "moral and political risk." In an era of absolute faith in the sanctity of balanced budgets, Peru had achieved balance only three times between 1915 and 1924. Yet published circulars on the bond issues omitted all unfavorable information. Baker offered no explanation.[45]

Since truth-in-securities legislation still lay in the future, National City broke no law, but it did offend the public's sense of fair play and social responsibility. Casualties appeared to be victims of crimes. By the time of the Pecora hearings, Rio de Janeiro had defaulted on $12 million in bonds to build a municipal slaughterhouse and the project was incomplete; the same was true of $25 million to electrify a Brazilian railroad and $90 million for unspecified purposes in Chile. As for value declines, $16.5 million "worth" of bonds of the Brazilian state of Minas Geraes sold in 1928 and 1929 at prices ranging from 87 to 97½; they had dropped to 21 by 1933.[46] The Senate hearings uncovered this information at the same time as they revealed abuses of publicity and writing-down of loans; the two inevitably mingled. Moreover, net profits of $24,757,003.47 hardly endeared the National City Company to a disillusioned public, especially to those citizens who had lost money.[47]

Mitchell, on the other hand, found these transactions irreproachable. He startled Pecora by insisting that the National City Company had never participated in "pools" or "syndicates" but had only taken part in "joint accounts" to stabilize rather than raise

---

45. SEP, pp. 2047–58, 2060–87, supplemented by pp. 2059–60, 2088–2118; Pecora, *Wall Street*, pp. 100–103; Allen, *Lords of Creation*, pp. 311–19; Werner, *Privileged Characters*, pp. 453–66. A full account of the Peruvian transactions appears in Levin, "Regulating the Securities Industry," pp. 220–23. Levin quotes extensively from agents' reports.

46. SEP, pp. 2119–40, 2151–70; Pecora, *Wall Street*, pp. 96–100.

47. Between 1914 and 1931, $14,883,000 worth of foreign securities were floated in the United States. As of March 1, 1934, $8,193,237,200 worth of foreign securities, both industrial and governmental, were outstanding, and of these $2,930,422,600 were in default. The National City Company made a total net profit of $13,393,502.21 on sales of the foreign securities which it managed, and a net profit of $11,363,501.26 on securities in the sale of which the National City Company participated as part of a syndicate. These profits were over the period 1919 to 1930, and during that time the National City Company managed issues totalling $1,171,955,000 and participated in issues totalling $3,260,407,000. Werner, *Privileged Characters*, p. 453.

prices on the New York Exchange. Pecora remembered that "towards all this, Mr. Mitchell maintained on the witness stand an unwavering opinion of its complete propriety."[48]

Throughout this questioning, Pecora apparently wanted the officers to admit that the National City Company was a mere *alter ego* for its affiliated bank, that the bank traded in bonds and stocks through the thin legalization of the company. Moreover, he attempted to show that the bank was trading in its *own* stock through the same affiliate. From bank President Gordon S. Rentschler, he learned that National City Company was the largest single trader in National City Bank stock, selling approximately 1,950,000 shares at $650 million. Company President Baker revealed that his company had even borrowed 15,000 shares of bank stock from chairman Mitchell on April 23, 1929, and another 15,000 shares on May 13, 1929 (all until July 10, 1929). According to Baker, the company needed the certificates to cover deliveries on stock purchases which were coming in from all parts of the world when shareholders used rights exercisable between January 15 and February 15, 1929. Pecora felt that the operation might be short-selling (that is, the sale of stocks which had not yet been acquired on the assumption that they could be purchased for delivery later for less than the sale price). Pressed on that point, Baker maintained that the company did not lack the stock altogether, only the certificates in hand for delivery; later when the certificates came in, more slowly than the orders, Mitchell's stock was returned. Company secretary Harry S. Law added that the company itself had exercised rights at that time to acquire approximately 51,000 shares of National City Bank stock for its own portfolio.[49] Both New York State and federal laws forbade a bank to deal in its own stock or that of any other bank. Technically, the National City Company traded National City Bank issues; yet the affiliate existed to circumvent those state and federal statutes. Two in law, one in practice—the twins offered an annoying ambiguity of ethics.

Morality rather than legality determined popular response. While National City's officers had done nothing in the operation of their twin enterprise which merited prosecution, they had been less

48. SEP, pp. 1841–63; Pecora, *Wall Street*, pp. 105–09.
49. SEP, pp. 1846, 1879–87, 1889–1919.

than candid on several matters. They had avoided laws, if not actually broken them, and worse, they had guessed wrongly on almost 5 percent of the items they had sold. Mitchell estimated that in the ten years before the hearings, the National City Company had sold issues valued at approximately $20 billion, of which about $1 billion was then in difficulty or default, including the Latin American investments.[50] Public opinion could forgive such mistakes in ordinary mortals, but the gods of finance must never violate infallibility. Nor should they ever slip into a position where they could be blamed, in most specific terms, for disaster.

Moreover, the Pecora hearings revived the story of Mitchell's "personal responsibility" for speculation prior to the stock market collapse of 1929, and its recounting at this particular moment fed public hostility. Mitchell had allegedly defied the Federal Reserve Board. In February 1929, on the eve of Hoover's inauguration, Federal Reserve Board Chairman Roy Young had issued two warnings against excessive speculation, urging banks to curtail brokers' loans. Shortly after the Board raised the rediscount rate in March, National City Bank threw $25 million into the call money market at rates of 16 percent and above, and Senator Glass indicted Mitchell as "Chairman of the Board of Saboteurs."

When he testified in 1933, Mitchell defended his 1929 action. He had interpreted the Reserve Board's warning, he said, as a curb upon banks borrowing from the Federal Reserve in order to lend that money to speculators, and proudly recorded that his bank had not done so. In fact, National City had never leaned on Federal Reserve credits while speculation was rampant but only after the break, when every New York bank was forced to go to the Reserve bank. Mitchell claimed that National City had actually prevented a crisis in 1929 by releasing money into the call loan market. There was no money available to lend, even at rates up to 15 or 16 percent, he said, and the legitimate borrower who needed money for short-term contracts could not find it. Far from supporting a speculative market, Mitchell asserted that he had forestalled a money panic—the moral responsibility of any man who could do so. Furthermore Mitchell claimed that he had never issued a statement for the newspapers in defiance of the Federal Reserve Board's warning, but had merely

50. Ibid., p. 1888.

discussed the matter with an apparently indiscreet reporter. He thought it a great "misunderstanding" that Senator Glass had interpreted his position as telling the Federal Reserve Board to go to hell. Commenting privately on this regurgitation of the Young-Mitchell-Glass confrontation, Federal Reserve Board member Charles Sumner Hamlin recalled that some members of the Board had felt that Mitchell was dangerously dominant at the New York Federal Reserve Bank and should have been removed from his position on its board in 1929.[51]

Highhanded public dealings would mean little to men who dallied with the internal financing of their own organization. The Senate hearings revealed that within the National City Company, and at the bank after Mitchell became president, a portion of annual profits was distributed among the officers; this "management fund" was established to compensate them for what they might have received as partners in private banking houses. Mitchell defined the management fund as "twenty percent of the net earnings after 8 percent of capital, surplus, and undivided profits have been deducted from the net operating expenses of the year." This sum was distributed by vote: each officer filed three unsigned ballots with the cashier; on the first he estimated that Mitchell should receive; on the second he apportioned the remainder of the fund among his colleagues, excluding himself; and on the third he nominated the half-dozen men other than eligible officers who should participate in the year's fund because of their contributions to the business. When the executive committee acted on these recommendations, Mitchell stipulated only that he should receive no more than the portion voted him by the officers, and felt that he was taking a bold step in making himself thus vulnerable to his subordinates.

Large sums went into the management funds. In addition to a uniform base salary of $25,000 per year for all executive officers including Mitchell, the distribution for 1927–1929 was approximately as follows:

	1927	1928	1929
Management fund, bank	$1,356,999.53	$1,401,585.47	$1,725,177.96
Mitchell's share	529,230.00	566,634.19	608,868.00

51. Ibid., pp. 1814–31; [Gilbert], *Mirrors of Wall Street*, pp. 150–51; Hamlin, Diary, 25 Feb. 1933.

Management fund, company	1,988,000.00	2,739,438.98
Mitchell's share	527,000.00	750,000.00
Total funds	3,344,999.53	4,141,024.45
Mitchell's total	1,056,230.00	1,316,634.19

As the figures were put on the record, acting committee chairman James Couzens commented that the senators had no wish to intrude upon the personal affairs of either Mitchell or the company but believed in "demonstrating publicly, if possible, that these unreasonable salaries and these bonuses lead to unsound banking and unsound sales of securities." Pecora asserted that the officers had "nothing to gain and everything to lose, individually, by a conservative policy," since their own participation began only after they had insured an 8 percent return on the stockholders' money.[52]

Executives enjoyed other privileges as well. In 1928 and 1929 officers bought into particular profitable flotations, such as aircraft stocks, while the same offerings were withheld from the public as "too speculative." When issues such as Boeing common and preferred turned downward, a suitable advertising campaign helped the National City men to unload with considerable gains.[53] The board of directors at the bank also established a fund of $2.4 million for "morale" loans (with and without security) to bank officers and employees to purchase their own bank's stock or to survive the 1929 debacle. On his own testimony, Hugh Baker bought 1,500 shares of stock in December 1931 with $75,000 borrowed from the Stock Purchase Corporation; at that time he was a director of the National City Bank and president of the National City Company. The loan was secured with the stock itself. (Baker then loaned those 1,500 shares to his brother, a partner in a stock brokerage house, to see him through the emergency.) In the case of officers, these loans were frequently written down when they could not be repaid; for example, one $285,000 balance became $65,000 and was eventually assumed by the National City Company.

Employees fared less well. Many bought National City Bank stock under the stock-purchase plan of February 15, 1927. Payments plus interest would be deducted from salaries, usually at a rate of

52. SEP, pp. 1769–79, 1782–88, 1878–79, 1965–66, definition on p. 1788; Pecora, Wall Street, pp. 113–21.
53. Pecora, Wall Street, pp. 123–26.

$200 to $220 per share. The employees were still paying at this rate in 1933 when the stock was selling at $40.[54]

Pecora admitted grudgingly that at least the officers of National City never sold their own stock short (despite the 1929 rights dispute) as had Albert Wiggin of the Chase National Bank. In fact, National City removed its stock from the New York Exchange, ostensibly to avoid manipulation.[55] In this, at least, the bank could not be criticized.

Moreover, Mitchell himself had purchased stock in the midst of the 1929 panic, to protect the shareholders' interest by sustaining its value, he said. Having suffered a greater individual loss on National City Bank stock than anyone else in the country, Mitchell recalled that throughout the panic he retained all his own stock and authorized the National City Company to buy up to $12 million of stock which shareholders wanted to unload at approximately $375 per share.[56]

Mitchell's stock transactions did bring him some discomfort, however. In 1929 when he had earned over $4 million, he sold stock to his wife at a loss of $2,872,305.50, thus paying no federal income tax for that year. Later, he repurchased the stock at the same price, despite a market drop. This revelation before the Pecora hearings led to his prosecution on a charge of tax evasion three months later. Vindicated in criminal proceedings, he was found guilty in civil court and ordered to pay $700,000 in back taxes. On December 28, 1938, the full sum of $1,384,222.92 in taxes, interest, and penalties was paid off.[57]

From February 21 to March 4, 1933, the Senate Banking and Currency Committee listened and the American public watched as Ferdinand Pecora and Charles Mitchell reviewed the last ten years of the National City Bank and the National City Company, the second largest bank and the largest investing house in the nation. Mitch-

54. SEP, pp. 1868–79, 1944–47; Pecora, *Wall Street*, pp. 127–30; Werner, *Privileged Characters*, pp. 483–85. Employees had also paid at the $220 rate earlier when the market quotation was $585 after a 5 to 1 split.

55. Pecora, *Wall Street*, pp. 110–12, 154–55.

56. SEP, pp. 1811–14.

57. Pecora, COHC, pp. 682–85; SEP, 1812–14; Pecora, *Wall Street*, pp. 189–205; Werner, *Privileged Characters*, pp. 485; Wilson, "Sunshine Charley," pp. 52–62.

ell had acquired a considerable reputation both as a banker and as a promoter; consequently, revelations of his misdeeds smeared the investment and commercial banks, of which his firms were leaders. By implication, the bankers—and especially Wall Street—were held socially irresponsible, meriting popular disapproval, even wrath. The public saw no reason to be impartial and even less to be forgiving.

Periodicals channeled and reflected this indignation. The disgruntled *Nation* quoted: "If you steal $25, you're a thief. If you steal $250,000, you're an embezzler. If you steal $2,500,000 you're a financier."[58] Heywood Broun commented that the bankers had only overlooked the roulette wheel in their solicitude for depositors, and while *Commonweal* admitted that Mitchell had been candid, it concluded that Al Capone was a bungler by comparison.[59] Certainly, as *Colliers* recorded, the revelations shocked the "moral sense of the nation," since a bank was, or should be, "a public trust."[60] Almost alone of the critics, the *Literary Digest* questioned the wisdom of these exposures: "Coming at the same time with the banking crisis in Michigan and elsewhere, it has led to questioning in Wall Street whether it was wise to unsettle national public confidence at this time, when banking troubles in some centers are serious enough without aggravation."[61]

If the Pecora investigation nourished such hostility, how much more damaging information still lay hidden? Speculation ran wild, and even insiders remained suspicious. A group of employees of the National City Bank wrote anonymously to President Roosevelt to tell him that, either intentionally or through ignorance, the government appeared willing "to punish one or two persons in order to let a larger and equally responsible group escape." Although "the Senate Committee meant well," its members "did not know what to ask questions about." The group urged further investigation into four areas: 1) lack of prosecutions by the National City Bank to recover loans to officers, for fear of what might be revealed in the courtroom; 2) unwarranted bond issues for Panama, with full knowledge of officials of the State Department; 3) the effect of National

58. *Nation* 136 (8 Mar. 1933): 248–49.
59. "Banking in the U. S. A.," *Commonweal* 17 (14 Mar. 1933): 535.
60. "Banksters Must Go," *Colliers* 91 (Apr. 1933): 50.
61. "Big Bankers' Gambling Mania," *Literary Digest* 115 (11 Mar. 1933): 11–12.

City Bank foreclosures of large Cuban sugar plantations and speculations by Mitchell and by Percy Rockefeller in such ventures as Consolidated Railroad of Cuba; and 4) revelations about certain National City directors in the Charles Evans Hughes report on postwar airplane contracts. Stockholders' groups were forming to prosecute the officers and publicly air their mismanagement, but the anonymous correspondents urged instead a single government-sponsored "amputation over with in one operation" in the interest of public confidence. They concluded: "It must be obvious to you that if we signed our names to this memorandum we would be signing our death warrants so far as employment is concerned."[62]

Others did perish. In the midst of testimony, on February 26, Mitchell and Baker withdrew from the National City organization; their resignations were accepted, effective the next day. (Rumor said that President-elect Roosevelt had advised the move.[63]) That same night an agent for National City telephoned Pecora to tell him of Mitchell's separation from the bank. "Of course, Mr. Pecora," he said, "under the circumstances, it won't be necessary for Mr. Mitchell to resume the stand." Pecora felt that it certainly would be necessary and that the subpoena was still in effect. He added that he was conducting a fact-finding inquiry, not a head-hunting expedition.[64] Mitchell completed his testimony.

If Charles E. Mitchell had been a hero in the 1920s, his rapid decline during the final days of February 1933 symbolized the plummeting reputation of commercial and investment bankers. Pecora himself saw the striking contrast as he watched Mitchell for the last time:

> I was standing with Senator Norbeck at a window that faced the plaza that intervened between the Senate Office Building and the Union Railroad Station in Washington . . . and I saw walking across the plaza towards the railroad station a man who was walking completely alone,

62. "A group of old timers in Wall Street" to FDR, 22 Mar. 1933, copy to Carter Glass, 28 Mar. 1933, Glass Papers, box 310. Roosevelt never saw the letter; his secretaries forwarded it to the senator for use in the Glass bill movement.

63. *New York Times*, 28 Feb. 1933.

64. Pecora, COHC, pp. 677–79; Colt and Keith, *28 Days*, pp. 32–34; National City Bank newsletter, Mar. 1933, Hamlin Papers, Scrapbook, v. 238; E. Francis Brown, "Roosevelt Takes Control," *Current History* 38 (Apr. 1933): 77–87.

whose shoulders seemed stooped, and as far as we could judge from his bearing, he was a man wrapped up in his own thought. . . . He had a piece of luggage in his hand. I recall the first day I put him on the stand, and he came into the hearing room attended by a retinue of officials and persons connected with the bank, carrying records and so forth. . . . The impression it made on me was of a person going into exile, and Senator Norbeck agreed with me.[65]

As Mitchell boarded his train, bankers across the nation fought to stay alive one more day—and many were losing the battle.

65. Pecora, COHC, pp. 685–87.

CHAPTER VI

Exit Hoover

THE FUNERAL of former President Calvin Coolidge on January 7, 1933, tolled requiem over the age of prosperity, laissez-faire, and voluntary action. Mounting bank failures and disillusioning publicity frightened depositors into withdrawing currency. When an impotent administration could not save the banking system of an entire state, the Michigan moratorium, as well as a disheartening recitation of bankers' sins before the Pecora hearings, unsettled a public confidence already trembling from bank closings and contraction of credit.

Each of these problems might have been avoided singly, but in concert they overwhelmed a regime which felt its lack of legitimacy deeply. Eugene Meyer called the last days of the Hoover administration "a period of going along as best you could from day to day. There was an inability to function, and the new people were standing aloof and the trouble was piling up."[1]

In facing heavy drains of gold and currency in addition to bank closings in Michigan, Maryland, and other states, Herbert Hoover believed that he needed the support of the incoming president, even when his closest advisers pleaded for emergency action. Hoover spent his last days in office seeking the cooperation of a man who held that no president could ever require the endorsement of any other person to follow a course of action he thought justified.

The depression had deepened. Industrial and financial activity did not enjoy even the brief upturn seen in the textile trades early in the summer of 1932. Nor did the presidential election results reassure businessmen; the *Commercial and Financial Chronicle* recorded that "gloom was still all pervading." The editors based their conclusion on "enormous shrinkages" of bank clearings in 1930, 1931, and 1932. That is, the rate of economic activity measured by the processing of checks through commercial banks and the clearinghouses fell to "figures that previously would have been regarded as unbelievable." Clearings decreased 25.4 percent in 1930 over 1929, 24.5 percent in 1931 over 1930, and 37.3 percent in 1932 over 1931. Moreover, each month of 1932 showed a lower total of clearings than the corresponding month of 1931, as did 1931 over 1930, and 1930 over 1929. Turnover of deposits, a measure of the rate at which money was being used, also declined drastically in 1932, hitting a a ten-year low, according to the Federal Reserve Board.[2]

Banks continued to retrench. Loans for securities and other purposes decreased by $250 million in the last quarter of 1932, despite a growth in reserve accounts which would have permitted more lending if business had been less pessimistic and more willing to borrow. Bankers still believed they had to protect themselves; for the first time in sixty-three years, national banks made no profits for their stockholders, and in eleven of the Federal Reserve districts they distributed almost their entire surplus as interest to depositors.[3] A study by the National Industrial Conference Board blamed this bank deflation for continued depression. "It is patent," the report said, "that the course of the present depression has been made deeper by the failure of the banking system at large to extend credit accommodation to industry and trade as a whole." It recommended a reestablishment of credit contacts between banks and their business customers.[4] Yet assets continued to dwindle, deposits declined, and bankers concentrated their resources in fewer institutions or sought increased liquidity.[5]

In 1932 more American banks failed than in any single year

1. Meyer, COHC, pp. 688–90.
2. *Commercial and Financial Chronicle*, 21 Jan. 1933, pp. 381–84; *Federal Reserve Bulletin*, Jan. 1933, pp. 1–5; Feb. 1933, p. 67.
3. *Federal Reserve Bulletin*, Jan. 1933, pp. 1–5.
4. *New York Times*, 1 Jan. 1933.
5. *Commercial and Financial Chronicle*, 14 Jan. 1933, p. 259; 18 Feb. 1933, p. 1147; *New York Times*, 15, 31 Jan. 1933; *Federal Reserve Bulletin*, Apr. 1933, pp. 209–12.

except 1931; 1,453 institutions with $730,426,000 in deposits closed their doors. Only a few New England states escaped suspensions. In 1931, 2,298 banks with $1,691,510,000 in deposits closed; in 1930, 1,345 institutions holding $864,715,000. In those three years, 20 percent of all banks in operation at the end of 1929 failed; during 1932 alone, 7 percent of the institutions open at the beginning of the year suspended.[6]

At first the largest number of closings involved small banks with minimal capitalization and resources. Increasingly, however, runs spread to San Francisco, New Orleans, Kansas City, and Nashville. Even large metropolitan banks felt their assets weakened and feared the unruly temper of their depositors.[7] For example, of the 41 banks in the District of Columbia, none failed in 1930 or 1931, but four went down in 1932 and fourteen in 1933; in the opinion of one analyst, these banks suspended primarily because of anxiety created in Washington residents by reports of bank difficulties in their home communities.[8]

Confidence suffered a major shock on February 4, 1933, with the Louisiana bank holiday and again ten days later when Michigan closed. Consequently, institutions in the interior withdrew money from their correspondent banks in New York City while depositors everywhere rushed to convert time and demand deposits to cash and especially to gold. Transfers of funds out of New York, drains of hoarded money, and further gold withdrawals for export to Europe forced a tightening of money rates in New York, and the New York Federal Reserve Bank decided to use its purchases of bills to pour funds into the market. Citizens apparently needed reassurance about money; in December 1932 many families increased the customary practice of giving gold pieces as Christmas gifts to children and servants.[9]

6. *New York Times,* 26, 27 Jan., 17 Feb. 1933.
7. *Federal Reserve Bulletin,* Apr. 1933, pp. 209–12; Henry Bruère, COHC, pp. 144–45; Upham and Lamke, *Closed and Distressed Banks,* pp. 9–12; Feis, *1933,* p. 12; Laurin L. Henry, *Presidential Transitions* (Washington, D. C.: Brookings Institution, 1960), pp. 343–45; *New York Times,* 30 Mar. 1933.
8. David M. Cole, *The Development of Banking in the District of Columbia* (New York: William-Frederick, 1959), pp. 450–53.
9. Memorandum of meeting, Board of Directors, New York Federal Reserve Bank, 23 Feb. 1933, Harrison Papers, binder 50; New York Federal Reserve Bank, *Monthly Review of Credit and Business Conditions,* Apr. 1931, p. 26; *Federal Reserve Bulletin,* Apr. 1933, pp. 209–12; Bird, *Invisible Scar,* p. 98.

In January 1933, 241 more banks failed; in February, 148— not counting places where banks were sealed by law to avoid failures. Newspapers underplayed bank closings[10] but found it difficult to bury other damaging news on the financial pages. Collapse of the Insull empire, Ivar Kreuger's suicide, the Dawes loan, Father Coughlin's denunciations of bankers, and dozens of similarly demoralizing reports contributed to the spiritual paralysis of the nation.

No blow, however, did so much damage as the publication of the names of banks which had received loans from the Reconstruction Finance Corporation. Despite opposition from the American Bankers Association, the Federal Advisory Council, and the Hoover administration, the House of Representatives on January 6, 1933, passed a resolution calling on the RFC to submit a report of its first five months' operations to become "a part of the public records." Under the terms of the Emergency Relief and Construction Act of 1932, the RFC had to report its loans to the Senate, but by agreement they had been kept confidential. Now the rescues became public, and as the administration feared, publicity exposed even saved banks to heavy withdrawals by frightened depositors.[11] Almost immediately Hoover tried to secure repeal of the noxious resolution, and on February 18, Senator Robinson introduced a bill to stop the practice,[12] but publicity continued until the next administration took office.

Other bad news further undermined the banks. For the last month of the Hoover administration, newspapers daily reported no success in reopening the moratorium-protected Michigan banks; depositors suspected "colossal blundering"—or worse.[13] At the same time, on the national scene the Senate Finance Committee and the Banking and Currency Committee were conducting investigations of the depression which elicited more harmful information and

10. Charles Michelson, *The Ghost Talks* (New York: Putnam's, 1944), p. 54–56.

11. John T. Flynn, "Inside the R.F.C.," *Harper's Magazine* 166 (Jan. 1933): 161–68; Thomas B. Paton to members of the American Bankers Association, 17 Jan. 1933, Hoover Papers, West Branch, Presidential Papers, box 1–G/981; Federal Reserve Board, Minutes, 23 Feb. 1933; *New York Times*, 27, 28 Jan. 1933; *Commercial and Financial Chronicle*, 14 Jan. 1933, p. 271; *Congressional Record*, 72d Cong., 2d Sess., 6 Jan. 1933, pp. 1361–62.

12. Hoover, *Memoirs* 3:198; David Burnett to F. Gloyd Awalt, quoted in *New York Times*, 31 Jan. 1933.

13. *Commercial and Financial Chronicle*, 15 Feb. 1933, p. 1066; Josephson, *Infidel in the Temple*, pp. 185–87.

opinions about bankers. Testimony by Nicholas Murray Butler of Columbia University, Alexander Dana Noyes of the *New York Times*, and Winthrop W. Aldrich of the Chase Bank highlighted the bankruptcy of business and banking leadership, while Ferdinand Pecora brought out a nine-day string of damaging evidence from Mitchell of the National City Bank.[14]

Depositors rushed to salvage their funds. One family taped a thousand dollars in large bills to their young son's chest rather than leave it in a savings account. Letters to newspapers also reflected popular distrust; one to the *New York Times* indicted bankers' training, saying that it did not generate the courage and vision essential to public leadership. Most Washington reporters saw the danger even more clearly; by late February, according to Arthur Krock, "it was only a question of when they would do it"—close the banks. Disillusionment even sparked a perverse humor. According to one story, a banker begged an old friend not to reveal his profession to his mother. "She thinks I'm playing the piano in a sporting house," he said. Senator Carter Glass of Virginia told another anecdote: "One banker in my state attempted to marry a white woman and they lynched him."[15]

Meanwhile, in the last two weeks before he left office, Hoover searched for a stopgap against the banking panic. The president accepted a joint resolution offered to Congress by Senator James Couzens, authorizing the Comptroller of the Currency to extend state emergency banking privileges to national banks. Although Congress rushed the measure through in only five days,[16] the Comptroller had no opportunity to use his new powers since no state could devise appropriate rescue or rehabilitation measures. At the same time, the Federal Reserve System continued its efforts to free credit and meet deflation; the Open Market Committee agreed to maintain the level of excess reserves, and the Board endorsed a lowering of the rates

14. *New York Times*, 22, 23, 24, 26, 28 Feb. 1933; Gilbert Seldes, *The Years of the Locust: America, 1929–1932* (Boston: Little, Brown, 1933), p. 275; "Washington and the Banks," *Business Week*, 8 Mar. 1933, pp. 3–4.

15. Bird, *Invisible Scar*, p. 103; Josephson, *Infidel*, pp. 173–74; *New York Times*, 6, 10 Feb. 1933; Krock, COHC, p. 14.

16. *New York Times*, 19–25 Feb. 1933; *Commercial and Financial Chronicle*, 18 Feb. 1933, pp. 1150–51; 25 Feb. 1933, p. 1304; 4 Mar. 1933, p. 1478; Ogden Mills to James Couzens, 18 Feb. 1933, Mills Papers, box 111; Hamlin, *Diary*, 17, 20, 21 Feb. 1933; O'Connor, *Banking Crisis and Recovery*, p. 144.

charged for advances to member banks from 5½ to 5 percent.[17] Congress, too, cooperated by extending for another year the provisions of the Glass-Steagall Act of 1932 making government securities eligible as backing for currency, deposits, and loans.[18] Despite this power, member banks continued to unload their holdings into demoralized markets. Simultaneously the nation resounded with a host of suggestions ranging from insurance of bank deposits to compulsory withdrawal and spending of 10 percent of all money in banks.[19] And pundits, including Walter Lippmann and vice-president-elect Garner, thought the emergency called for a great concentration and use of administrative and ministerial powers.[20]

In the absence of really effective national action, the states tried to solve their own banking problems. Nevada, Louisiana, and Michigan had already declared moratoriums. Banks in New Jersey, Maryland, and New York, as well as the District of Columbia, reduced interest rates on savings deposits. Many states and localities prepared legislation to prevent additional failures; New Jersey, Pennsylvania, Indiana, Ohio, Delaware, West Virginia, and Arkansas authorized state banks to limit withdrawals, and increasing numbers of institutions took advantage of the privilege. As suspicion spread, mayors in Huntington, Indiana, and Mt. Carmel, Illinois, suspended banking, while communities in North Carolina, Iowa, Michigan, Tennessee, and Illinois permitted their banks to issue scrip. On February 23, Indiana declared a bank holiday; Maryland followed on February 25, Arkansas on February 27, and Ohio on February 28. In each case the governor justified his action as a protection for the banks to prevent depleting withdrawals in reaction to the Michigan suspension.[21]

17. Federal Reserve Board, Minutes, 5 Jan. 1933; Hamlin, Diary, 24, 27 Feb. 1933; Commercial and Financial Chronicle, 7 Jan. 1933, pp. 2–4.

18. Federal Reserve Bulletin, Feb. 1933, pp. 59–60; Annual Report of the Federal Reserve Board, 1933, pp. 36–37.

19. J. M. Cunningham to FDR, 23 Feb. 1933; Spurgeon Bell to Senator Robert J. Bulkley, copy to FDR, 28 Feb. 1933, FDRL:OF 230; New York Times, 3 Jan., 23 Feb. 1933; New York Journal of Commerce, 21 Feb. 1933.

20. Lippmann, Interpretations: 1933–1935, p. 11.

21. New York Times, 19, 22, 24–29 Feb., 1–4 Mar. 1933; New York Journal of Commerce, 8 Feb. 1933; Newark News, 1 Feb. 1933; Baltimore Sun, 1 Feb. 1933; Commercial and Financial Chronicle, 4 Feb. 1933, p. 703; 11 Feb. 1933, pp. 933–38; 18 Feb. 1933, p. 1063; Federal Reserve Bulletin, Mar. 1933, p. 113.

Moratoriums increased pressure on the great banking houses in New York. Banks in that city felt they had cooperated fully to combat the depression in 1931 and 1932 through the National Credit Corporation, the Federal Reserve Banking and Industrial Committee, a $100 million bond pool to sustain prices, and a $50 million Commodities Finance Corporation. But with the crisis in Michigan and other interior states, out-of-town banks withdrew half a billion dollars from New York, creating almost overwhelming demands on individual New York banks and on the Federal Reserve Bank there.[22]

Meanwhile, President Hoover watched this deterioration with anguish, believing that he could do nothing to stop it without the sanction of his successor and some assurance that Congress would endorse his movements.

Herbert Hoover and Franklin Roosevelt wasted no affection on one another. Hoover felt a natural bitterness after losing the election, and he resented Roosevelt's polite but resolute refusal to become involved in national policies during the interregnum. Most of all, Hoover believed Roosevelt criminally remiss in not revealing the intentions of the incoming administration, particularly about money; uncertainty, he thought, was encouraging hoarding of currency and runs on the banks. For his part, Roosevelt could not help but disapprove—as a member of the Woodrow Wilson school of practical politics—of Hoover's refusal to use the full prerogatives of his office for effective leadership. Nor did he want to make a commitment to the rejected policies of the Hoover administration; not only did Roosevelt disagree with his predecessor's approach to the depression, but he did not relish assuming office burdened with Hoover's unpopularity.[23] The first encounter of president and president-elect, over the World War I debts and plans for a world monetary and trade conference, failed to produce any agreement for continuity between

22. *Federal Reserve Bulletin,* Apr. 1933, pp. 209–11.

23. Hoover, *Memoirs,* 3:176–77; Max Freedman, ed., *Roosevelt and Frankfurter: Their Correspondence, 1928–1945* (Boston: Little, Brown, 1967), pp. 64–67; Grace Tully, *F. D. R.: My Boss* (New York: Scribner's, 1949), pp. 57, 59–60; Raymond Moley, *27 Masters of Politics: In a Personal Perspective* (New York: Funk and Wagnalls, 1949), pp. 26–27; Rexford G. Tugwell, *The Democratic Roosevelt: A Biography of Franklin D. Roosevelt* (Garden City, N. Y.: Doubleday, 1957), p. 263.

the two administrations.[24] Neither could accept the other's position; neither saw any room for compromise.

Domestic economic concerns early in February drove Hoover to seek cooperation from Roosevelt on banking issues. In the first half of the month, gold dwindled dangerously and banks suffered heavy withdrawals in the wake of RFC publicity. On February 12 the president thought the banking crisis sufficiently volatile to change the topic of his Lincoln's birthday address in order to avoid further panic. While Michigan tottered on February 13 and 14, he begged Democratic leaders to influence Roosevelt to reassure the nation by revealing the anticipated currency policies of the incoming administration. Apparently Hoover expected some reciprocal gesture to his speech at the National Republican Club in which he pledged support to his successor in promoting the public welfare.[25]

Roosevelt also knew of the critical situation. When Secretary of State Stimson approached him to relay details about Michigan, he discovered that "the Texas gentleman of the R.F.C." (Jesse Jones) had already delivered a briefing. Moreover, the "big guns" of Wall Street had exerted all possible pressures on Roosevelt to avert a panic, but he saw no reason to bail out the bankers and "responded breezily" to Stimson and others who urged him to be more amenable to Hoover.[26] Hoover himself attempted to contact Roosevelt on February 6 only to be told by his advisers that he could not be reached. Roosevelt was then on a fishing trip aboard Vincent Astor's yacht.

On February 18, Hoover sent Roosevelt a hand-written appeal, delivered by a Secret Service agent during a banquet at the

24. FDR, introductory note to "Between Election and Inauguration–November, 1932 to March 4, 1933," Rosenman, *Public Papers*, p. 871; Tugwell, Diary, 20 Dec. 1933, FDRL: Group 80; Myers and Newton, *Hoover Administration*, pp. 277–302; Feis, *1933*, pp. 32, 35; Tully, *F. D. R.*, p. 60; Moley, 27 *Masters*, p. 23; idem, *First New Deal*, pp. 21–46.

25. Hoover, *Memoirs*, 3:202; Myers and Newton, *Hoover Administration*, pp. 317–20; Joslin, *Hoover Off the Record*, pp. 355–58; Arthur Krock, COHC, pp. 12–13; Showan, "Hoover-Roosevelt Relationship," p. 46; Broadus Mitchell, *Depression Decade: From New Era through New Deal, 1929–1941* (New York: Holt, Rinehart and Winston, 1947), pp. 129–30; Harris Gaylord Warren, *Herbert Hoover and the Great Depression* (New York: Oxford University Press, 1959), pp. 279–87.

26. Tugwell, Diary, 18 Feb. 1933; Stimson, Diary, Yale University, 17 Feb. 1933; Feis, *1933*, p. 81.

Hotel Astor in New York. "The major difficulty," the president said, "is the state of public mind—for there is a steadily degenerating confidence in the future which has reached the height of general alarm." Hoover then defended the policies of his own administration, claiming that recovery had proceeded smoothly until the fall of 1932 when Roosevelt's election engendered a "natural and inevitable hesitation all along the economic line pending the demonstration of the policies of the new administration." This uncertainty, together with the failure of budget balancing, inflationary proposals, publication of RFC loans, bank runs, hoarding, congressional spending, and talk of a dictatorship demoralized both borrowers and lenders, he said. Hoover therefore asked Roosevelt to clarify the public's mind with a "prompt assurance that there will be no tampering or inflation of the currency; that the budget will be unquestionably balanced even if further taxation is necessary; that the government credit will be maintained by refusal to exhaust it in issue of securities." He also wanted Roosevelt to announce the name of his new secretary of the Treasury to implement liaison between the two administrations.[27]

If it had been consciously planned—and it was not—Hoover could not have devised a worse approach to Roosevelt. To begin by blaming the current crisis on the very man whose help he wanted required a peculiarly Hooverian logic—the same mental processes that justified his contention that those who elected Roosevelt in November distrusted him soon afterward and regretted that they would not continue to enjoy the stability of the Hoover administration which they had foolishly rejected. Moreover, in the review and defense of his own policies, Hoover implied that he expected Roosevelt to adopt the same program he had successfully opposed in the campaign. A few days later, the president wrote to Senator David A. Reed, "I realize that if these declarations be made by the President-elect, he will have ratified the whole major program of the Republican Administration; that is, it means the abandonment of ninety per cent of the so-called new deal. But unless this is done, they run a grave danger of precipitating a complete financial debacle. If it is precipitated, the responsibility lies squarely with them for they have

27. Hoover to FDR, 18 Feb. 1933, FDRL:PPF 820; Hoover, *Memoirs*, 3:203–04; Myers and Newton, *Hoover Administration*, pp. 338–40; John S. West to W. H. Moran, 19 Feb. 1933, Mills Papers.

had ample warning—unless, of course, such a debacle is part of the 'new deal.' " Raymond Moley commented that the Hoover letter "assumed that Roosevelt would succeed—where Hoover had repeatedly failed—in hornswoggling the country with optimistic statements which everyone knew weren't justified."[28]

Hoover could not have written to Roosevelt in this vein with any realistic estimate of the latter's personality or political philosophy—not if he expected to be considered seriously. Yet he believed that his successor could not miss the obvious truths he cited.

At the banquet, Roosevelt received Hoover's letter calmly. He passed it unobtrusively to Raymond Moley and other companions while he continued to enjoy the Inner Circle dinner apparently unconcerned. Later, at his residence, he discussed the appeal with his aides; Moley wondered at the lack of annoyance with Hoover's blundering self-righteousness. Perhaps Roosevelt did not understand the gravity of the banking panic; perhaps he was persuaded by Louis Howe's constant citation of optimistic human interest news stories from Detroit. In observing Roosevelt during the days following Hoover's letter, Moley "detected nothing but the most complete confidence in his own ability to deal with any situation that might arise."[29] Probably Roosevelt merely dismissed Hoover's explanation of the crisis, believing that depositors feared their own banks rather than the New Deal. Apprehension of the discredited bankers, he felt, fostered a deep mistrust of the entire system, with ensuing runs and depletion of currency. At least one Roosevelt adviser believed that the ideas and words in Hoover's appeal were those of Treasury Secretary Mills and the big bankers: "None of them would face the fact that their own policies during the previous decade had fostered the depression. They were taking refuge in the belief that the soundness of their policies and actions would be proven if only the President-elect and the inflationist members of Congress and other groups would stop scaring the American people."[30] Roosevelt

28. Myers and Newton, *Hoover Administration*, p. 341; Moley, *After Seven Years*, pp. 140–42.

29. Moley, *After Seven Years*, pp. 140–43; idem, *First New Deal*, p. 349; Hoover, *Memoirs*, 3:215; Tugwell, *Democratic Roosevelt*, pp. 262–64; idem, "The Protagonists: Roosevelt and Hoover," *Antioch Review* 13 (Dec. 1953): 420–21.

30. Feis, *1933*, p. 82.

accordingly could not believe that the American people feared *him*.

Above all, he held that Hoover remained president until noon on March 4 and required no outsider's support so long as he chose to use his official prerogatives. Roosevelt, a private citizen until he took the oath of office, had no obligation to act for or against the current administration—courtesy, in fact, required that he keep silent. He would neither comply with Hoover's request for a statement, since to do so would make him a pseudo-Hoover, nor would he refuse outright and run the risk of being labelled a saboteur. Roosevelt therefore followed the proper and prudent course—he did nothing.

Meanwhile, Hoover waited silently for an answer and worried about the lack of direction in his successor's approach to office. He importuned several senators and party leaders to try to convince Roosevelt that he must cooperate. To each, Hoover made the same case: fear of the policies of the new administration was plunging the country into a financial disaster and only a commitment to Hoover's ideas could save it. At no time, however, did he make his request to Roosevelt public, believing that any such acknowledgment by him of the true gravity of the situation would only increase panic.[31] Other prominent men, including Bernard Baruch and Melvin Traylor, publicly called for a commitment to sound money; the Federal Advisory Council passed a formal resolution to the same effect; and many New York bankers pleaded with the president-elect to reveal his intentions.[32]

The president-elect also failed to cooperate with Hoover by announcing his cabinet appointees early. Because of the critical situation, Roosevelt might have announced his choices for the State and Treasury departments to establish contacts with the outgoing administration. Instead, his delay minimized communications between the two regimes and even encouraged speculations like Hoo-

31. Hoover to David A. Reed, 20 Feb. 1933; Hoover to Simeon D. Fess, 21 Feb. 1933; Myers and Newton, *Hoover Administration*, pp. 341, 351–56; Hoover, *Memoirs*, 3:204–09; Joslin, *Hoover Off the Record*, pp. 361–62; Wolfe, *Hoover*, pp. 347–48; Moley, *First New Deal*, pp. 142–43; Feis, *1933*, pp. 82–83; Henry, *Presidential Transitions*, pp. 348–49.

32. Mark Sullivan, memorandum, 21 Feb. 1933; unsigned memorandum, 21 Feb. 1933—both in Hoover Papers, West Branch, box 1-G/981; Hamlin, Diary, 21 Feb. 1933; Stimson, Diary, 22 Feb. 1933; Ernest Burham to Roosevelt, 26 Feb. 1933, FDRL:OF 230; Lindley, *Half Way with Roosevelt*, p. 94.

ver's about the Roosevelt administration's forthcoming policies.

During January and February, Roosevelt's lieutenants negotiated with Senator Carter Glass for the Treasury post. Certainly the senator was the logical choice since he had held the office under President Wilson and as "father" of the Federal Reserve System was the Democratic party's man of orthodoxy on banking and finance; thus, his appointment would have reassured those who worried about the nation's shaky credit structure. But as the talks proceeded, Glass repeatedly expressed reservations about his own precarious health, his desire to have Russell Leffingwell of the House of Morgan as under-secretary, and his concern over inflation. Roosevelt refused to accept Leffingwell and would give no guarantees about money. Raymond Moley, who conducted most of the conversations about the appointment, came to realize that Glass's acceptance would be disastrous for all concerned; Roosevelt's capricious views on fiscal and monetary affairs would, he was sure, inevitably lead to a clash and Glass's resignation. Glass must have reasoned along the same lines, since he refused the post, using his health as an excuse to avoid a public statement of his fears.[33]

With Glass out of the running and his gesture made to the party, Roosevelt could look for a more pliable secretary. On February 21 he announced the appointment of William Woodin, a Republican manufacturer who had contributed generously to the Roosevelt campaign fund. Indeed, long before Glass bowed out, Moley and Louis Howe had advanced Woodin's candidacy. They felt that his temperament would permit him to accomodate himself to whatever monetary and banking measures Roosevelt chose to try, and his position in the business community would salve fears there as well. They wired Roosevelt in code, "Prefer a wooden roof to a glass roof over swimming pool." As soon as Glass formally refused the job, therefore, Roosevelt offered it to Woodin, who accepted almost immediately.[34] Roosevelt at once attached Moley

33. A. W. Terrell to Glass, 2 Feb. 1933; Glass to Governor Harry F. Byrd, 4 Feb. 1933; Glass to Roosevelt, 7 Feb. 1933; Glass to Moley, 6 Feb. 1933—all in Glass Papers, box 6; Moley, First New Deal, pp. 73, 80–84; idem, After Seven Years, pp. 118–23; Hoover, Memoirs, 3:204; Baltimore Sun, 18 Feb. 1933; New York Times, 18 Feb. 1933; Commercial and Financial Chronicle, 25 Feb. 1933, pp. 1304–05; Smith and Beasley, Carter Glass, pp. 329–38.

34. Moley, First New Deal, pp. 84–85; idem, After Seven Years, pp. 121–22; Tugwell, COHC, pp. 35–36; James A. Farley, Behind the Ballots: The Personal

to Woodin, and the two men scarcely parted company for the next two weeks.

To the Hoover administration, Woodin's appointment offered another possibility for liaison with Roosevelt. Secretary Stimson had pressed the president-elect to announce his cabinet choices for precisely this reason. "The trouble was so serious," he said, "that it seemed to be a matter which could not be handled by intermittent intercourse between us and him, but could only be properly carried on by direct, continuous conference between the men who will be responsible for this after the 4th of March and those who are responsible for it now."[35]

Ogden Mills, Hoover's secretary of the Treasury, descended on his successor almost immediately. On February 23, 25, and 27, Mills bombarded Woodin with evidence of mounting bank withdrawals, currency hoarding, and gold famine. George Leslie Harrison of the New York Federal Reserve Bank also pressed Woodin and Moley to extract a commitment from Roosevelt. Woodin replied for Roosevelt that Hoover was still responsible and should act on his own authority in whatever manner he felt justified. Neither Roosevelt nor Woodin intended to issue any statement.[36] On March 1 Hoover instructed Mills to offer "full cooperation of the administration to the President-elect in any line of sensible action which will meet the present banking situation." But he added, "It would be futile to present anything unless the President-elect will publicly declare that it is his desire that it should be undertaken."[37] Again Roosevelt's answer was no.

On February 28, Hoover had taken the direct approach again

History of a Politician (New York: Harcourt, Brace, 1938), p. 206; Michelson, *Ghost Talks*, pp. 54–55; Lindley, *Roosevelt Revolution*, pp. 54–56, 285–86; Tugwell, *Democratic Roosevelt*, p. 264; Roger W. Babson, *Washington and the Revolutionists* (New York: Harper, 1934), pp. 231–39; Alfred B. Rollins, Jr., *Roosevelt and Howe* (New York: Knopf, 1962), p. 373.

35. Stimson, Diary, insert memorandum of conversation with FDR, 17 Feb. 1933.

36. Hoover to Mills, 22 Feb. 1933, Hoover Papers, West Branch, box 1–G/981; Myers and Newton, *Hoover Administration*, pp. 343–44, 355, 356; Hoover, *Memoirs*, 3:204; Henry, *Presidential Transitions*, p. 350; Moley, *First New Deal*, pp. 86, 144–45; Feis, *1933*, p. 83; Harrison, memoranda of conversations with Owen Young, Woodin, and Moley, 17, 18, 19 Feb. 1933, Harrison Papers, binder 46.

37. Hoover to Mills, 1 Mar. 1933, Hoover Papers, West Branch, box 1–G/981; Myers and Newton, *Hoover Administration*, p. 361.

by writing to Roosevelt. Because of economic declines since the first letter, he repeated his request for some declaration from the president-elect and now asked for a special session of Congress to meet soon after inauguration. As before, the president's letter was confidential. At a White House meeting the day before, Hoover had reviewed the situation with his advisers. Some urged him to make a public request for a reply from Roosevelt in order to fix responsibility where it belonged, but Hoover said that he would not play politics with the national welfare.[38] This approach was in line, too, with his previous secret efforts to counteract the depression, such as his meetings with the bankers in 1931 to establish the National Credit Corporation.

Finally, on March 1, Roosevelt replied to Hoover's letters. By a secretary's oversight, Roosevelt said, a letter written on February 20 had never been sent to Hoover. (He did not explain why he himself had never questioned why the letter was not offered for his signature, nor what remarkable foresight allowed him to write on February 20 in a tone unjustified by events of that date, but wholly in keeping with conditions ten days later.) The February 20 response would have done Hoover no good in any case, since it merely expressed concern over "the gravity of the present bank situation" and asserted that no mere statement could counteract the real trouble, namely, "that on present values very few financial institutions anywhere in the country are actually able to pay off their deposits in full, and the knowledge of this fact is widely held."[39] Roosevelt continued to regard Hoover as wholly free to do whatever he chose to meet the banking panic, while Hoover persisted in believing that he could do nothing without Roosevelt.

What did Roosevelt want? Did he understand the crisis? Could he possibly desire a total crack-up of the American banking system before he took office? On February 25, in a conversation with James Rand, Rexford Tugwell of the Brains Trust claimed that the Roosevelt group was fully aware of the impending collapse and worried

38. Hoover to FDR, 28 Feb. 1933, FDRL:PPF 820; Myers and Newton, *Hoover Administration*, pp. 358–60; Stimson, Diary, 28 Feb. 1933.

39. FDR to Hoover, 20 Feb., 1 Mar. 1933, FDRL:PPF 820; Hoover Papers, West Branch, box 1–G/981; Hoover, *Memoirs*, 3:206; Myers and Newton, *Hoover Administration*, p. 360; Moley, *First New Deal*, pp. 143–44, 211–13; idem, *After Seven Years*, p. 142; idem, *27 Masters*, p. 27; Feis, *1933*, p. 84; Schlesinger, *Crisis of the Old Order*, pp. 477–78.

only about "rehabilitating the country on March 4th."[40] Tugwell never denied making the statement, which his biographer later judged a serious tactical error, even if he was merely trying to avoid giving information to Rand. Tugwell's talkativeness, his biographer concluded, "was attributable to a lapse in self-control or a miscalculation at the moment, carelessness, or extreme naivete, or all of these."[41] But Tugwell's position on economic matters frequently fell to the left of Roosevelt's early in 1933. Hence he may have been stating his own hopes that the banking structure would crumble around Hoover's ears, allowing the incoming administration to revamp the system—a procedure Tugwell would suggest less than two weeks later. Raymond Moley, who still had Roosevelt's ear in that period, later claimed that the president-elect never told him that he intended to gamble with the nation's security. "It deserves to be said, however," Moley later commented, "that if he had so calculated, his conduct would have been exactly what it was."[42]

Henry Stimson, after a meeting with Roosevelt, decided that the president-elect "had put it all up on to Hoover, and evidently to get the benefit of having matters as bad as they can be now before he comes in."[43] More directly, Roosevelt told one of his own group, "Let them bust; then we'll get things on a sound basis."[44]

When the banks went down, they would fall on Hoover; Roosevelt would inherit neither the crisis nor Hoover's limitations. Since he believed that the banks would collapse anyway of internal causes, a statement to the contrary from him would only dissipate his own prestige fruitlessly.

By March 1, therefore, the old and the new administrations had reached a standstill. Hoover feared repudiation too much to take the risk that his last official act would blot what he regarded as an otherwise upright record. Roosevelt, on the other hand, saw no reason to rescue either Hoover or the bankers; their salvation would

40. James Rand to Theodore Joslin, memorandum of telephone conversation, 25 Feb. 1933, confirmed in Hoover to Rand, 28 Feb. 1933, Hoover Papers, West Branch, box 1–G/981; Hoover, Memoirs, 3:214–15, 357; Stimson, Diary, 3 Mar. 1933.
41. Bernard Sternsher, Rexford Tugwell and the New Deal (New Brunswick, N. J.: Rutgers University Press, 1964), pp. 73–75.
42. Moley, 27 Masters, p. 24.
43. Feis, 1933, pp. 86, 104.
44. Roosevelt to Feis, quoted in John T. Flynn, The Roosevelt Myth (New York: Devin-Adair, 1948), pp. 24, 31–32.

not improve his position and their fall could offer him some interesting opportunities. In the last analysis, however, no one—neither Hoover, nor Roosevelt, nor the bankers—produced a concrete program to correct either the banking or the gold panic until it was too late to put such measures into effect.

By the end of February, popular confidence had collapsed. Michigan, Maryland, and Tennessee suspended banking entirely; seventeen other states had legislation waiting to limit withdrawals or close state banks. On March 1, Alabama and Louisiana declared mandatory holidays; Kentucky and West Virginia left closing to the discretion of individual banks; Idaho gave its governor power to proclaim holidays; and Minnesota sanctioned a fifteen-day suspension whenever the commissioner of banking thought it justified. The next day six more states—Arizona, California, Mississippi, Oklahoma, Oregon, and Nevada—closed their banks. Attention still centered on Detroit, where continuing conferences failed to reopen Michigan's banks, and on Baltimore, where the holiday was extended day by day after February 25. In the District of Columbia and several states, savings banks required depositors to give sixty days notice of withdrawals. New York considered similar action. In that state, savings depositors stood in long lines to get cash: $732 million in a single week. New York's commercial banks lost over $750 million to out-of-town correspondents, and even the largest institutions had to sell short-term paper to get cash. Domestic hoarders and foreign earmarkers took gold out of circulation; the stock market remained in the doldrums; government securities and railroad and utility bonds fell.[45]

Top government officials, recognizing the danger, asked Hoover to assume special powers. On February 20 Senator David Reed of Pennsylvania relayed suggestions from Democratic senators that the president restrict gold exports and forbid banks to give out gold in exchange for paper money; he promised Senate support. Hoover could have acted under the World War I Trading-with-the-Enemy Act to control transactions in foreign exchange and hoarding

45. E. A. Goldenweiser to Theodore Joslin, 2 Mar. 1933, Hoover Papers, West Branch, box 1–G/981; Restrictions on Deposit Withdrawals, memorandum by Statistical Division, U. S. Treasury Department, FDRL:OF 21; *New York Times*, 1, 2, 3 Mar. 1933.

of silver, gold, and currency. Secretary of the Treasury Ogden Mills and Undersecretary Arthur Ballantine, as well as Adolph Miller of the Federal Reserve Board, urged Hoover to use those prerogatives. Both the Justice Department and the Senator Glass, however, advised against such a course on grounds that the original act had been amended and partially repealed; they also cited the risk in using a wartime law during peacetime.[46]

Even after Roosevelt's letter of March 1, the president continued to seek his successor's approval. He sent Mills to Woodin again to ask for a joint plea to Congress to pass special banking legislation. When Roosevelt arrived in Washington for his inauguration, Woodin presented this latest appeal, but no one—neither Mills, nor Woodin, nor Senator James Byrnes—could convince him to cooperate. And Hoover still would not act alone.[47]

Mounting crisis and dimming hopes of cooperation drove Hoover to the Federal Reserve Board for a solution to the banking panic. He wrote to the Board on February 22 asking whether "any measures should be undertaken at this junction and especially what, if any, further authority should be obtained."[48] Hoover may have hoped to share laibility for the almost inevitable crash. If so, the Board evaded that trap by sending a conservative answer on February 25, despite serious deterioration in the New York and Cleveland districts. In the main, the Board cautioned against adopting any of the current proposals without weighing whether they might bring on even greater disturbances; it offered no specific recommendation for additional measures or authority but promised to continue to consider carefully "all aspects of the situation."[49]

46. Tugwell, Diary, 27 Feb. 1933, pp. 123–25; Krock, COHC, p. 34; Hamlin, Diary, 13 Nov. 1932; Hoover, Memoirs, 3:205, 212–13; Myers and Newton, Hoover Administration, pp. 240, 365–66; Moley, After Seven Years, p. 144; idem, First New Deal, pp. 146–48; Schlesinger, Crisis of Old Order, p. 479; Henry, Presidential Transitions, pp. 347–48.

47. Farley, Behind the Ballots, pp. 206–07; Moley, First New Deal, pp. 145–48; Hoover, Memoirs, 3:213; New York Times, 2–4 Mar. 1933; James F. Byrnes, All in One Lifetime (New York: Harper, 1958), pp. 70–71.

48. Hoover to Federal Reserve Board, 22 Feb. 1933, Federal Reserve Board files; Myers and Newton, Hoover Administration, pp. 354–55; Hoover, Memoirs, 3:210; memoranda of meetings, Board of Directors and Executive Committee, New York Federal Reserve Bank, 16, 20 Feb. 1933, Harrison Papers, binder 50.

49. Eugene Meyer to Hoover, 25 Feb. 1933, Federal Reserve Board files; Federal Reserve Board, Minutes, 23, 25 Feb. 1933; Myers and Newton, Hoover Administration, p. 357; Hoover, Memoirs, 3:210.

By February 28, Hoover had narrowed the alternatives and again approached the Board for its opinion. Ogden Mills offered the idea of a temporary federal guarantee of free assets in banks in order to keep most banks open and functioning. Adolph Miller, however, urged that banks be allowed to meet the demand for funds by issuing pseudo-money in the form of clearinghouse certificates and scrip, particularly in areas under moratoriums. Should he adopt either of these suggestions or permit continued drift, Hoover asked The Board knew that most local bankers, especially those in New York and Washington, opposed scrip, although most of the Reserve banks had scrip plans ready. The New York Reserve Bank had devised a guarantee program calling for 50 percent Reserve backing of deposits, but the Board learned that Roosevelt would not support a guarantee. To make their dilemma worse, reports came in from New York of debilitating drains, and the Board had to induce the Reserve bank in Chicago to lend money to New York.[50]

When Governor Meyer replied for the Board on March 2, therefore, he ruled out any form of guarantee, evaded the scrip question, and concluded that the essential issue was not one of drift, "but whether any other step can be properly taken now which would produce better results" than the "sporadic state and community solutions now in progress."[51] The Federal Reserve Board wanted responsibility no more than did Hoover; each hoped that the other would decide what to do.

Frustrated in his proposals for a deposit guarantee, Mills now urged Hoover to use the Trading-with-the-Enemy Act to declare a national banking holiday, but the attorney general still questioned its authority and recommended that the president obtain prior consent from the incoming administration. In the light of extraordinarily large currency payments in all Federal Reserve districts and reports that many banks could not keep within their reserve margins and hence could not survive, the Reserve Board, too, recommended to Hoover that he proclaim a holiday for March 3, 4, and 6 on the

50. Hoover to Federal Reserve Board, 28 Feb. 1933, Federal Reserve Board files; Myers and Newton, *Hoover Administration*, pp. 359–60; Federal Reserve Board, Minutes, 28 Feb., 1 Mar. 1933; Hoover, *Memoirs*, 3:210–11; Hamlin, Diary, 1, 2 Mar. 1933.

51. Meyer to Hoover, 2 Mar. 1933, Hoover Papers, West Branch, box 1–G/981; Federal Reserve Board, Minutes, 2 Mar. 1933; Hoover, *Memoirs*, 3:211–12; Myers and Newton, *Hoover Administration*, pp. 361–63.

understanding that an emergency session of Congress would pass enabling legislation no later than March 7. Hoover asked the Board for a formal recommendation and draft proclamations, but he made it clear that he did not want to close the banks and would prefer a guarantee. If the Board would go on record as advising him and if Roosevelt would publicly approve the action, he would use the war power to restrict withdrawals and suspend trading in gold; in his opinion, a holiday would then be unnecessary.[52]

By March 3, 5,504 banks with deposits of $3,432,000,000 had closed their doors. New York and Chicago faced acute gold losses. Federal Reserve banks reported that they could not support member banks indefinitely, especially those drained by Michigan, Maryland, and Ohio. Governors in Georgia, New Mexico, Utah, and Wisconsin declared holidays; North Carolina, Virginia, and Wyoming limited withdrawals. At the end of the day eighteen states had mandatory restrictions; five others suffered widespread closings under statute; and thirteen plus the District of Columbia had scattered voluntary restrictions.[53] Ogden Mills thought conditions so serious that he advised a banker planning a trip to Bermuda, "If you go, don't get a round trip ticket—when you're ready to return, there'll be nothing worth returning to."[54]

March 3 was Herbert Hoover's last day in office. As failing banks inundated the outgoing administration, Hoover decided to give Roosevelt one last chance to join him in a rescue action. At the traditional formal call of the president-elect on the retiring president that afternoon, Hoover got through the amenities quickly and then called in Eugene Meyer and Ogden Mills. Roosevelt, forewarned, summoned Raymond Moley. The president repeated his request for endorsement, this time of his use of the Trading-with-the-Enemy Act to control foreign exchange and gold withdrawals. The president-elect replied mildly that his own attorney general had

52. Federal Reserve Board, Minutes, 2 Mar. 1933, 9:30 p.m.; Hamlin, Diary, 2 Mar. 1933; Hoover to Federal Reserve Board, 2 Mar. 1933, Federal Reserve Board files; copy in Hoover Papers, West Branch, box 1-G/981; Walter Wyatt to Raymond Moley, 16 Mar. 1966, quoted in Moley, First New Deal, pp. 146-47.
53. George W. Norris to Meyer, 3 Mar. 1933, Adolph Miller Papers, Federal Reserve Board, box 9; "Summary of Restrictions on Deposit Withdrawals through March 3, 1933," Statistical Division, U. S. Treasury Department, FDRL:OF 21; memorandum, n.d., Comptroller's files, NA: RG 101, box 6; New York Times, 3, 4 Mar. 1933.
54. Byrnes, All in One Lifetime, pp. 70-71.

found the act adequate and that he himself accepted its authority but he would not formally go further. He departed, telling Hoover that he would wait at his hotel for the president's decision.

Ike Hoover, head usher at the White House, said later that President Hoover had had no intention of inviting his successor at all, regardless of precedent, and issued the invitation only after the usher "in sheer desperation" told him that he must give "the President-elect an opportunity to pay his respects." He also relayed Roosevelt's desire to forego the customary dinner in favor of afternoon tea. In fact, neither William Howard Taft nor Woodrow Wilson had entertained their successors at dinner; tea was the usual practice when a new political party was coming in. Roosevelt did, however, have some cause for resentment at the meeting. Hoover kept him waiting for half an hour, an extremely uncomfortable time for a man to stand in braces; and at the end of the social exchange when Roosevelt graciously told Hoover that he did not expect him to return the call, Hoover replied that when Roosevelt had been in Washington as long as he had, he would learn that "the President of the United States calls on no one." Roosevelt's son later recorded his desire to punch Hoover in the nose.[55]

The Federal Reserve Board, meanwhile, continued to insist on a holiday. Conditions had become so grave that the Board suspended reserve requirements for thirty days. It also drafted an executive order declaring a national bank holiday and two joint resolutions for Congress, one ratifying the presidential proclamation, and another independently ordering the holiday under congressional authority. Since the Senate had already adjourned, only Hoover could effect the closing which the Board now regarded as the sole way of saving the nation's banks. Governor Meyer telephoned this information to the president, and the Board decided to send him a formal letter making its request for the record. Simultaneously Adolph Miller tried unsuccessfully to see Roosevelt at the Mayflower Hotel. When he later reached Roosevelt by phone, neither

55. Hoover, *Forty-Two Years*, p. 227; Tully, *F. D. R.*, pp. 63–64; James Roosevelt with Sidney Shalett, *Affectionately F. D. R.: A Son's Story of a Lonely Man* (New York: Harcourt, Brace, 1959), pp. 204–06; James C. Young, *Roosevelt Revealed* (New York: Farrar and Rinehart, 1936), pp. 5–6; Moley, *After Seven Years*, pp. 144–46; idem, *First New Deal*, pp. 148–49; Henry, *Presidential Transitions*, pp. 353–54; Wolfe, *Hoover*, pp. 355–56; Myers and Newton, *Hoover Administration*, pp. 365–66; Hoover, *Memoirs*, 3:213.

his urgings nor two calls from Hoover moved the president-elect. Hoover said finally that he would do nothing unless Roosevelt specifically asked him. At midnight president and president-elect retired to their respective bedchambers. The impasse held. At 1 a.m. on March 4 a secretary slipped the Federal Reserve Board's letter and drafts under Hoover's door; still he did nothing.[56]

Moley later tried to sort out the several versions of Hoover's critical 11:30 call to Roosevelt. From Roosevelt's end of the conversation, which he had overheard, and the summary immediately afterward, Moley questioned the official version of the Hoover group, namely, that Roosevelt told Hoover that Senator Glass had advised against a holiday and recommended instead nationwide scrip. Rather, Moley stressed the later conversation between Glass and Roosevelt in which the president-elect made it clear that he intended to use the Trading-with-the-Enemy Act to close all the banks, despite Glass's reservations as to its legality and ultimate effect. Moley did not accept Hoover's argument that he failed to issue the proclamation because Roosevelt told him that he wanted nothing done on the eve of the inauguration.[57]

A sleeping president could not help New York and Chicago. Banks in both cities had remained open throughout March 3, despite an old-fashioned money panic. New York in particular had to withstand a two-fold run of local depositors and out-of-town banks and corporations. With the city under siege, the state legislature had been working on plans against the day when the community would have no banking facilities. Only the pleas of the commercial bankers had prevented the savings banks from employing the sixty-day notice clause on March 2. The next day Governor Herbert Lehman cancelled his trip to Washington for the inauguration of his former chief. Instead Lehman, himself a banker, met at his New York City apartment with the state superintendent of banks, representatives

56. Federal Reserve Board, Minutes, 3 Mar. 1933, noon, 3 p.m., 9:15 p.m.; 4 Mar. 1933, 12:05 a.m.; Hamlin, Diary, 3, 4, 8 Mar. 1933; Hamlin's notes in Federal Reserve Board files; Wolfe, *Hoover*, pp. 354–55; Myers and Newton, *Hoover Administration*, p. 363; Henry, *Presidential Transitions*, pp. 351–52; Walter Wyatt to Raymond Moley, 16 Mar. 1966, quoted in *First New Deal*, pp. 147–48; Meyer to Hoover, 3 Mar. 1933, Hoover Papers, West Branch, box 1–G/981.

57. *First New Deal*, pp. 149–51; *After Seven Years*, pp. 146–47; Hoover, *Memoirs*, 3:213–14; Smith and Beasley, *Carter Glass*, pp. 340–42; Henry, *Presidential Transitions*, pp. 354–55.

of the House of Morgan and the clearinghouse banks, and Harrison of the New York Federal Reserve Bank. Harrison reported that despite suspension of reserve requirements, directors at the Reserve bank believed their only choice was suspension of specie payments or a banking holiday. At their request Harrison had telephoned Hoover to ask for a national closing, but the president had told him to convince Lehman to declare a moratorium for the state. Harrison relayed these facts to the local meeting, repeating that his directors preferred a nationwide closing but did not expect to get it. He therefore used the weight of the Reserve bank to urge Lehman to close down the state. William Woodin and Raymond Moley called from the Treasury Department offices in Washington to second that request. Lehman felt that he could not comply without a formal appeal from the clearinghouse banks, but the bankers—hoping to avoid the onus of having asked to have their banks closed—tried to force the governor to act independently. He refused, and they finally handed him a petition. So at 2:30 a.m. on March 4, Lehman suspended banking in the State of New York through March 6.[58] Riding to the inauguration that morning, Ogden Mills told Henry Stimson of the events of the preceding night; Mills said that in case Lehman had not yielded and the banks had opened on Saturday, by Sunday they "would have gone bust, and the fault would have been lain at the President's door."[59] Ironically, Franklin Roosevelt's former lieutenant governor had spared Hoover that ignominy.

One hour after Lehman's action, the governor of Illinois took the same step. Chicago banks had weathered the post-Michigan strain well, but suffered a decline in deposits at the end of February.

58. Memorandum of special meeting, Board of Directors, New York Federal Reserve Bank, 3 Mar. 1933, Harrison Papers, binder 50; Joseph A. Broderick (commissioner of banks), memorandum of events leading up to banking holiday, sent to Lehman, 14 Dec. 1933; supported by Henry Bruère (president, Bowery Savings Bank), 15 Oct. 1935, based on diary notes for Mar. 1933, Lehman Papers, Columbia University, School of International Affairs, Special Subject Personal File; Bruère, COHC, pp. 145–47; list of participants, clearing house request, memorandum of legal basis for closing banks, and draft proclamation, Lehman Papers, Governorship Papers, microfilm reel 8; George Leslie Harrison to Charles Sumner Hamlin, 15 Aug. 1933, Federal Reserve Board files; *New York Times*, 4, 5 Mar. 1933; *Commercial and Financial Chronicle*, 1 Mar. 1933, pp. 1666–70; Allan Nevins, *Herbert H. Lehman and His Era* (New York: Scribner's, 1963), pp. 135–37; Moley, 27 *Masters*, pp. 188–89; idem, *After Seven Years*, pp. 147–48; idem, *First New Deal*, pp. 151–53.

59. Stimson, Diary, 4 Mar. 1933.

Moreover, on March 1 under pressure from the Federal Reserve Board, the Chicago Reserve Bank reluctantly loaned $105 million to New York to support declining reserves. Although the great Loop banks still appeared strong, Chicago bankers, in communication with Washington, concluded that they should conserve their resources. On March 3 runs developed, and Chicago had to refuse to discount another $150 million from New York. Chicago bankers, like their counterparts in other states, hoped to avoid asking Governor Horner for a holiday proclamation. But when word came that Lehman had closed New York, at 3:22 a.m. at the request of the bankers the governor signed a declaration calling for a three-day holiday with restrictions on bank operations during the following week.[60] The Federal Reserve Board immediately warned the other ten Reserve banks against inevitable runs.[61]

Herbert Hoover left office on March 4, 1933, without closing the nation's banks. Action by the governors of New York and Illinois safeguarded the two largest banking centers from complete collapse. Hoover replied to the Federal Reserve Board's request for a holiday by pointing out that no national closing was necessary since the two governors had acted. He petulantly repeated that Roosevelt had tied his hands and chided the Board for sending its proposal when it knew of the declarations in New York and Illinois.[62]

Although thirty-four states had no banking facilities or only partial ones, Hoover maintained to the end of his life that the United States was not "in ruins" on March 4, that it suffered instead from "an induced hysteria of bank depositors" terrified at the portents of the New Deal.[63] His own grim expression riding to the inaugural ceremonies, however, reflected the mood of a country depleted and disappointed. The United States had never stood so desperately in need of rescue as on that bleak March morning.

60. James, *Growth of Chicago Banks*, pp. 1059–67; Chester Morrill to Charles Sumner Hamlin, 22 Aug. 1933, and Eugene M. Stevens to Hamlin, 11 Aug. 1933, Federal Reserve Board files; *Chicago Tribune*, 4 Mar. 1933; *New York Times*, 4 Mar. 1933.

61. Wyatt to Moley, 16 Mar. 1966, in Moley, *First New Deal*, pp. 147–48, 151–53.

62. Hoover to Meyer, 4 Mar. 1933, Hoover Papers, West Branch, box 1–G/981; Hamlin Diary, 4, 5, 12 Mar., 14, 21 Aug. 1933.

63. Hoover, *Addresses upon the American Road: 1933–1938* (New York: Scribner's, 1938), pp. 87–91, 142–45.

CHAPTER VII

Enter Roosevelt

AT 1:06 on the afternoon of Saturday, March 4, 1933, during a near-total banking eclipse, Franklin Delano Roosevelt took the oath of office as president of the United States. Despite the closing of over 5,000 banking institutions since 1931, Roosevelt refused to slink into the presidency as the inheritor of Hoover's tragedy. He rejected the idea of cancelling the inaugural parade, choosing instead to adopt Hoover's own theme of confidence and to make it work for him. As the two men rode together to the Capitol, Hoover sat immobile before the cheering crowd; Roosevelt, at first embarrassed by his predecessor's silence, finally decided not to cheat the expectant throngs and began to smile and wave.

On the platform Roosevelt stood in heavy braces to repeat the oath and then began an inaugural address which told the nation to take heart. "So first of all," he said resolutely, "let me assert my firm belief that the only thing we have to fear is fear itself—nameless, unreasoning, unjustified terror which paralyzes needed efforts to convert retreat into advance." Addressing himself to the crisis, Roosevelt excoriated the bankers for their incompetence and lack of vision. "The money changers have fled from their high seats in the temple of our civilization," he said. But the new president proposed to restore that temple according to "social values more noble than mere monetary profit." Unhesitatingly he assumed that leadership which Hoover and the business community had abdicated, all but ordering Congress to give him "broad executive power to wage a war against the emergency." Nor would he limit his options, as Hoover had done. "Our constitution is so simple and practical," he pointed out, "that it is possible always to meet extraordinary needs by changes in emphasis and arrangement without loss of essential form."[1]

The United States was entering its forty-first month of continuing deflation. In most areas business merely marked time. National income had fallen 53 percent below 1929; the budget remained unbalanced; and the national debt had increased to 20.7 percent above 1929. Federal Reserve ratios had dropped critically from 69.5 percent on March 3, 1929, to 45.3 percent on the same date in 1933. Hoarding had pulled money out of circulation and depleted monetary gold stocks. Bank loans had contracted to 59 percent of 1929 figures; banks refused any but the surest risks. Net profits had declined in 500 test companies to 76 percent of 1929 levels, while security prices had dropped to approximately one-fourth of 1929. The usually strident centers of finance and industry now lay under a terrifying quiet.[2] One historian regarded the banking crisis as the "terminal trough" of the depression; of forty measures of economic activity, twelve hit bottom in the second half of 1932 and twenty-four about March 1933. Two other analysts pointed out that this was a double crisis: the immediate emergency created by financial breakdown and the multiple economic and social factors of business stagnation, unemployment, failure of distress relief, and widespread unrest.[3] Morale had ebbed to the point where the former holders of economic power now appeared as helpless as their clients. This discovery, said one reporter, had "shaken the faith of a people whose cathedrals are banks." She went on to analyze the disillusionment: "The average citizen always suspected the morals of the financial hierarchy," she said, "but now his distrust goes deeper; he doubts its intelligence." And Senator William Gibbs McAdoo at

1. Rosenman, ed., *Public Papers and Addresses of Franklin D. Roosevelt,* 2:11–15.
2. Daniel C. Roper, "Statement of Conditions in the United States," 1 May 1933, FDRL:PPF 1820; *New York Times,* 4, 5 Mar. 1933.
3. Wecter, *The Age of the Great Depression: 1929–1941* (New York: Macmillan, 1948), p. 66; W. C. Mitchell and A. F. Burns, "Production during the American Business Cycle of 1927–1933," *National Bureau of Economic Research Bulletin,* (1936), p. 2; Charles A. Beard and George H. A. Smith, *The Future Comes: A Study of the New Deal* (New York: Macmillan, 1934), pp. 16–17.

the same time told the Senate Finance Committee, "Our entire banking system does credit to a collection of imbeciles."[4]

Disaster did open some new options, however. Any dynamic individual offering direction out of, or even away from, the morass stood an excellent chance of being heard. Moreover, even in ordinary times, a new chief executive enjoys refreshing freedom of action, and in the depth of a panic he was released from many of the usual restraints on his prerogatives. Probably Roosevelt could have done anything he wanted with the banking crisis on March 4, 1933. He had the power; he had a mandate; and his inaugural address stated clearly that he intended to use them.[5]

To his new tasks the president brought a limited knowledge of economics but great political sense. He held to no particular orthodoxy but adopted and rejected ideas as they suited his current needs. Certainly his formal education offered little preparation for meeting the problems of the Great Depression. Roosevelt attended Groton preparatory school where the curriculum concentrated on English and the classics. He did, however, study political economy under a classical economist who derived his main theories from Ricardo, Say, Malthus, and Mill. On currency, he learned that "gold is stable, silver is unstable; therefore, gold is the only suitable standard of value." Later, at Harvard University, his introduction to economics followed traditional lines and remained middle-of-the-road, although a few advanced courses mentioned reforms in the economics of corporations and transportation. His money and banking professors emphasized sound money, stable prices, and the gold standard.

Outside the academic sphere, Roosevelt's early experiences with Progressivism sharpened his awareness of the political impact of economic problems. But in his own financial dealings, he gambled with the rest during the speculative 1920s' often disastrously. As governor of New York from 1928 to 1932, he emphasized social welfare but did little to preserve or reform the banks, only endorsing

4. Anne O'Hare McCormick, "Main Street Reappraises Wall Street," *New York Times*, 28 Feb. 1933; Schlesinger, *Crisis of the Old Order*, pp. 4–5, 474; Rexford G. Tugwell, "The New Deal in Retrospect," *Western Political Quarterly* 1: (Dec. 1948): 380–81.

5. Mowry, *Urban Nation*, p. 93; Shannon, *Between the Wars*, pp. 150–53; Harold B. Hinton, *Cordell Hull: A Biography* (Garden City, N. Y.: Doubleday, Doran, 1942), pp. 219–20.

change when the closing of the Bank of United States in 1930 underscored his failure to act when the City Trust had collapsed a year before.

By 1932, however, he had graduated from the simple *noblesse oblige* of his ancestors to acceptance of society's responsibility to those who have suffered economic misfortune. Moreover, he understood the political advantage of endorsing a strong, positive role for the federal government in promoting the public welfare. His convictions still reflected the general climate of opinion, and he remained free from any reflective economic philosophy or group interest, making him receptive to the improvisations which might prove necessary in March 1933.[6] Frances Perkins later commented that "Roosevelt took the status quo in our economic system as much for granted as his family. They were part of his life, and so was our system; he was content with it."[7] One of Roosevelt's advisers doubted that either he or the president could have passed an elementary college economics examination but claimed that this limited expertise operated to their advantage since it permitted them to escape the advice of the New York banking community and other traditional authorities and gave them "a broad view of the national scene."[8]

Thus equipped, Franklin Roosevelt assumed the presidency amid pleas for a nationwide banking moratorium to supercede the state closings.[9]

6. Fusfeld, *Economic Thought of Franklin D. Roosevelt*, pp. 16–116, 251–57; Frank Freidel, *Franklin D. Roosevelt: The Apprenticeship* (Boston: Little, Brown, 1952), pp. 5, 32, 41; Tugwell, *Democratic Roosevelt*, pp. 54–55.

7. Perkins, *The Roosevelt I Knew*, pp. 34, 328–31; Richard Hofstadter, "Franklin D. Roosevelt: The Patrician as Opportunist," in *The American Political Tradition and the Men Who Made It* (New York: Knopf, 1948), pp. 311–47; David M. Potter, "Sketches for the Roosevelt Portrait," *Yale Review* 39 (Sept. 1949): 39–53.

8. Moley, *First New Deal*, pp. 224–25.

9. State limitations on banking stood as follows: Alabama, closed until further notice; Arizona, closed until March 13; Arkansas, closed until March 7; California, mostly closed until March 9; Colorado, closed until March 8; Connecticut, closed until March 7; Delaware, closed indefinitely; three banks in the District of Columbia had limited withdrawals to 5 percent and nine savings banks invoked sixty days' notice; Florida, restricted withdrawals to 5 percent plus $10 until March 8; Georgia, banks closed at their own option until March 7; the same in Idaho until March 18; Illinois, closed until March 8, then 5 percent restrictions for seven days; Indiana, half restricted to 5 percent indefinitely; Iowa, closed "temporarily"; Kansas, restricted to 5 percent withdrawals

The new president received strong advice on banking from both his own and his predecessor's advisers. His secretary of the treasury, William Woodin, and close counsel Raymond Moley had spent the night of March 3–4 in conference with retiring Secretary Ogden Mills and Undersecretary Arthur Ballantine, who had agreed to remain at the Treasury during the period of crisis to assist their successors. In addition, F. Gloyd Awalt retained the job of Acting Comptroller of the Currency, and the membership and staff of the Federal Reserve Board continued in office. Since Woodin had no time to get used to his new post before he was called upon to make critical decisions and plans, the presence of these men minimized the difficulties which necessarily came from his lack of familiarity with the department. Moreover, their influence would help to shape policies and solutions in the days of the panic. Both Woodin and Moley later expressed their relief and gratitude for this gesture by the Hoover men. They particularly praised Ballantine, who acted as liaison between the two administrations, for his "patriotism" and "indispensable" contributions to the ultimate solution. Moley stated flatly that "except for the expertness, the information, and the plans at the lower levels of the Hoover Administration, the crisis could never have been surmounted."[10]

---

indefinitely; Kentucky, mostly restricted to 5 percent withdrawals until March 11; Louisiana, closed mandatorily until March 7; Maine, closed until March 7; Maryland, closed until March 6; Massachusetts, closed until March 7; Michigan, closed; Minnesota, closed "temporarily"; Mississippi, restricted to 5 percent indefinitely; Missouri, closed until March 7; Montana, closed until further notice; Nebraska, closed until March 8; Nevada, closed until March 8; New Hampshire, closed subject to further proclamation; New Jersey, closed until March 7; New Mexico, mostly closed until March 8; New York, closed until March 7; North Carolina, partially restricted to 5 percent withdrawals; North Dakota, closed temporarily; Ohio, mostly restricted to 5 percent withdrawals indefinitely; Oklahoma, closed until March 8; Oregon, closed until March 7; Pennsylvania, closed until March 7 except Pittsburgh banks (Andrew Mellon); Rhode Island, closed March 4; South Carolina, on banks' own initiative some closed and some restricted; Tennessee, some closed and others restricted until March 9; Texas, mostly closed but some restricted to withdrawals of $10 per day until March 8; Utah, mostly closed until March 8; Vermont, closed until March 7; Virginia, closed until March 8; Washington, some closed until March 7; West Virginia, restricted to 5 percent monthly withdrawals indefinitely; Wisconsin, closed until March 17; and Wyoming, withdrawals restricted to 5 percent indefinitely.

10. Woodin to Ballantine, 14 June 1933, quoted in Moley, *First New Deal*, pp. 214–17; *New York Times*, 3, 19 Mar. 1933.

On the morning of his inauguration, Roosevelt learned that the joint consultations of these men at the Treasury Department had produced a consensus on three points. They recommended that the president: 1) close all banks in the nation uniformly by proclamation under the authority of the Trading-with-the-Enemy Act; 2) call a special session of Congress to validate this order, extend the holiday if necessary, and pass legislation to reopen the banks at its conclusion; and 3) summon the important bankers of New York, Chicago, Philadelphia, Baltimore, and Richmond for consultation in Washington on Sunday, March 5.[11]

Roosevelt approved the general outlines of this plan but wanted several details resolved before he would act to close the banks. Woodin settled the question of the meeting of Congress by promising to have emergency legislation ready by March 9; the bankers' conference on Sunday formally requested a holiday; and Attorney General Homer Cummings affirmed that the Trading-with-the-Enemy Act remained in force and that a closing order would be legal under it.

The enabling provision of the Trading-with-the-Enemy Act stated "that the President may investigate, regulate, or prohibit, under such rules and regulations as he may prescribe, by means of licenses or otherwise, any transactions in foreign exchange, and the export, hoarding, melting, or earmarking of gold or silver coin or bullion or currency." Officers at the Treasury Department had been aware of the act since early in 1932 and began considering it as the basis for a nationwide bank holiday in January 1933. On March 2, Ogden Mills and Eugene Meyer had urged it upon Hoover without success.

Roosevelt himself said that he began discussing the authority two months before he used it. After Rene Leon suggested the act to Raymond Moley in January, the Roosevelt group had sent Rexford Tugwell to Washington to verify its powers. Through an economist in the Treasury Department, Tugwell secured a marked copy of the act and asked Senator Key Pittman to determine how much of it had been repealed. Tugwell personally believed the authority dubious but

11. Moley, *First New Deal*, pp. 160, 165–66; Rollins, *Roosevelt and Howe*, p. 382; Hamlin, Diary, 4–5 Mar. 1933.

thought the power appealed to Roosevelt when he learned that "Mills and Hoover obviously had taken a good look at this."[12]

Given Cummings's verification, and his own acceptance of the powers of the 1917 law, Roosevelt decided that the act provided justifiable authority. Moreover, he was "fully convinced that the drastic action of closing the banks was necessary in order to prevent complete chaos on Monday morning." As soon as the Federal Reserve Board agreed to close the Reserve banks (a decision which may indeed have been outside the president's sphere) Roosevelt proceeded with plans for the bank holiday. As Raymond Moley later recalled, Eugene Meyer said that the Board would close the Reserve banks on its own authority. The Board did not act, however, and the Reserve banks came under the "all banking institutions" phrase of the president's order.[13]

On Monday, March 6, Roosevelt proclaimed the suspension of "all banking transactions" until Thursday, March 9, "throughout the United States and its territories." Because of "heavy and unwarranted withdrawals of gold and currency from our banking institutions for the purpose of hoarding" and "continuous and in-

12. Walter Wyatt to Raymond Moley, 16 Mar. 1966, quoted in Moley, *First New Deal*, pp. 157–60; Roosevelt, *On Our Way*, pp. 3–5; Tugwell, *Democratic Roosevelt*, pp. 271–72; Tugwell, Diary, 27 Feb. 1933, pp. 123–25, FDRL: Group 80; Tugwell, COHC, pp. 36–40; Tugwell, "Transition: Hoover to Roosevelt, 1932–1933," *Centennial Review* 9 (Spring 1965): 186–87; Joseph Alsop and Robert Kintner, *Men around the President* (New York: Doubleday, Doran, 1939), pp. 30–31; Leuchtenburg, "The New Deal and the Analogue of War," p. 107.

Of course, President Hoover continued to regard the entire procedure as unnecessary, and many of Roosevelt's critics held it was unconstitutional. Hoover, *Memoirs*, 3:214; Flynn, *Roosevelt Myth*, p. 27. A District of Columbia judge, however, upheld the order and the authority in a decision handed down on 3 Nov. 1933 (*Daly Brothers, Inc.,* v. *Thomas P. Hickman* [conservatory for the Franklin National Bank]). *New York Times*, 4 Nov. 1933. Moreover a series of decisions rendered between 1933 and 1940 continued to uphold the constitutionality of section 5 (b) of the Trading-with-the-Enemy Act and the proclamations and orders issued under it. James W. Shay to Walter Wyatt, 8 Aug. 1941, Federal Reserve Board files.

13. Franklin D. Roosevelt, Diary, 5 Mar. 1933, FDRL; Roosevelt, *On Our Way*, pp. 3–5; Moley, *First New Deal*, pp. 160–61; idem, *After Seven Years*, p. 148; Henry, *Presidential Transitions*, pp. 359–60; Hamlin, Diary, 5 Mar. 1933; Harold L. Ickes, *The Secret Diary of Harold L. Ickes: The First Thousand Days, 1933–1936* (New York: Simon and Schuster, 1953), p. 3; Ickes, "My Twelve Years with F. D. R.," *Saturday Evening Post* 220 (12 June 1948): 34; *New York Times*, 5 Mar. 1933; Wyatt to Moley, 16 Mar. 1933, quoted in *First New Deal*, pp. 160–61.

creasingly extensive speculative activity abroad in foreign exchange," the decree directed that no banking institution should "pay out, export, earmark, or permit the withdrawal or transfer in any manner or by any device whatsoever, of any gold or silver coin or bullion or currency, or take any other action which might facilitate the hoarding thereof." Nor should such banks "pay out deposits, make loans or discounts, deal in foreign exchange, transfer credits from the United States to any place abroad, or transact any other banking business whatsoever." It did, however, authorize the secretary of the Treasury to permit usual banking functions, issuance of scrip, and creation of special accounts for new deposits where necessary.[14]

In closing the nation's banks, Roosevelt merely confirmed the existing situation. Almost every bank in the country had already suspended, either by failure or on state authority. He even used a pre-existing draft proclamation of the moratorium, one prepared for Hoover. His predecessor's attorney general had dictated a preliminary draft on March 2, which was revised by Federal Reserve officials before the Reserve Board sent it to Hoover on the night of March 3. Ogden Mills and Arthur Ballantine also worked on the text, and through them it passed to the Roosevelt group on March 4. During the next day, Roosevelt, Woodin, Cummings, Moley, and Walter Wyatt of the Federal Reserve worked over the draft, but its final form hardly differed from the decree intended for Hoover.[15]

Roosevelt's issuance of the edict represented a coup in timing, tone, and impact, however. Using the prestige he had refused to waste on Hoover, he now galvanized popular support and turned disaster into heartening revival. His moratorium replaced a long period of wavering confidence and demoralizing bickering over the fate of the country's banks with direct executive leadership. Roosevelt acted vigorously on the strength of an unquestionable mandate for action on the depression from his election victory and Hoover's failure during the interregnum. While he padlocked the banks, he avoided alarm

---

14. Proclamation, FDRL:OF 230; Rosenman, *Public Papers*, 2:26–29; *New York Times*, 6 Mar. 1933; Federal Reserve Board circular letter to governors and chairmen, 6 Mar. 1933, in Federal Reserve Board files.

15. Moley, *First New Deal*, pp. 156, 161, 208–09; idem, *After Seven Years*, p. 149; *New York Times*, 7 Mar. 1933; Arthur Krock, COHC, p. 34; idem, "Reminiscences," *Centennial Review* 9 (Spring 1965): 226; Arthur F. Mullen, *Western Democrat* (New York: Wilfred Funk, 1940), pp. 312–13.

by limiting the initial moratorium to four days—fully intending to extend it later—because he thought it unwise to suspend banking indefinitely in the first instance.[16] In addition, he and members of his administration reassured the nation that the step was meant to avert catastrophe. "We are at the bottom now. We are not going any lower," said Secretary Woodin when he asserted that the United States would remain on the gold standard.[17]

Hope replaced fear in the mind and heart of America. From the first vibrant lines of the inaugural address, the nation adopted a new spirit; gloom evaporated in the face of Roosevelt's offer of leadership. Editorials commended his "spirit of high purpose," and praised him as "a leader who believes he knows what ought to be done and who had the will to do it."[18] One rabbi said, "The confidence which the people place in the new President is an expression of its own self-confidence."[19] At the same time businessmen advertised: "I trust my government. I trust our banks. I do not expect the impossible. I shall do nothing hysterical."[20] Alfred P. Sloan, Jr., of General Motors informed Roosevelt that his company stood ready to accept whatever losses might result from "this program of facing the facts." Some observers even cautioned against a possible wave of speculation because of holiday-inspired confidence.[21]

Former President Hoover broke his retirement silence to urge support for his successor.[22] A conference of governors, meeting at the White House on March 6, passed resolutions of confidence in the president and issued a statement calling on "our united country to cooperate with him in such action as he shall find necessary and desirable in restoring banking and economic stability."[23] Even

---

16. Roosevelt, *On Our Way*, pp. 17–18.
17. *New York Times*, 6 Mar. 1933.
18. *Kansas City Star*, 4 Mar. 1933; *St. Louis Globe Democrat*, 4 Mar. 1933.
19. Rev. Dr. Samuel Shuman, sermon at Temple Emmanu-el, *New York Times*, 5 Mar. 1933.
20. Advertisement by Jesse I. Straus of R. H. Macy, *New York Times*, 6 Mar. 1933; Charles B. Dulcan of Hecht Co. to FDR, 10 Mar. 1933; and Louis Howe to Dulcan, 14 Mar. 1933—all in FDRL:OF 172. Bankers, bar associations, and private citizens telegraphed support to the president.
21. Sloan to FDR, 11 Mar. 1933, FDRL:PPF 144; Lionel P. Kristeller, secretary, Essex County (N. J.) Bar Association, to FDR, 7 Mar. 1933; Loren N. Wood to FDR, 6 Mar. 1933; and FDR to Morris Sheppard, 6 Mar. 1933—all in FDRL:OF 230; Professor Sumner H. Slichter, Harvard University, *New York Times*, 13 Mar. 1933.
22. *New York Times*, 7 Mar. 1933.

radio's "Amos 'n' Andy," Freeman Gosden and Charles Correll, offered to devote their broadcasts to an explanation of the moratorium.[24]

Individuals responded good-naturedly to the banking holiday. Suspension of all banking at least gave some respite from depressing reports of bank failures. Moreover, solution to banking problems by the new administration would be worth some temporary inconveniences. America, therefore, set out to live for a few days without banks. In some localities unusual items replaced currency: a pair of trousers paid one man's fare on a Salt Lake City trolley; a Philadelphia department store permitted customers to charge streetcar tokens on their credit accounts; ten bushels of wheat bought a year's subscription to the Lewiston, Montana, *Democrat-News*; Alaskan miners used gold dust for small change; and when an Oklahoma City hotel agreed to accept payment of guests' bills in "anything we can use in the coffee shop," the first patron presented a pig. Princeton and Vassar students devised their own scrip; Harvard fed commuter students on credit. Few travellers suffered from the lack of real money: railroads accepted checks for passenger and freight charges; most Florida tourists remained on vacation, sustained by postal money orders and $50 advances from the American Express Company. Visitors in Washington, D.C., for the inauguration paid hotel bills by check—fortunately for some like the governor of Pennsylvania, who had only ninety-five cents in his pockets.

On the legal scene, Reno, Nevada, suspended divorce proceedings when clients could not pay filing fees. The governor of California deferred two hangings because "a bank holiday was no time to hang a man." Men scheduled to leave reformatories in New York State had to remain until the end of the moratorium because they could not cash the checks they received on their release. Courts did very little business, and attorneys petitioned for waiver of documentary fees.[25]

---

23. Roosevelt, Diary, 6 Mar. 1933; Rosenman, *Public Papers*, 2:18–23; *New York Times*, 7 Mar. 1933; *Commercial and Financial Chronicle*, 11 Mar. 1933, pp. 1660–61.

24. Gosden and Correll to FDR, 5 Mar. 1933; Stephen Early to Gosden and Correll, 6 Mar. 1933; Gosden and Correll to Early, 6 Mar. 1933—all in FDRL: PPF 3795.

25. *New York Times*, 7, 11 Mar. 1933; Cornelius Wickersham to Herbert H. Lehman, 9 Mar. 1933, Lehman Papers, Governorship Papers, microfilm reel 8.

The holiday also drew people together. A New York banker borrowed pennies and nickels from a newsboy to pay his bus fare from Connecticut; the boy refused to take the banker's check, which he could not cash. Churches received IOUs, checks, and large unchangeable bills in the Sunday offerings, then conversely received requests for change from local businesses Monday morning. Senator Huey Long offered reporter Arthur Krock $3,000 of the $15,000 he normally carried. Comedian Groucho Marx divided $50 four ways with his famous brothers. Across the nation parents robbed their children's piggy banks for cash.[26] The president's wife was anxious about sending her sons back to school without money but learned "that there were certain things one need not worry about in the White House."[27]

National life continued although banks of all kinds closed or performed only the most essential services. Savings banks allowed small withdrawals—some up to $10—to meet urgent personal needs. Commercial banks opened to make change. Depositors generally responded calmly to the closing announcement, small crowds dispersing quietly from the front of banks when the order was explained. Holders of safety deposit boxes used them no more than usual. At postal savings windows, deposits exceeded withdrawals. Bank checks went unquestioned, and Internal Revenue collectors accepted checks in payment of federal taxes, which remained due despite the holiday. Even gold began to flow back into banks, probably in response to rumors that Secretary Woodin planned to fine large hoarders twice the value of the gold they held; a Brooklyn doctor deposited $2,000 in gold "as a manifestation of confidence in the banks and in the present administration," and in Mississippi a Negro farmer brought in $4,000 in bills over fifty years old because, as he said, "I hear the guv'ment wants all the old money."[28]

26. New York Times, 4–13 Mar. 1933; Tugwell, "Franklin D. Roosevelt on the Verge of the Presidency," Antioch Review 16 (Mar. 1956): 49; Commercial and Financial Chronicle, 11 Mar. 1933, p. 1677; Robert Bendiner, Just around the Corner: A Highly Selective History of the Thirties (New York: Harper and Row, 1967), pp. 31–33; Krock, COHC, pp. 16–18; idem, Memoirs: Sixty Years on the Firing Line (New York: Funk and Wagnalls, 1968), p. 173; Josephson, Infidel in the Temple, pp. 172, 174–77, 180–81.

27. Eleanor Roosevelt, This I Remember (New York: Harper, 1949), p. 79.

28. New York Times, 5, 8, 11, 12, 15 Mar. 1933; Commercial and Financial Chronicle, 11 Mar. 1933, pp. 1670, 1676–78; Friedman and Schwartz, Monetary History, pp. 349–50, 428–34.

Ordinary citizens showed unprecedented interest in the situation. The economics division of the New York Public Library had to post a "Standing Room Only" sign and issued a ready reference list on banking materials. The list included *America Weighs Her Gold*, by James Harvey Rogers; *The ABC's of the Federal Reserve System*, by Edwin Kemmerer; *Behind the Scenes of International Finance*, by Paul Einzig; *The Economics of Branch Banking*, by Bernhard Ostrolenk; *Financial Organization of Society*, by Harold G. Moulton; and *Principles of Money and Banking*, by Russell D. Kolbourne.

Business, too, held on. Wholesalers and producers granted customers credit, and prices remained generally constant at the retail level. The New York and other stock exchanges closed for the duration, and brokerage firms retained only skeleton staffs, although some dealers maintained an unofficial market. An unusual number of firms omitted their quarterly dividends, but on the whole business clung to at least the outward forms of normal operations and seemed little worse than during the preceding weeks of bank failures.[29] Bank closings hit hardest at life insurance companies, causing runs on these institutions in states which did not declare moratoriums on surrender values and policy loans. But the insurance companies endured, meeting claims and permitting longer grace periods for payment of premiums.[30]

Two analysts concluded that "the sudden nationwide holiday performed the same function for the bank panic as may a sharp slap in the face for a person gripped by unreasoning hysteria. By arresting all banking functions, government removed the sources on which fear might thrive; and it gave the people time to collect themselves."[31]

The national response to Roosevelt's inauguration and first actions in office proved Herbert Hoover wrong in his belief that the country feared Roosevelt. On the other hand, the great freedom of options enjoyed by the new administration underscored Rexford

29. *New York Times*, 11, 13 Mar. 1933.
30. George S. VanSchaick, COHC, p. 82; *New York Times*, 5, 7–11, 15 Mar. 1933; *Commercial and Financial Chronicle*, 11 Mar. 1933, pp. 1601–05; Lorry Jacobs to Marvin H. McIntyre, 6 Mar. 1933, and McIntyre to Jacobs, 8 Mar. 1933, FDRL:OF 121.
31. Charles A. Beard and George H. A. Smith, *The Old Deal and the New* (New York: Macmillan, 1941), pp. 78–81.

Tugwell's wisdom in preferring that the system collapse around Hoover, leaving a clear path for Roosevelt as savior. As Walter Lippmann said, "Every crisis breaks a deadlock and sets events in motion. A bad crisis is one in which no one has the power to make good use of the opportunity, and, therefore, it ends in disaster. A good crisis is one in which the power and the will to seize the opportunity are in being. Out of such a crisis come solutions." He identified the banking crisis of 1933 as a good crisis.[32]

President Roosevelt possessed the power and the will to deal with the banking crisis; all he needed now was an acceptable solution. Strong, magnetic, and totally at ease in command, the new chief executive delivered a virtuoso performance during his first forty-eight hours in office. He issued a proclamation which halted deterioration and demoralization, thus checking the immediate crisis in confidence. There is no reason to believe, however, that the president himself had any idea of where to proceed from there. As Secretary Woodin said, "The main problem was to work out a plan for the restoration of normal banking."[33]

While the administration looked for that solution, however, Woodin faced the immediate task of governing the operations of banks and financial institutions during the emergency. Accordingly, he issued thirty-two regulations, twelve instructions to Federal Reserve banks, and twelve interpretations permitting restricted banking functions and regulating the handling of money during the crisis. On March 5, with the holiday not yet declared, Walter Wyatt, counsel to the Federal Reserve Board, had drafted recommendations for limited banking operations during the moratorium. Most of his suggestions became the basis for Woodin's subsequent regulations.[34]

On March 6, the first day of the national closing, Woodin exempted the Canal Zone, Guam, American Samoa, the Philippine Islands, and the Virgin Islands from the terms of the president's proclamation. He then authorized banking institutions affected by

32. Lippmann, *Interpretations: 1933–1935*, pp. 17–20.

33. William Woodin to Joseph T. Robinson, 15 Mar. 1933, Treasury Secretary's correspondence, Banks and Banking, 1933, NA(Suitland).

34. "Skeleton Outline" and "Suggested Permissive Operations during Bank Holiday," 5 Mar. 1933, Federal Reserve Board files. Wyatt claimed responsibility in a letter to Moley in 1966, quoted in Moley, *First New Deal*, pp. 169–71.

the moratorium to make change, allow access to safety deposit boxes, cash checks drawn on the treasurer of the United States, accept payments for obligations, and create special trust accounts for receipt of new deposits. The emergency regulation providing for the segregation of deposits reflected a simple and practical solution to the problem of the banks' accepting money from those who had it available for deposit but feared that it would become as frozen as that already in the moratorium-sealed banks, although bankers opposed the device as favoring hoarders over other depositors, on the premise that the only people who had cash to deposit were those who had drained the banks in the last days of February.

At the same time, Woodin informed the Federal Reserve banks that they could purchase gold or gold certificates and could exchange gold or currency for small denominations, but payments "in gold in any form" required a license from the secretary of the Treasury. Woodin cautiously saw to housekeeping details on the first day—nothing more. He established especially strict control over the flow of gold, a key point in the president's decree.

By the second day of the suspension, the secretary acted more freely in making funds available. In response to many requests,[35] regulations permitted settlement of checks drawn before March 4, allowed the issuance of clearinghouse certificates against sound assets of banks to provide a temporary medium of exchange, and authorized delivery of documents and securities held for safekeeping. In particular, Emergency Banking Regulation No. 10 stated that a national or state banking institution could exercise "usual banking functions to such extent as its situation shall permit and as shall be absolutely necessary to meet the needs of its community." Of course, the authorization cautioned against hoarding and unnecessary withdrawals of currency and still prohibited payment in gold. While the decree defined "needs of the community" as food, medicine, and "other necessities of life," it also provided for "relief of distress" and "payment of usual salaries and wages." Depositors could now withdraw small sums in cash if they demonstrated sufficient need to their bankers, and could hope to obtain some portion of their wages in currency as well. Moreover, on the following day

---

35. Lehman to Woodin, 7 Mar. 1933, Lehman Papers, Governorship Papers, microfilm reel 8; James, *Growth of Chicago Banks*, pp. 1077–78.

the Treasury Department ordered release on demand of deposits held in segregated accounts during the holiday.[36]

By these temporary ordinances and with the cooperation of state banking authorities, Woodin maintained skeleton banking during the moratorium while he and his advisors worked on an emergency banking act. The states followed suit; in New York, for example, Governor Lehman issued a statement on March 7 applying the secretary's regulations to banks under the authority of the state Banking Department.[37]

Meanwhile, as the nation waited optimistically for a solution to the banking crisis, advocates of all forms of banking change recognized the opportunities inherent in the moratorium and emergency bill to press for their individual plans. The movement for federal guarantee of deposits gained strength as Vice-President Garner, Jesse Jones of the RFC, and Senators Key Pittman, Robert M. La Follette, Jr., and Edward Costigan, as well as a host of academics, bombarbed President Roosevelt on behalf of insurance schemes.[38] Others endorsed greater government supervision of banking through the Federal Reserve System or even unification of banking, with elimination of small banks.[39] The plan submitted by economists of the University of Chicago to Secretary of Agriculture Henry A. Wallace is typical of the recommendations offered at this time. Its provisions included 1) federal government ownership and management of Federal Reserve banks, 2) Federal Reserve guaran-

36. The first fifteen regulations and ten instructions appeared on 6, 7, and 8 Mar.; the remainder primarily facilitated reopening of the banks and were issued between 10 and 30 Mar. Copies of the regulations are in the Comptroller's files, the secretary of the Treasury's files, and FDRL:OF 21 Treasury Department. They were issued as press releases through Woodin's office. *New York Times*, 6–30 Mar. 1933; O'Connor, *Banking Crisis and Recovery*, pp. 117–32.

37. Lehman Papers, Governorship Papers, microfilm reel 8.

38. Timmons, *Jones*, pp. 187–88; Pittman to FDR, 2 Mar. 1933, FDRL:PPF 745; La Follette and Costigan to FDR, 8, 9 Mar. 1933, FDRL:OF 230; University of Minnesota faculty plan, *New York Times*, 8 Mar. 1933. For a discussion of Roosevelt's reactions to the guarantee proposals at this time and after, see Chapter 9, below.

39. Charles R. Whittlesay, economist, Princeton University, quoted in *New York Times*, 19 Mar. 1933; John Dewey, educator, quoted in ibid., 19 Mar. 1933; J. H. Taggart and L. D. Jennings, University of Kansas School of Business, plan submitted by Dean Frank T. Stockton to Ernest K. Lindley, 7 Mar. 1933; Ernest A. Lowe, University of Georgia, to Louis Howe, 7 Mar. 1933; Malcolm H. Bryan to Howe, 10 Mar. 1933—all in FDRL:OF 230.

tee of deposits in all member banks open for business on the last day preceding any moratorium, 3) authority for issuance of Federal Reserve notes in any amount necessary to meet demands for payment by member-bank depositors, 4) these notes to be full legal tender, 5) loans by the Reserve banks and/or the RFC to relieve nonmember banks, 6) liquidation of failed member banks, and similar measures.[40] Many of the proposals reiterated ideas submitted during the Glass bill debates, but now even bankers accepted them. Winthrop W. Aldrich of the Chase Bank called publicly for separation of securities affiliates from parent commercial banks, and said so in an interview with President Roosevelt.[41]

Not everyone presented orthodox solutions, however. In the wake of the February collapses, the old order appeared discredited and the banking community impotent. Attention shifted from New York to Washington, particularly as President Roosevelt's assumption of emergency powers and the repeated analogies to a wartime situation broadened his options and lessened the separation of powers.[42] Moreover, the energy released by Roosevelt's early actions might be directed into almost any kind of solution.

Some, therefore, went so far as to demand socialization of banking, the pooling of assets of both strong and weak banks into a government-owned and -operated banking system; the Socialist Party in New York City was loud among the ranks of this faction.[43] Even some presidential advisers were reported in favor of nationalization of banking; Rexford Tugwell, for example, had argued since early in 1932 that the government could be a more effective banker than private groups.[44]

40. G. V. Cox *et al.* to Henry A. Wallace, 16 Mar. 1933, and Wallace to FDR, 23 Mar. 1933, FDRL:OF 230.

41. *New York Times*, 9, 10, 12 Mar. 1933; *Commercial and Financial Chronicle*, 11 Mar. 1933, p. 1653; Arthur M. Johnson, *Winthrop W. Aldrich: Lawyer, Banker, Diplomat* (Boston: Harvard University, Graduate School of Business Administration, 1968), pp. 149–53.

42. Clinton L. Rossiter, "War, Depression, and the Presidency, 1933–1950," *Social Research*, 17 (Dec. 1950): 417–40.

43. Henry J. Rosner, "Nationalize the Banks," *World Tomorrow* 16 (22 Mar. 1933): 279–81; Charles Albert Hawkins, "Our Present Banking Situation and the Remedy. . . ," mimeographed, FDRL:OF 230; *New York Times*, 5 Mar. 1933.

44. Moley, *First New Deal*, pp. 177–80; Tugwell, "Roosevelt on the Verge," pp. 46–79; idem, "The Compromising Roosevelt," *Western Political Quarterly* 6 (June 1953): 334; idem, "New Deal in Retrospect," pp. 380–81; Sternsher, *Tugwell and the New Deal*, pp. 124–25.

President Roosevelt never considered nationalization seriously, however. Although he enjoyed broad opportunities in proposing a solution to the crisis of 1933, he chose to avoid radical solutions, seeing no reason to embrace socialization when a more conventional approach would serve as well. He listened to conservative advisers, such as Moley, and—with one exception—left the problem in the hands of Woodin and his colleagues at the Treasury, where Mills and Ballantine retained a large measure of influence. Roosevelt had no plan of his own for opening the banks, but in calling on this particular set of advisers, he apparently took an orthodox solution for granted, believing that the financial system could be made to grind on with only minor corrections to avoid another general breakdown. The man who found it politically profitable to castigate the money changers in his inaugural address was not prepared to bar them from the temple entirely. Admitting as much to a friend, he remarked wryly, "They'll make a banker of me yet."[45]

The "revolution" of nationalizing American banking was not even stillborn, for it was never really conceived at any level where it might have been brought about. Indeed, Socialist Norman Thomas saw the New Deal "revolution" as exactly the reverse; "it has re-established a banking system when it was on the verge of ruin," he said.[46]

Since the chief problem involved restoration of normal banking, therefore, conferences seeking that remedy had begun at the Treasury Department even before the president issued his moratorium edict. In practice, the meetings were merely carryovers from the harried session of the night of March 3 to 4 when the Mills-Ballantine forces and the Woodin-Moley contingent cooperatively secured the New York and Illinois closings. The same group continued to work together now, and the greater influence inevitably fell to the more experienced men: Mills, Ballantine, Awalt, and Wyatt, on whom Woodin increasingly depended in the endless hours ahead.

At ten o'clock on the morning of March 5, these officials met at the Treasury with representative bankers from New York, Chi-

45. Quoted by Felix Frankfurter in memorandum of visit to Roosevelt, 8 Mar. 1933, in Freedman, *Roosevelt and Frankfurter*, pp. 110–11.
46. *New York Times*, 20 Aug. 1933.

cago, and other financial centers; Professor Moley and his young colleague at Columbia University, Adolf Berle, were also present. For more than three hours, the bankers tried to work out an answer to the problem of reopening. Their conversations, however, became hopelessly bogged down in discussions of deposit guarantees and recriminations about the arbitrary behavior of the New York and Chicago Reserve banks during the previous week in bypassing Reserve Board control. Another long session in the afternoon got no further, and Moley wondered that Woodin was not "totally confounded" by the deafening "babble of tongues."[47] Finally, the secretary appointed a subcommittee in hopes that a smaller group could agree on a plan.

The subcommittee commenced its meeting on March 6 with a vote "that something must be done" but spent the day with no decision about what that "something" should be. Discussion continued to center on a guarantee, and the conference resolved its differences sufficiently to offer two plans, both limited. Some members, especially George Leslie Harrison and a group within the Comptroller's office, favored a 50 percent guarantee backed by Reserve or RFC loans where necessary. Another segment, headed by Melvin Traylor, preferred a sliding scale guarantee whereby banks would be classified according to worth and their deposits insured in proportion to that evaluation. Berle attempted to work these two alternatives into a consensus report, but the subcommittee remained so divided that he could only declare a majority in favor of the proportional plan and a strong minority for the 50 percent plan. These distinctions were academic, however, since President Roosevelt had strongly rejected any kind of guarantee whatsoever. At the conclusion of two full days of bickering, the bankers had produced nothing.

The only point on which all participants agreed was the tension and confusion of those two days. Traylor blew up several times and was once reduced to tears; Moley and Berle, fellow Brains Trusters, snapped at one another; and several members of the subcommittee scurried frequently to Woodin with complaints about the conduct of their colleagues. Charles Michelson, who arrived from

47. Moley, *First New Deal*, p. 149.

the White House to act as a press aide, hardly smoothed the hostility; he later recalled, "My declaration (with no authority) that no statements should be issued that I could not understand almost provoked an earthquake."[48]

Woodin finally dismissed the subcommittee with thanks for its observations but remarked that the policy decision would have to rest with him, the president, and their advisers.[49] The bankers went home still helpless.

Fortunately, Woodin had a plan in reserve, a proposal submitted by Ogden Mills on the afternoon of March 4 which became the basis for reopening the banks and solving the banking crisis. Mills presented a program based on the assumption that not all banks could be opened at the same time and that some banks presently closed should remain so. Therefore, he divided the banks of the country into three categories: 1) those of complete solvency and adequate liquidity, capable of immediate reopening if not hindered by fears of the collapse of weaker institutions; 2) banks whose capital structures based on present values were impaired, or were insolvent, or not liquid, or any combination of these, but capable of reorganization; and 3) banks so hopelessly insolvent that they should not be permitted to reopen at all. Nothing could be done for the last group except to make whatever payments were available to depositors.

For the other two classes, however, Mills suggested staggered openings based on soundness. The first set, which he called Class A banks, should resume operations as soon as possible, with assurances from the government "that they are capable of meeting all of the demands of their depositors." Some might have to be supplied with adequate currency to meet those withdrawals, but Mills

48. Moley, *First New Deal*, pp. 169–71; idem, *After Seven Years*, pp. 149–50; Bird, *Invisible Scar*, pp. 114–15, based on Berle's notes; Michelson, *Ghost Talks*, pp. 54–56.

49. George Leslie Harrison, confidential memorandum re 4–7 Mar. 1933, dictated 12 Mar. 1933, Harrison Papers, binder 46; memoranda, unsigned, undated, re guarantee plans; "A Suggested Plan for Consideration of the Committee Appointed by the Secretary of the Treasury to Recommend a Plan to the Advisory Committee," from comptroller's office, 5 Mar. 1933; Berle, "Memorandum on the Sub-Committee Plan," and "Sub-Committee Report"– all in Secretary Woodin's files on Bank Holiday, Comptroller's files, NA: RG 101, box 6; Hamlin, Diary, 5, 6, 7 Mar. 1933; Jackson Reynolds, COHC, pp. 166–67.

believed that this action would free approximately 26 percent of the banking resources of the country, and he hoped that at least one Class A bank could reopen to serve each geographic area of the nation. Moreover, the public's experience with these reopened sound banks would, in his opinion, go far towards restoring confidence. Then Class B banks could reopen gradually after reorganization and restoration of their capital. Mills felt that the government could afford to supplement capital where needed through purchase of preferred stock, probably by the RFC. In some cases, such as Detroit or Cleveland, where no Class A banks would be available and the B status of existing institutions remained questionable, he suggested that the secretary of the Treasury offer to establish a new bank; the government would buy preferred stock to furnish capital, and the new institution could take over assets of the old banks in return for assumption of a percentage of their deposit liabilities.[50]

Even if the banks reopened under Mills's plan, however, many still faced an acute shortage of cash.[51] On the first day of the moratorium, Woodin had announced his intention "to get a medium of exchange into circulation throughout the country so that the necessary business may be transacted."[52] If sound banks reopened, they would still need a supply of money to pay out to customers.

To most observers, the money question rapidly resolved itself into whether or not scrip should be issued as it had been during past banking emergencies. Bankers and clearinghouse associations, especially in New York, wanted clearinghouse certificates, like those employed in 1907 to facilitate interbank transactions. This pseudo-currency would be backed not by gold but by clearinghouse obligations based on sound banking assets. A memorandum to the same effect circulated at the Treasury Department, proposing "special currency" like the Aldrich-Vreeland bills a generation earlier to make bank assets liquid to meet withdrawals.[53] Some businesses already paid employees in certificates of obligation; the *Chicago Tri-*

50. Mills to Woodin, 4, 6 Mar. 1933, Mills Papers, box 59; Woodin's file in Comptroller's files, NA: RG 101, box 6; Mills to Hoover, 13 Mar. 1933, Mills Papers, box 59; Reynolds, COHC, pp. 170–72; Moley, *First New Deal*, pp. 166–69.

51. For currency substitutes during the holiday, see pp. ooo–oo, above.

52. *New York Times*, 7 Mar. 1933.

53. Unsigned memorandum, Woodin's file in Comptroller's files, NA: RG 101, box 6.

bune distributed facsimile "dollars" picturing President Theodore Roosevelt.[54] Railroads and retailers announced that they would accept scrip; paper mills and printers prepared to supply the new "money"; and Will Rogers confidently announced, "The psychology of the stuff not being actual money is going to make everyone want to buy something."[55] Cities and bankers' groups had already arranged for certificates: Philadelphia banks took $50 million in scrip and circulated $8 million of it; Chicago struggled through the first day of the holiday on a cash basis and then decided to issue scrip backed by bank deposits;[56] communities in New Jersey, Delaware, Kentucky, Connecticut, Georgia, California, and other states did the same while their legislatures considered enabling laws and stiff penalties for forgery.[57]

New York assumed the lead in the movement for scrip. As soon as Governor Lehman issued his closing proclamation, he promised "rehabilitation of the banking mechanism so that the essential needs of the people of this State may be satisfied."[58] Immediately the New York Clearing House Association Committee met and adopted a plan for distribution of certificates based on sound assets of the member banks, at a rate of $1 in scrip for $1.25 in good holdings. The bankers agreed to set up machinery for the issue, but they delayed positive action pending approval from Washington. The governor, however, believed that the Clearing House Association could not serve the needs of the entire state since it could benefit only a limited number of communities. Instead, he suggested a single type of state currency to be issued against "securities of all corporations under the Banking Law of the state," with restrictions on the total amount of such currency and the amount to be paid out against specific collateral. Secretary Woodin tentatively approved the plan, subject only to its being superseded by a national program. On March 7, the New York State legislature amended the banking

54. They used plates left over from 1907. Bendiner, *Just around the Corner*, p. 32.
55. Bird, *Invisible Scar*, p. 121; *New York Times*, 7 Mar. 1933.
56. James, *Growth of Chicago Banks*, pp. 1075–76; *Chicago Tribune*, 5, 8 Mar. 1933.
57. *New York Times*, 6–11 Mar. 1933.
58. Lehman, statement, 5 Mar. 1933, Lehman Papers, Governorship Papers, microfilm reel 8; *Commercial and Financial Chronicle*, 11 Mar 1933, p. 1670.

law to authorize statewide scrip, and Lehman set up the Emergency Certificate Corporation at once, naming as its chairman former governor Alfred E. Smith. The corporation obtained estimates and specimens of work from bank note printers and stood ready to begin distribution as soon as the federal Treasury gave final approval.[59] On March 8, however, Woodin revoked his earlier permission on the grounds that a nationwide solution had evolved.[60]

Washington officials proved less enthusiastic for scrip than did the bankers. Governor Eugene Meyer of the Federal Reserve Board dismissed the entire idea as "a phony lot of words thrown together and called a plan." He argued that the existence of Federal Reserve currency had rendered scrip obsolete nearly twenty years earlier.[61] Directors at the New York Reserve Bank agreed, noting in alarm that "the scrip idea would give encouragement to those in Congress and elsewhere who think a lack of currency is our trouble and who want currency inflation."[62]

President Roosevelt also considered an alternative to scrip. He called in Woodin and proposed that all government bonds—$21 billion worth—become immediately convertible into cash at par, no matter what maturity date they carried. This bold gesture might have encouraged the general public, but bankers and Treasury officials turned livid at the thought of such outrageous inflation. They persuaded Woodin to talk the president out of his scheme on the grounds that it would completely destroy the credit of the United States government and offered no means of contracting currency after the emergency. "No gentleman makes a bet he can't pay," said one.[63] Jackson Reynolds, who claimed that he held Woodin's hand throughout the crisis, told the secretary to tell the president the

59. Lehman, statement of 5 Mar. 1933, memorandum on scrip corporation, message to legislature, draft text of enabling act, memorandum to George Burr, 7 Mar. 1933—all in Lehman Papers, Governorship Papers, microfilm reel 8; Joseph A. Broderick to Lehman, 14 Dec. 1935, Lehman Papers, Special Subject Personal File; *New York Times*, 4–8 Mar. 1933; *Commercial and Financial Chronicle*, 11 Mar. 1933, pp. 1670, 1674–76; Andrew W. Mills, Diary, Columbia University, 4–5 Mar. 1933.

60. James Douglass to Lehman, 8 Mar. 1933, Lehman Papers, Governorship Papers, microfilm reel 8; *New York Times*, 9 Mar. 1933.

61. Meyer, COHC, p. 687.

62. Meeting of the Executive Committee, Federal Reserve Bank of New York, 7 Mar. 1933, Harrison Papers, binder 50, pp. 103–06.

63. Reynolds, COHC, pp. 167–70.

story of two philosophers, a Stoic and an Epicurean, who had argued for hours without changing their respective convictions. Finally, the Epicurean clinched his case by pointing out that many Stoics had been converted to Epicureanism but never the reverse. The Stoic countered that he had also heard of many roosters becoming capons but never a capon who became a rooster. "If the President does this job," Reynolds concluded, "he'll be a capon all right and he'll never get back to be a rooster."[64]

On the currency question as well as the reopening plan, Hoover's men finally rescued the Roosevelt administration with a workable but orthodox solution. George Leslie Harrison had remained at the Treasury after the collapse of the bankers' conferences. He, among others, heard Roosevelt's bond proposal with horror. In urging Woodin to dissuade the president from the mad scheme, Harrison offered an alternative which he hoped would satisfy all parties. He proposed to make cash available to holders of government bonds, but with controls against inflation. Federal Reserve banks would be authorized to make loans to individuals, firms, or corporations on their own ninety-day notes backed by pledge of government securities; the Reserve banks could, if necessary, limit inflation by raising rates to put pressure on borrowers to liquidate their notes. In conjunction with Mills's reopening plan, Harrison added that Federal Reserve bank notes might also be loaned to member banks against their sound assets. Mills, Ballantine, and Meyer endorsed the idea, which Woodin took to the president. Roosevelt agreed to the entire prospectus and authorized the drafting of enabling legislation.

Historians have generally assumed that Secretary Woodin originated the idea of using Federal Reserve notes instead of scrip, because Raymond Moley credited the exhausted secretary with that inspiration when he told the story in 1939. Woodin had returned to his hotel room on the night of March 6 to read, think, and play his guitar for respite from the haggling at the Treasury. While he was so engaged, the answer supposedly "came" to him, and he decided to issue currency against the sound assets of the banks. "The Reserve Act lets us print all we'll need," he told Moley the next morning.

64. Harrison, memorandum of 4–8 Mar. 1933, Harrison Papers, binder 46.

"And it won't frighten people. It won't look like stage money. It'll be money that looks like money." But Moley later corrected the impression that Woodin had thought of the note idea himself; instead, he had merely accepted "a recommendation already made to him by Mills and Ballantine." Since the plan went out under Woodin's authority, it was naturally credited to him.[65]

As soon as Roosevelt accepted Mills's plan for reopening and Harrison's currency device, Woodin began work on the Emergency Banking Act of 1933. He summoned Walter Wyatt to compose the bill; Wyatt had worked for the Federal Reserve Board throughout the crisis and had written the official language of many of the interim regulations. He labored from 11 o'clock on Tuesday evening, March 7, until 3 o'clock on Thursday morning to evolve the final draft, while Moley and others ran liaison to the Board, the White House, and various congressional leaders to obtain approvals and modifications. Senator Glass in particular demanded substantial changes, including exclusion of nonmember state banks from the section of the act dealing with licensing to reopen. In addition, the drafters met great resistance from Jesse Jones of the RFC over the clause whereby his agency would purchase preferred stock in national banks when so requested by the secretary of the Treasury, a feature for which Jones later claimed credit. By the morning of March 9, the day on which the new Congress would meet, however, the exhausted Treasury men had an acceptable bill in hand.[66]

As they filed into their places in the House and Senate chambers, few among the legislators at the special session knew the details of the forthcoming bill, but all realized they were there to pass a banking act. Senate and House leaders had already taken steps to expedite emergency legislation by binding their followers to vote in a bloc the way a majority of the party caucus decided. Both houses had designated their leaders and selected committee members in order to avoid delays with housekeeping details.

65. Ibid.; Moley, *After Seven Years*, pp. 150–52; idem, *First New Deal*, pp. 171–76; *New York Times*, 8–13 Mar. 1933; *Commercial and Financial Chronicle*, 11 Mar. 1933, pp. 1680–81.
66. Walter Wyatt to Arthur Ballantine, 1 Aug. 1944, and Wyatt to Moley, 16 Mar. 1966, quoted in Moley, *First New Deal*, pp. 174–77; Hamlin, Diary, 9, 10 Mar. 1933; Jones, *Fifty Billion Dollars*, p. 188.

The Senate of the Seventy-third Congress convened at noon and thirty-seven minutes later heard the president's message calling for immediate action. In it he asked for executive control of banks for the protection of depositors, authority to open sound banks at once and others as rapidly as possible, and amendments to the Federal Reserve Act to provide needed additional currency. With the message, he sent the draft bill.[67] At 1:40 the bill was formally introduced and referred to the Banking and Currency Committee, where Senator Glass and Walter Wyatt explained its provisions to the committee. Acting Comptroller Awalt testified that only 2,600 national banks could open without this legislation, but 5,000 could resume operations with the support it offered. By 4:10 the Senate committee had approved the bill and sent it to the full Senate, where debate began at 4:30. Senator Huey Long of Louisiana interrupted the proceedings at this point with an amendment authorizing the president to declare state banks members of the Federal Reserve System and therefore covered by the act. Long argued heatedly for the "little county seat banks," charging that Senator Glass and others wanted to open only 5,000 banks and keep 14,900 closed. Glass explained that the bill closed no banks and that state authorities could open any institution under their jurisdiction whenever they chose. Long's amendment fell by voice vote. At 7:23 that evening, by a roll-call vote of 73 to 7, the Senate passed the banking bill and adjourned.[68] (Senators Borah, Carey, Costigan, Dale, La Follette, Nye, and Shipstead voted against the bill. Borah explained that he feared the bill would destroy the state banks and chiefly benefit those in New York City.)

Meanwhile, the House had also convened and confirmed its leaders, and at 2:55 began consideration of the bank legislation. Members did not even have copies of the bill—at one point it was represented by a folded newspaper—and the majority leader forbade amendments. The minority leader noted that such procedures were "entirely out of the ordinary" but saw no practical choice. "There

67. Rosenman, *Public Papers*, 2:45–47; Samuel I. Rosenman, *Working with Roosevelt* (New York: Harper, 1952), p. 81; Roosevelt, *On Our Way*, p. 15; *New York Times*, 7, 9, 10 Mar. 1933.

68. *Congressional Record*, 73d Cong., 1st Sess., Mar. 1933, pp. 52–67; Beasley, *Carter Glass*, pp. 343–45; Williams, *Huey Long*, p. 627; Moley, *First New Deal*, pp. 177, 181–88; *New York Times*, 11 Mar. 1933.

is only one answer to this question," he said, "and that is to give the President what he demands and says is necessary to meet the situation." The bill passed by voice vote at 4:05. As soon as a duplicate law got through the Senate, the Speaker signed the House copy, and the emergency act went to the president.

At 8:36 that evening—seven hours and fifty-nine minutes after his message asking for immediate action—President Roosevelt signed the Emergency Banking Act of 1933. Two hours later he issued a proclamation extending the holiday indefinitely.

The Emergency Banking Act approved the holiday and provided the legal basis for reopening the banks. Title I validated the March 6–9 moratorium, confirming the authorization in the 1917 Trading-with-the-Enemy Act. It also amended that act to give the president power in time of national emergency to regulate or prohibit operations in member banks of the Federal Reserve System, paying particular attention to movements of gold. Title II, called the "Bank Conservation Act," followed Mills's plan for reopenings. National banks with impaired assets would not be liquidated as previously required; now the Comptroller of the Currency could appoint a "conservator" (a new variant on receivership) to release money from a closed bank as he felt it safe; meanwhile the conservator would prepare reorganization plans which would go into effect when approved by the Comptroller, the courts, and three-quarters of the bank's creditors. Title III authorized national banks to issue preferred stock for sale to the public or the RFC in order to rehabilitate their capital structure. Title IV broadened the Federal Reserve Act permitting Reserve banks to make advances to member banks on security of any acceptable assets. All direct obligations of the United States became eligible as collateral and many other bonds, bills, drafts, and acceptances were made temporarily eligible. Moreover, the Reserve banks could make similar advances to any individual, partnership, or corporation on its promissory note secured by United States bonds. Finally, Title V appropriated $2 million for carrying out the act.[69]

69. Emergency Banking Bill, typewritten text, FDRL:OF 230; summary of the bill, Glass Papers, box 311; memorandum for Mr. Harlan, Woodin's file, Comptroller's files, NA: RG 101, box 6; Woodin to Joseph T. Robinson, "Resume of Handling of the Banking Situation," 15 Mar. 1933, Treasury Secretary's

Swift passage of the Emergency Banking Act encouraged those who sought prompt release from the crisis,[70] but it also alarmed those who feared "panic legislation" and abdication of congressional power to the president.[71] In effect, Roosevelt had issued autocratic orders to Congress and had gotten exactly what he wanted—broad discretionary powers.[72] The plan he submitted, however, represented the best efforts of both his own and the preceding administration. Its provisions remained much more orthodox than many of those considered during the emergency. And it was so broadly drawn that its effect would depend primarily on how it was administered.

Perhaps presidential aide Louis Howe best summarized the mood of America on March 9, 1933. "Oh hell," he said, "any country that has for its theme song 'Who's Afraid of the Big Bad Wolf' isn't going to be too scared of what Franklin is trying to do."[73]

correspondence, NA(Suitland); Federal Reserve Board, *Annual Report, 1933,* pp. 37–38; Moley, *After Seven Years,* pp. 152–53; idem, *First New Deal,* p. 189; *New York Times,* 10, 11 Mar. 1933.

70. *New York Times,* 10 Mar. 1933; *Hartford Courant,* 10 Mar. 1933; *Atlanta Constitution,* 10 Mar. 1933; *Cleveland Plain Dealer,* 10 Mar. 1933.

71. John J. Murphy to Missy LeHand, 19 Mar. 1933, FDRL:OF 230; Peter Norbeck to O. W. Coursey, 28 Apr. 1933, Norbeck Papers; Joseph A. Gavagan, COHC, p. 37; James Walcott Wadsworth, COHC, pp. 398–99; Felix Frankfurter to Walter Lippmann, 11, 15 Mar. 1933, quoted in Freedman, *Roosevelt and Frankfurter,* pp. 114–19.

72. Anne O'Hare McCormick, " 'Let's Try It!', Says Roosevelt," *New York Times,* 26 Mar. 1933; U. V. Wilcox, *The Bankers Be Damned* (New York: Daniel Ryerson, 1940), pp. 22–23.

73. Lela Stiles, *The Man behind Roosevelt: The Story of Louis McHenry Howe* (Cleveland: World, 1954), p. 244.

CHAPTER VIII

Reopening

FRANKLIN ROOSEVELT had acted rapidly to save banking in the short run. In less than one week, the president closed the nation's banks, promised that they would reopen, provided interim services, and went to the Congress with enabling legislation. At the same time, he revived confidence in the government and offered reassurances about his economic policies. During his first press conference, on March 8, Roosevelt stated clearly that the gold standard was safe, that the nation would have an adequate but sound currency, and that, although the government would not guarantee bank deposits, it would try "to keep the loss in the individual banks down to a minimum."[1] The following day, newspapers previewed a new book by the president,[2] in which he stressed individual freedom of action, the sanctity of private property, and the role of government as a counterbalance to oligarchy—all tenets inclined to encourage the country while it waited for more specific information on the fate of its banks.

The Congress cooperated in the restoration of confidence by rushing through the Emergency Banking Act of March 9, endorsing the president's actions of the past week and outlining a framework for reopening. It remained for the government to superintend the reopening of the banks which had closed under the president's moratorium proclamation.

The new administration went about reopening the banks with almost as much dispatch as it had exhibited in closing them. Under the authority of the Emergency Banking Act, Roosevelt issued an executive order on March 10 directing the secretary of the Treasury to license any member of the Federal Reserve System which could obtain endorsement of its soundness from its district Reserve bank; state banking authorities could reopen sound nonmember banks at their discretion. The following day, he released a statement to the press outlining the reopening procedure in more detail. Resumption of banking would take three days, the president said. On Monday, March 13, licensed banks in the 12 Federal Reserve cities would reopen, the 250 cities having clearinghouse associations would follow on March 14, and other areas could begin operations again on March 15. At the same time, Roosevelt announced that he would address the nation over the radio on Sunday evening, March 12, at ten o'clock, to explain the banking situation to the people. That statement quieted critics who believed that banks should have reopened the morning after the Emergency Banking Act was passed.[3]

Roosevelt spoke to sixty million listeners in that first presidential fireside chat. He had used the intimate radio talk while governor of New York; now, as president in an emergency, he hoped to reach those "who had everything they owned in the world in the form of a money deposit in some local bank and who wondered if they would ever see their money again."[4]

"I want to talk for a few minutes with the people of the United States about banking," the president began. Then he briefly explained the mechanics of banking, why banks could not lay their hands on cash to meet runs, and why governors had suspended banking in a closing which the president had made uniform for the nation. (He made no effort to justify these actions, assuming that the reasons were self-evident.) "No sound bank," he went on, "is a dollar worse off than it was when it closed its doors last Monday." These safe institutions would be the ones to reopen, with currency made available through Federal Reserve bank issues against their good assets; he specifically stated that this currency would be real money

1. Rosenman, *Public Papers*, 2:30–45; Elmer E. Cornwell, "The Presidential Press Conference: A Study in Institutionalization," *Midwestern Journal of Political Sciences* 4 (Nov. 1960): 370–89; Tully, *F. D. R.: My Boss*, pp. 89–91.

2. *Looking Forward.*

3. Rosenman, *Public Papers*, 2:56–57, 59–60; *New York Times*, 11, 12 Mar. 1933; Smith and Beasley, *Carter Glass*, pp. 345–46.

4. Roosevelt, *On Our Way*, p. 26.

and would be printed in sufficient volume to meet all needs. Of course, not all banks would reopen immediately, because the government wanted no repetition of the past epidemic of failures. Therefore, only those banks would reopen which had been "found to be all right" by Treasury Department examination. The other banks could resume business eventually, after reorganization, "in exactly the same status as the bank that opens tomorrow. . . . There is nothing complex, or radical, in the process," he affirmed; government was merely disentangling safe banks from the chaos created by the unsound. And he concluded, "Confidence and courage are the essentials of success in carrying out our plan. You people must have faith."[5]

Roosevelt persuaded the nation to accept the reopening procedure. Ogden Mills of the Hoover administration had created the original solution, and his assistant, Arthur Ballantine, drafted the president's fireside chat. Although Charles Michelson, formerly of the Democratic National Committee, had written a preliminary draft, Raymond Moley got Ballantine to submit a new summary, based on the Mills reopening plan. This became the text for the radio address, altered only by the president's own direct and clear style.[6] According to Louis Howe, Roosevelt revised the speech while watching workmen tearing down the inauguration scaffolding, and wrote the speech for them. Will Rogers later remarked that it was so simple that even bankers understood it.[7]

It took the new president to translate the program devised by the old order into terms which the average man, on whom its success depended, could understand. The public responded enthusiastically; hundreds of letters poured into the White House congratulating and thanking him, frequently concluding with a fervent "God bless you."[8] More concretely, when banks reopened the

5. Rosenman, *Public Papers*, 2:61–66; *New York Times*, 13 Mar. 1933; *Commercial and Financial Chronicle*, 18 Mar. 1933, p. 1809.

6. Michelson, *Ghost Talks*, pp. 56–57; Ballantine, memorandum, n.d., Woodin's file, Comptroller's Banking Emergency Records, NA: RG 101, box 6; Moley, *After Seven Years*, p. 155; idem, *First New Deal*, pp. 172–74, 193–96.

7. Stiles, *Man behind Roosevelt*, p. 245; Rollins, *Roosevelt and Howe*, p. 384; Rosenman, *Working with Roosevelt*, pp. 92–94, 259.

8. Telegrams included one from the Rev. Mr. Charles Coughlin, commending the president as "a natural born artist" of the radio; FDRL:PPF 200B, 7 file boxes; Farley, *Behind the Ballots*, p. 210.

next morning as promised, currency deposits far exceeded withdrawals.[9]

Underlying this record of success, however, were five days of feverish activity at the Treasury Department. Before any banks could reopen, all closed institutions had to undergo evaluation and classification as to soundness. The Mills plan stipulated that banks must be divided into three categories: those whose assets equalled deposits so that they could resume unrestricted activity at once, those so obviously insolvent that they must remain closed permanently and be liquidated under supervision, and those which might be restored to full activity after reorganization. Harried Treasury officials labored over these designations from the time the plan was first accepted until—and in many cases after—the first banks opened on March 13.

The Emergency Banking Act and the president's executive order named the secretary of the Treasury as sole licensing agent for Federal Reserve member banks. For practical administration, Secretary Woodin asked the help of Acting Comptroller of the Currency Awalt, who supervised all national banks; he also requested the twelve Federal Reserve banks to pass on license applications for state-chartered member banks in their districts. Thus, evaluation began with officials who had immediate knowledge of the soundness and liquidity of individual banks. In licensing, the secretary did not usurp control from the Comptroller or the Reserve but relied on the same cooperation he had enjoyed since taking office.

In calling on the Reserve banks to certify non-national member institutions for reopening, Woodin in effect asked the Federal Reserve to stand behind these banks. At the same time, Awalt convinced him that judgments should be fairly liberal in order to effect the fullest possible restoration of banking facilities to troubled communities. As former Secretary Mills put it, "anyone anything like all right will be allowed to come in."[10] A preliminary list of national banks showed 2,494 with total deposits of $10,393,766,000 abso-

9. George W. Norris to FDR, 16 Mar. 1933, FDRL:PPF 200B; *New York Times*, 13–16 Mar. 1933; Moley, *First New Deal*, pp. 196–99; Mitchell, *Depression Decade*, p. 135; Lippmann, *Interpretations: 1933–1935*, pp. 34–37.

10. Ogden Mills-Herbert Hoover telephone conversation, 10 Mar. 1933, memorandum, Hoover Papers, West Branch, Post-Presidential Papers, 1933–1946, AG 6.

lutely sound; a second classification, twenty-four hours later, added 1,477 banks with deposits of $2,077,000,000. (The new total represented 66 percent of deposits in national banks.)[11] Woodin wanted the Reserve banks to be just as free in their estimates. Since both the president and the secretary had stated publicly that only sound banks would reopen, the Federal Reserve Board protested the acceptance of banks which might not be wholly sound and argued that the Reserve System should not have to take on this burden of approval.[12] Woodin, however, continued to demand that the Reserve banks submit their lists of approved banks and that they follow the broad classifications begun by Awalt.

The twelve district banks were perplexed. They had been asked, in confidence, to send in lists of banks which might be reopened, yet they had no clear information on whether or how those lists might be used. Nor did they have a specific formula for judging banks, since national and state examiners used different standards of evaluation; and at best, they had only the information in the last report on each bank—all precrisis and some almost a year old. Moreover, the Reserve banks could not find out at first whether the Treasury Department intended to limit reopening to institutions which could resume on a 100 percent basis or would also permit partial openings. In New York, the directors of the Reserve bank decided to classify all institutions under their jurisdiction in three categories: those clearly able to open 100 percent immediately, those which could open on some basis less than 100 percent, and those which should not be opened at all. The Board agreed, feeling that this solution would throw the final decision back to the Treasury.[13]

If they were to reopen banks on a liberal basis, authorities had to make generous determinations on assets of member banks, both for estimates of solvency and for establishing collateral for rediscounts or issues of Federal Reserve notes. Many member banks would have to remain closed if their assets for such advances were

---

11. Awalt to Ballantine, 8 Mar. 1933, and Awalt to Woodin, 9 Mar. 1933, Comptroller's files, NA: RG 101, box 5.

12. Federal Reserve Board, Minutes, 8, 9 Mar. 1933; Hamlin, Diary, 8, 9 Mar. 1933; Moley, *After Seven Years*, p. 154; idem, *First New Deal*, pp. 190–91.

13. George Leslie Harrison, memorandum of special meetings, Board of Directors, New York Federal Reserve Bank, 8, 10 Mar. 1933, Harrison Papers, binder 50, vol. 3:107–10, 118–25.

judged at current market prices. To reassure Reserve officials, therefore, Woodin confidentially distributed a letter from the president
admitting that some losses on the rediscounts and note issues would
be inevitable, but promising to "ask the Congress to indemnify any
of the 12 Federal Reserve Banks for such losses" if they would
evaluate members' holdings more freely than at current prices.[14]
Thus the president lifted the moral and financial burden on the
Reserve banks, making it easier for them to submit liberal reopening recommendations. "Under the new circumstances of today," said
one director, "liberality probably would cost us less than severity
in judgment."[15]

Not only did the Reserve banks now accept their new responsibility, but they became instantly jealous of its prerogatives.
The New York bank urged Secretary Woodin not to license any
member bank unless it had first been cleared through its Reserve
bank, since "the principle burden of taking care of such banks as are
reopened will be ours."[16] At the same time, the Reserve banks decided not to change the rediscount rate. Woodin also persuaded them
to cooperate in an informal arrangement to discount eligible paper
acquired from nonmember banks, so that all categories of banks
might reopen as soon as possible.[17]

Thus, the secretary of the Treasury quickly established the
method of licensing Reserve member banks. If a state member institution could convince its district Reserve bank or if a national
bank could convince the Comptroller of its soundness, it would be
licensed by the secretary to perform usual banking functions, except as limited by presidential order or Treasury regulations, particularly the decree forbidding dealings in gold.[18]

14. FDR to Woodin, 11 Mar. 1933, Comptroller's files, NA: RG 101, box 7;
Woodin to Harrison, 11 Mar. 1933, Harrison Papers, binder 54; Federal Reserve
Board, Minutes, 9, 10, 11 Mar. 1933; Hamlin, Diary, 11 Mar. 1933; Frederic H.
Prince to FDR, 10 Mar. 1933, FDRL:OF 230.

15. Harrison, memorandum of special meeting, Board of Directors, New
York Federal Reserve Bank, 11 Mar. 1933, Harrison Papers, binder 50, vol.
3:126–29.

16. Harrison to Woodin, 12 Mar. 1933, Harrison Papers, binder 54.

17. Harrison, memorandum of special meetings, Board of Directors, New
York Federal Reserve Bank, 9, 13, 16, 23 Mar. 1933, Harrison Papers, binder 50;
Federal Reserve Board, Minutes, 11 Mar. 1933.

18. A. K. Cherry, memorandum, 18 Sept. 1933; "Termination of Procedure
for Licensing Member Banks by Secretary of Treasury," 5 Dec. 1945–both in
Federal Reserve Board files.

State nonmember banks, however, fell outside this procedure. At first, Treasury officials wondered who should rule on the solvency of these institutions. Since all banks in the nation had closed under the president's moratorium proclamation, were all banks to be treated similarly in reopening? Powerful members of the House and Senate Banking and Currency Committee opposed vesting this part of the licensing authority in the secretary of the Treasury, although Woodin stated that he was ready, if necessary, to take it on. They argued that the president had not even had Constitutional power to close state nonmember banks and that only the grave emergency had justified that action. Now, judgment on the soundness of those banks should revert to state banking boards and commissioners.[19] Simultaneously, state governors, such as Herbert Lehman of New York, protested any reopening decisions regarding state banks—members or nonmembers—without consulting the state superintendents of banking.[20] On the other hand, the governors did not want state banks to suffer discrimination, and they obtained Woodin's agreement to treat state institutions equally with member banks, particularly in benefiting from supportive loans and rediscounts at the Reserve banks.[21] The federal authorities decided that their proper role in reopening the state banks would be to offer this kind of assistance but to leave the actual licensing decisions to state authorities. (Roosevelt included this division of jurisdiction in the Executive Order of March 10; a further decree on March 18 permitted state banking authorities to name conservators for state nonmember banks which remained closed.) The men in Washington hoped, however, that the state boards would not open institutions which could not meet standards set for member banks.[22]

With the procedures established, the actual decisions on reopening required prompt, decisive, but judicious action. Bankers everywhere pressed for rapid reopenings. On March 10 alone, the Chicago Reserve bank received applications from ten city banks and sixteen others in the district. Within three days, they endorsed the

19. Senator Glass argued particularly strongly for this solution. Hamlin, Diary, 8, 9 Mar. 1933.

20. Lehman to FDR, Woodin and Meyer, 9 Mar. 1933, Lehman Papers, Governorship Papers, microfilm reel 8.

21. For the Robinson-Steagall Act of 24 Mar. 1933 which made this equity a matter of law, see below, pp. 197–201.

22. Harrison to Governor Seay, 10 Apr. 1933, Harrison Papers, binder 54.

licensing of five giant Loop banks and twenty-nine smaller institutions—only 10 percent of Chicago's financial institutions, but those reopened held 97 percent of the city's banking resources.[23]

Some banks, anxious to receive licenses, obtained the cooperation of local authorities or political representatives in presenting their applications. The superintendent of banking in New York personally went to the New York Federal Reserve Bank to plead for a group of large upstate banks on the grounds that failure to reopen them would wreck their communities. The Reserve bank directors resisted, believing that approval of banks known to be unsound would undermine the strength of their endorsement of truly safe institutions.[24] Senators found their offices flooded with requests for aid; many politicians obliged with frequent trips to the Treasury on behalf of local institutions. In a number of cases, they failed. Senator Tom Connally of Texas could not obtain licenses for several banks in his constituency; subsequently, they withdrew from the Federal Reserve System and received permission to reopen from the state bank superintendent.[25]

Although the reopened institutions usually received licenses because of their liquidity and financial strength, as liberally judged by competent men, in a few instances bankers and politicians were able to overcome objections of the district Reserve bank and persuade Secretary Woodin to grant licenses, as in the case of the giant Bank of America in California.

As soon as he learned of the licensing procedure, Amadeo P. Giannini applied directly to Secretary Woodin to reopen the 410-branch Bank of America. The governor of the San Francisco Reserve bank, however, refused to certify the complex as sound. Giannini charged prejudice since the two men had clashed in the past. He offered more recent figures to supersede the evidence of the Reserve bank, and contacted California's senators, Hiram Johnson and William Gibbs McAdoo, as well as a representative of the Hearst

23. Walter J. Cummings, to Woodin, 10 Mar. 1933, Treasury Secretary's correspondence, NA(Suitland); *Chicago Tribune*, 13, 14 Mar. 1933; James, *Growth of Chicago Banks*, pp. 1084–86.

24. Harrison, memorandum of special meetings, Board of Directors, New York Federal Reserve Bank, 11, 12, 13 Mar. 1933, Harrison Papers, binder 50, vol. 3:130–34, 137–43.

25. Connally, with Alfred Steinberg, *My Name is Tom Connally* (New York: Crowell, 1954), p. 149; Hamlin, Diary, 21, 23 Mar. 1933.

newspapers, to act as his lobbyists in presenting those figures in Washington. They convinced Woodin to ask the Acting Comptroller to investigate, and Awalt ruled in favor of Giannini. Woodin then telephoned the governor of the Reserve bank and in strong language persuaded him to agree to license the banking complex. The Secretary asked if the Reserve bank would assume responsibility for keeping the bank closed, thus denying banking facilities to San Francisco and many other communities. The governor would not take on that burden, so Woodin directed that a license be issued. The Reserve bank then proceeded to reclassify all other banks under its jurisdiction, believing that almost every bank in its district was as sound as the Bank of America.[26]

When all government authorities had made their determinations, the banks fell into the three prescribed categories: 1) about half, with 90 percent of total resources in the country, were judged wholly safe and capable of reopening by March 15; 2) another 45 percent were to be placed under conservators (25 percent to open partially and pay out a percentage of deposits; 20 percent, whose assets would not justify any present payments on old deposits, to be saved through reorganization); and 3) the remaining 5 percent, perhaps 1,000 banks, had to be closed permanently.[27]

On Monday, March 13, banking resumed in the United States. Licensed institutions in each of the twelve Federal Reserve cities opened with full facilities and sufficient supplies of Federal Reserve notes. State authorities licensed banks under their jurisdiction to open simultaneously with member banks. In New York City, for example, all but nine banks reopened the first day. The public showed remarkable confidence in its reopened banks. Although operations had been restricted for at least a week in most places—and in some for almost a month—deposits far exceeded withdrawals. The Federal Reserve Bank of New York paid out $18 million to member banks but took in $27 million, of which $15.5 million was in coin or

26. Giannini to Jesse Jones, 14 Mar. 1933; Marvin McIntyre to Giannini, 15 Mar. 1933; Giannini to McIntyre, 15 Mar. 1933 – FDRL:OF 230; Hamlin, Diary, 12, 13, 21 Mar., 26 Apr. 1933; Moley, *After Seven Years*, p. 154; idem, *First New Deal*, pp. 191–93; Thomas M. Storke, *California Editor* (Los Angeles: Westernlore, 1958), pp. 344–45; James and James, *Biography of a Bank*, pp. 368–74, 379; Jones, *Fifty Billion Dollars*, p. 37.

27. Mitchell, *Depression Decade*, pp. 134–35; J. F. T. O'Connor, radio broadcast, 19 July 1933, mimeographed text, FDRL:OF 21B.

currency and $11.5 million in gold certificates.[28] The next two days repeated the first, and Secretary Woodin had to plead for patience in face of the flood of license applications; he repeated the president's guarantee that banks which did not resume activities on the first day could eventually be reopened "in exactly the same status as the bank that opens tomorrow."[29] By March 29, a majority of banking institutions across the nation were open for business; many areas reported almost completely normal operations. The Associated Press survey of bank operations by states found, for example, that 292 of the 338 banks in California were virtually normal, while most others operated under restrictions. All 160 state and 53 member banks in Connecticut were operating under varying restrictions. All national and two-thirds of the 353 state banks in Kentucky were open and normal. And only 20 banks remained closed in Tennessee.[30]

By the end of March, 5,387 members of the Federal Reserve System had been licensed to reopen and 1,307 remained closed. Thereafter, member banks opened gradually at an average rate of sixty per month (thirty-five national and twenty-five state members) for the rest of the year. As of June 1, 91 percent of deposits in member banks had become available.[31] Meanwhile, 7,654 of a total of 11,435 state-chartered institutions opened the first month, and further licensing followed, although at a slower rate than with Reserve member banks.[32]

Bank reopenings sparked business activity as well. The New York Stock Exchange and most other markets—suspended for the duration of the national moratorium—resumed operations on March 15. Stock prices rose steadily; increases in market value averaged 15 percent over the March 3 closing, and volume of trading in New York exceeded any day since September 22, 1932. Government bonds, corporate bonds, and basic commodities shared in the gains. Retail

28. Roy Robert (editor, *Kansas City Star*) to FDR, 13 Mar. 1933, FDRL:OF 230; Henry Stimson to FDR, 14 Mar. 1933, FDRL:PPF 20; *New York Times*, 12–15 Mar. 1933; "The Banks Reopen," *Business Week*, 22 Mar. 1933, pp. 3–4.

29. *Federal Reserve Bulletin*, Mar. 1933, p. 130; *New York Times*, 16 Mar. 1933.

30. *New York Times*, 15 Mar. 1933.

31. *Federal Reserve Bulletin*, 1933, pp. 216, 274, 341, 453, 517, 578, 658, 721, 776; *New York Times*, 15, 17, 19, 26 Mar., 15, 28 Apr., 2, 26 June, 17, 20, 21 Aug., 2, 20 Sept., 25 Oct., 7 Dec. 1933.

32. *New York Times*, 15 Apr. 1933; weekly reopenings reported in *Commercial and Financial Chronicle*.

trade was reported near normal, although production in such key industries as automobiles and public construction remained slow.[33]

The banking crisis of 1933 had been surmounted. Roosevelt had arrested the avalanche of failures and restored banking to the nation, rapidly and without radical change.

Treasury officials, however, could not regard the crisis as neatly solved with the first spate of reopenings. They also had to disentangle banks which had not been licensed, reorganize institutions which would eventually resume operations, and liquidate those which would not. After the first rush of licensing, freeing 90 percent of the nation's banking resources, officials decided to follow a very cautious policy in permitting more banks to reopen. "It seems to me fundamental," Awalt wrote, "that we should be very rigid, both in examination and requirements, from now on in order to keep these banks sound."[34]

The Emergency Banking Act provided that unlicensed national banks be placed under conservators; a later executive order permitted state banking authorities to name similar officials for state institutions. Ordinarily, closed banks were supervised by "receivers," administrators who managed the liquidation of insolvent institutions. Since many of the unlicensed banks were not hopelessly insolvent, however, conservators would administer them during reorganization pending eventual reopening.[35] Conservators had two sets of duties. In the short run, they must make some portion of deposits available for necessities of life, and at the same time provide depository services to the community by accepting "trust deposits" which would be separate from old assets and payable on demand. Additionally, conservators were to prepare their banks to reopen. Since both of these functions required a working knowledge of the community and its needs, the Comptroller frequently appointed one of a bank's own officers to serve as its conservator.[36] During 1933,

---

33. "The Figures of the Week" and "The Financial Markets," *Business Week*, 22 Mar. 1933, pp. 28–30; 29 Mar. 1933, pp. 28–31; *Federal Reserve Bulletin*, Apr. 1933, p. 219; *New York Times*, 9–18 Mar. 1933.

34. Awalt to Woodin, 24 Mar. 1933, Comptroller's files, NA: RG 101, box 5.

35. Jones, *Fifty Billion Dollars*, pp. 20–21; Timmons, *Jones*, pp. 188–89; Woodin, statement, 14 Mar. 1933, *Federal Reserve Bulletin*, Mar. 1933, p. 130; *New York Times*, 10, 13 Mar. 1933.

36. J. F. T. O'Connor, "Trust Department Operations and the Bank Holiday,"

the Comptroller named 1,105 conservators to oversee banks with almost $2 billion in deposits.

Wherever possible, authorities tried to strengthen local banking structures while they rehabilitated individual banks or groups of banks, since small, weak, nonmember institutions had precipitated the crisis. In Washington, D. C., for example, only one institution, of the thirteen placed under conservators, eventually reopened without merging with any other bank; even that became a national bank. By the time the Comptroller's office had restored banking in the District of Columbia, depositors had eighteen fewer banks but were dealing with larger, safer, national corporations more closely regulated by the Comptroller. At the same time, the banking laws were changed to prohibit any corporation from engaging in banking or fiduciary business in the District of Columbia without the Comptroller's approval or without meeting reserve requirements prescribed for national banks.[37]

Where banks were to be saved, they needed reorganization plans. Unlicensed national banks were rehabilitated and reopened under three major plans: capital correction, creditor waiver, and "Spokane sale."

Capital correction applied to banks in need of refinancing. If losses and unacceptable assets did not exceed the total of capital, surplus, and undivided profits, the bank could use its capital accounts to pay off liabilities and then restore its capital through new stock sales to the present stockholders or other interested parties. In many cases, bankers turned over their own fortunes to such rehabilitation plans; local businessmen often voluntarily invested funds to aid banks which had served their communities. Even the federal government assisted through the RFC.[38]

Under the terms of the Emergency Banking Act, the Reconstruction Finance Corporation could invest in preferred stock or capital notes of commercial banks and trust companies. A year earlier, a prominent Chicago banker had complained that banks were

Trust Companies, Sept. 1933, pp. 259–63; idem, *Banking Crisis and Recovery*, pp. 28–36; Upham and Lamke, *Closed and Distressed Banks*, pp. 48–53; *New York Times*, 14, 29 Mar. 1933; Homer Cummings to FDR, 21 Mar. 1933, FDRL:OF 21B.

37. Cole, *Development of Banking*, pp. 450–69.
38. O'Connor, *Banking Crisis and Recovery*, pp. 42–43.

too small and required the strength of size. "Our banks don't need loans," he said, "they need more capital."[39] Until March 9, 1933, no federal agency was permitted to contribute to a bank's capital structure because opponents feared government control of the banking system. Mass closings, however, revealed greater capital needs than voluntary contributions could supply. The president's advisers therefore decided to include in the reopening program an amendment to the Reconstruction Finance Corporation Act empowering the RFC to buy preferred stock. Where necessary, states revised their banking statutes to make state banks eligible for preferred stock and capital note purchases.[40] A further federal law revoked double liability of shareholders, thus making preferred stock a more attractive investment for the RFC.

The agency began buying immediately. On March 13, with powers less than four days old, the directors invested $2 million in a Minnesota bank. It also supported institutions in Maryland, Utah, and Texas, and especially Detroit.[41] In some cases, the RFC used its stock purchases to do more than add to a bank's capital. When it bought $50 million worth of preferred stock in the Continental Illinois Bank and Trust Company in Chicago, the purchase agreement gave the agency veto power over appointment of officers and directors of the bank. It used this influence to secure the election of its candidate as chairman of the board of directors because, in the RFC's judgment, the bank's staggering losses of the past two years—$50 million in 1932 and $60 million in 1933—came from unwise management.[42]

For a long time, bankers remained reluctant to seek RFC help. Large and powerful members of the American Bankers Association had little sympathy for weakened banks and were cool to government offers of aid; they also did not welcome RFC influence

39. Melvin Traylor, quoted in Jones, *Fifty Billion Dollars*, p. 133.
40. Herbert Lehman to FDR, Woodin, Robert Wagner, Royal S. Copeland, and Joseph T. Robinson, 14 Mar. 1933; F. F. Sisson to Lehman, 17 Mar. 1933; Robinson to Lehman, 21 Mar. 1933—all in Lehman Papers, Governorship Papers, microfilm reel 8; memorandum to Woodin, 14 Mar. 1933, FDRL:OF 230; *New York Times*, 17, 18 Mar., 1 Apr. 1933.
41. Jones, *Fifty Billion Dollars*, pp. 33–37.
42. *Chicago Daily News*, 14 Oct., 1, 8 Dec. 1933; *Chicago Journal of Commerce*, 14 Oct., 21, 30 Dec. 1933, 5, 9 Jan., 1934; *Chicago Tribune*, 1, 4 Jan. 1933; James, *Chicago Banks*, pp. 1086–90.

over their officers and directors. Jesse Jones, head of the RFC, addressing an ABA meeting in the fall of 1933, delivered an off-the-record blast. "Half the banks represented in this room are insolvent," he thundered, "and those of you representing those banks know it better than anyone else." Jones claimed that speech sparked a rush of small banks to the RFC, sometimes at a rate of a hundred per day. By the end of the year, the agency was even buying preferred stock in huge New York banks, including National City and Chase National.[43]

Between 1933 and 1938, 522 of the 1,417 banks licensed after reorganization issued a total of $68,069,250 in preferred stock, of which $19,467,850 was purchased by local interests and $48,601,400 by the RFC. Through its purchase of preferred stock, capital notes, and debentures, the RFC invested more than $1,171,000,000 (the equivalent of one-third of the total capital of all banks in the United States in 1933) in over 6,000 institutions in eighteen years of operations; it lost only $13,660,000, and only 206 of the banks it helped were later compelled to close.[44]

The more complex "creditor waiver" plan of reorganizing banks (applied in 565 cases) also involved capital correction. Where the appraised value of a bank's assets or resources was less than its liabilities, exclusive of its capital structure, conservators not only had to supply new capital but also had to eliminate that portion of liabilities which exceeded assets. To accomplish this balance, they persuaded the bank's creditors to sign waivers of a percentage of their deposits or other claims; in return, trustees would take over and liquidate the undesirable assets and distribute the proceeds to those executing the waiver agreements, as well as to the old shareholders. Carrying value of these assets equalled the amount of waived deposits plus the old capital structure of the banks. Then the conservator restored the capital structure, sometimes by contributions from the old stockholders, or from some old and some new shareholders. In many cases, creditors themselves bought new stock with the funds released to them through the reorganization.

43. Jones, *Fifty Billion Dollars*, pp. 26–30, 33–37; Timmons, *Jones*, pp. 199–205.

44. Jones, *Fifty Billion Dollars*, pp. 21, 25–26, 34; O'Connor, *Banking Crisis and Recovery*, pp. 56, 92–93; Friedman and Schwartz, *Monetary History*, pp. 426–28.

Here, too, the RFC helped with preferred stock purchases and made loans on sound assets to speed up distribution of funds.[45]

If neither capital correction nor creditor waiver could handle the volume of a bank's liabilities, the Comptroller's office reorganized the bank by a Spokane sale. (The procedure had been in use since 1928 but took its name from the first widely-publicized use of the sale plan for the Exchange National Bank of Spokane, Washington in 1929.) In 257 of the 1,417 unlicensed national banks, the amount of acceptable assets would provide less than 50 percent in immediate returns to creditors, but the existing banking facilities were adequate for community needs and justified keeping the banks in existence. Assessments on the shareholders would not provide enough cash to pay off the creditors. Therefore, with the approval of the Comptroller and a local court, conservators arranged the sale of desirable assets in bulk (at face or book value plus interest on notes, market value of securities, and appraised value of real estate, furniture, and fixtures) to an existing bank or a bank newly organized for that purpose. Creditors received dividends at once from the proceeds of this sale. In almost every case, the RFC assisted Spokane sale reorganizations with both stock purchases and loans. After the sale and distribution, a receiver could liquidate the old bank and collect stock assessments. Perhaps the most widely publicized use of this device involved the reopening of the Detroit banks, closed since the governor's proclamation on February 14.[46]

For three weeks, Detroit had endeavored to reopen its banks. Local, state, and federal authorities, as well as the bankers themselves, members of the business community, and even outsiders struggled to save the two giant Detroit banks. The law would not allow their first plan—segregation of old assets and partial operation based on new deposits—and enabling legislation could not be passed soon enough. Another plan failed when the Detroit bankers would not accept merger of the two local banks into a single institution with New York capital and control. At the same time, RFC officials continued to refuse loans until the Detroiters could raise sufficient funds to counterbalance their inadequate collateral. Nor did Henry Ford's offer of capital for two banks work out be-

45. O'Connor, *Banking Crisis and Recovery*, pp. 43–45.
46. Ibid., pp. 46–48.

cause supplementary loans fell through. The best Detroit could accomplish was a release of 5 percent of deposits held in closed banks. Thus, it entered the period of national moratorium no better off than when the state closed the banks. After March 6, however, restoring Detroit's banks became part of the nationwide reopening problem.[47]

The Detroit banks were not among those that reopened on March 13. Awalt opposed licensing them because, in his judgment, examinations during 1932 plus reports by Federal Reserve and RFC investigators proved the banks insolvent, although not so helpless as to require receivership. On March 13, he named conservators for the two banks. Both Awalt and Woodin realized that so large a city as Detroit could not get along with the banking facilities offered by the few state institutions which had opened; yet the Detroiters themselves had been unable to develop an effective reopening proposal. Thy concluded that Washington must take a larger part in the reorganizations in this case, and accordingly appointed Jesse Jones to negotiate a settlement. Jones first arranged for a release of cash. He convinced a group of large depositors to assign a portion of what they would eventually receive to pay off small accounts in full—116,000 accounts under $1,000 in one bank, 600,000 under $300 in the other.

On the larger question, that of opening the banks, Jones tried to persuade the Fords and General Motors to establish a new bank (or two) to replace the old institutions. Ford would not agree, but General Motors agreed to purchase all common stock in a new bank for $12.5 million, with the RFC subscribing to an equal amount of preferred stock. On March 21, Jones and Alfred P. Sloan of General Motors issued a joint statement officially announcing the new bank; the National Bank of Detroit received a charter the following day and began business on the morning of March 24. The new institution took over the assets and liabilities of the two closed banks under a Spokane sale arrangement, and on April 24 distributed another 30 percent of holdings to the old depositors. A month later, receivers began liquidation of the two old banks.[48] Thus, federal

47. For the history and circumstances of the Michigan moratorium, see Chapter 4.

48. Awalt, SEP, pp. 5840–41; Ballantine, ibid., p. 5803; W. R. Milford to Awalt, 13 Mar. 1933; Awalt to Ballantine, 15 Mar. 1933; Roy Chapin to Ballan-

authorities, armed with new laws and powers, accomplished in one week what Detroit could not do in a month.

Not all Detroiters supported the government's action, however. Newspapers campaigned for loans to preserve the existing banks. Two separate depositors' committees, one headed by the police commissioner, journeyed to Washington to ask Treasury officials to save the old banks; they were treated politely but their suggestions were ignored. Creditors feared that too speedy liquidation would destroy most of the real value of the banks' assets. And one embittered bank official, in a self-serving gesture, compiled a denunciation of "collusion, fraud, and official tyranny" in the delivery of Detroit banking into the hands of Wall Street by way of the New York-controlled motor companies.[49] Federal authorities, however, relied on examiners' reports which showed the perilous condition of the two banks; they saw no alternative to a Spokane sale reorganization, supplemented by capital contributions from the RFC and the local community.

Announcement of the "Detroit plan" brought a flood of applications for similar relief and reopening. The Treasury Department, assisted by the RFC, authorized a total of 257 such renovations. None, however, involved so large a community or so dramatically swift a solution as Detroit.

Almost 5 percent of the nation's banks remained outside any of these rehabilitation plans. Under the Mills formula, banks not licensed to reopen or classified for reorganization would cease operations, and their remaining assets would be liquidated. Receivers, appointed by the Comptroller of the Currency for national banks and by state authorities in all other cases, supervised the closing out of these banks; the same procedure applied to liquidations of old banks replaced by new institutions under Spokane sale. The receiver collected all unused resources of the insolvent bank, determined the amount and character of the liabilities, and then dis-

tine, 17 Mar. 1933; Sloan-Jones statement, 21 Mar. 1933—all in Comptroller's files, NA: RG 101, box 6; Jones, *Fifty Billion Dollars*, pp. 66–67; Timmons, *Jones*, pp. 190–93; *Detroit Free Press*, 12–25 Mar. 1933; *New York Times*, 13–17 Mar. 1933.

49. Taylor, "Detroit Banking Tragedy of 1933," pp. 58–97; D. F. V. to Ernest Kanzler, 29 June 1933, Dodge Papers; K. [Henry M. Kanne], memorandum, 23 Mar. 1933, FDRL:OF 259.

tributed assets to the creditors on a *pro rata* basis.[50] Officials took great pains to insure a fair allotment of these funds, so that no creditors would receive preferential treatment.[51] Between June 1933 and June 1935, receivers paid out approximately $103 million from closed national banks.

They also tried to make the fullest possible payments to depositors, assisted where possible by outside contributions. The Harriman National Bank, for example, belonged to the New York Clearing House Association, which had boasted in newspaper advertisements that no depositor ever lost a dollar in any of its member banks. Government authorities, therefore, tried to convince large and secure members of the association—including J. P. Morgan and Company and the Guaranty Trust Company—to contribute to a fund of $22 million needed to pay the Harriman's depositors in full. All refused, saying that they would not know how to explain such a subscription to their own depositors and stockholders. The Comptroller's office began liquidation but eventually forced the clearing-house members to honor their obligation by threatening court action to collect an assessment. In the end, the Harriman's creditors recovered eighty-nine cents per dollar of their deposits, a net loss of only $2 million.[52]

When liquidations dragged on, depositors grew restless to receive some portion of their money and called on government to deliver funds. The National Depositors' Committee and the Committee for the Nation particularly agitated for large-scale release of frozen deposits through mass reopenings or mass liquidations. The president's advisers briefly considered a currency issue to facilitate release but rejected the idea as inflationary. Roosevelt himself favored coordination of federal lending agencies and had the Comptroller and the Federal Reserve establish a joint relief committee. All agencies agreed, however, that the RFC would be the best hope for immediate dispersal of money.

50. O'Connor, *Banking Crisis and Recovery*, pp. 61–79; Upham and Lamke, *Closed and Distressed Banks*, pp. 17–29.

51. Awalt to Woodin, 16 Mar. 1933, Comptroller's files, NA: RG 101, box 4.

52. Harrison, memorandum of conversation with Thomas W. Lamont, S. Parker Gilbert, and W. C. Potter, 28, 29 Mar. 1933, Harrison Papers, binder 46; Jones, *Fifty Billion Dollars*, pp. 23–25; Timmons, *Jones*, pp. 193–94; "Wall Street vs. Woodin," *Business Week*, 9 Apr. 1933, p. 18.

The RFC had only to expand its lending function from open to closed banks to free frozen funds. It became the basis for an emergency federal liquidation corporation which made loans to insolvent banks on their good assets so that they, in turn, might pay out money to their depositors much sooner than if they had to wait for the bank's holdings to be sold. The practice also permitted the bank's assets to be held until the markets revived, thus raising their liquidating values. From its establishment in October 1933 until 1937, the deposit liquidation division of the RFC authorized $284,-322,734.75 in loans to 1,433 banks.[53]

Licensing solvent banks did not end the government's obligations, however; it also had to keep them open. President Roosevelt had stated categorically in his fireside chat that only sound banks would be opened; two weeks later, he promised prompt attention and fully publicity on any irregularities in reopened banks.[54] For the safety of the system, however, such problems could not be permitted to arise. If any licensed banks closed again, another and worse series of failures would inevitably result. The government had little choice but to stand behind every bank it reopened or face the dire consequences of public disillusionment.

Liberal licensing policies complicated the problem. Federal and state authorities had shown great concern for restoring full banking facilities to communities across the nation. Consequently, the Comptroller of the Currency had increased by 60 percent his original list of national banks permitted to resume operations in mid-March; most state superintendents were even more generous. President Roosevelt underwrote this program by promising that the Treasury would repay Federal Reserve banks for any losses incurred in reopening banks freely.

Federal officials acknowledged their responsibility to keep

---

53. Woodin, White House memorandum, 30 Sept. 1933, FDRL:OF 21B Miscellaneous; Bruère, COHC, pp. 153–55; Eugene M. Stevens to FDR, 20 June, 1933, FDRL:OF 230; Stevens to Adolph Miller, 20 June 1933, Miller Papers, Federal Reserve Board, box 9, envelope 4; FDR to Black, 2 Aug. 1933; Black to FDR, 7 Aug. 1933; Black to Jones, 8 Aug. 1933–all in Federal Reserve Board files; Hamlin, Diary, 10, 15, 16 Aug. 1933; Rosenman, *Public Papers*, 2:396–404; *Literary Digest*, 28 Oct. 1933, p. 11; *New York Times*, 25, 29, 30 Sept., 4, 10–17, 23 Oct., 12 Nov. 1933.
54. *New York Times*, 27 Mar. 1933.

banks open,[55] but could not agree on which agencies should perform the government's duties to those banks. Under the terms of the Emergency Banking Act, both the Federal Reserve banks and the RFC had powers which might be used to shore up weakened banks: the Reserve could make loans on an expanded list of collateral, while the RFC could lend on the same assets or buy preferred stock in reorganized banks. Directors of the RFC suggested that the Reserve banks could handle needs of reopened banks and even make loans to member institutions to liquidate RFC indebtedness. Reserve authorities dismissed this idea and added that if a member bank's assets were good enough to justify reopening, those same holdings should satisfy the RFC.[56] Some at the Federal Reserve favored joint efforts of the Reserve banks and the RFC to support reopened banks; loans could be authorized on a 50–50 basis, the two agencies sharing risks equally. Opponents pointed out that the Federal Reserve might be sacrificing the president's promised reimbursement if the Reserve banks passed off 50 percent of the loss burden. If so, the Reserve banks probably could not afford the risk.[57] Rather, let the Reserve take care of its members and the RFC lend to nonmember banks.

The Emergency Banking Act made no direct provision for nonmember state banks. Only national banks and state institutions within the Reserve System benefited from new Federal Reserve note issues and rediscounting of eligible paper. State authorities complained about the "sacrifice" of their banks, questioning whether state banks could survive under such discrimination. Governors of more than a dozen states pleaded with the president and the secretary of the Treasury to treat state banks equally with national institutions, particularly in supportive Reserve loans and rediscounts.[58]

55. Harrison, memorandum on joint meeting of Federal Reserve Board, governors' conference of the Federal Reserve System, directors of the Reconstruction Finance Corporation, and representatives of the Treasury Department and office of the Comptroller of the Currency, 26 Apr. 1933, Harrison Papers, binder 54; 28 Apr. 1933, box 12, miscellaneous folder.

56. Federal Reserve Board, Minutes, 19, 20 Apr. 1933; Harrison, memorandum of executive session, Executive Committee, New York Federal Reserve Bank, 24 Apr. 1933; memorandum of meeting of Board of Directors, 27 Apr. 1933, Harrison Papers, binder 50, vol. 3:158–64, 165–67.

57. Harrison, memorandum of meeting, Board of Directors, New York Federal Reserve Bank, 4 May 1933, Harrison Papers, binder 50, vol. 3: 177–80.

58. Oscar K. Allen (La.), I. C. Blackwood (S.C.), J. C. B. Ehringhaus (N.C.),

New York was already considering a separate state corporation to represent state nonmember banks in obtaining loans and funds in case they might not be accommodated at the Reserve banks.[59] Woodin had already agreed to an informal arrangement during the first phase of reopening, and the Federal Reserve Board directed district banks to cooperate.[60]

Keeping these nonmember banks open, however, required a broader commitment, one which the Reserve System did not welcome. Most Reserve officials believed that only members who had contributed to the System should participate in its benefits. Several state organizations accepted this logic and proposed compulsory membership for both commercial and savings banks in order to bring them within the responsibilities and protection of the System.[61] The idea did not win wide support, however, because most state institutions could not meet Federal Reserve requirements. Senator Huey Long attempted to bypass this difficulty by amending the Emergency Banking Act to empower the president to declare state banks members of the Reserve System and thus entitled to benefit from the law, but Senator Glass effectively opposed such arbitrary inclusion of banks without careful consideration of their qualifications for membership.[62] Extensive evaluation was required before state banks could become members, even if they wanted to join. In the meantime, some of these institutions still needed reinforcing in order to remain in business.

Congress and the administration proposed, therefore, to make nonmember banks eligible for Federal Reserve rediscounts without joining the System. Senator Joseph T. Robinson, Democratic

Miriam A. Ferguson (Tex.), Clyde L. Herring (Iowa), Henry Horner (Ill.), Ruby Laffoon (Ky.), Hill McAllister (Tenn.), Paul V. McNutt (Ind.), Guy B. Park (Mo.), John Garland Pollard (Va.), Gifford Pinchot (Pa.), Albert C. Ritchie (Md.), C. Ben Ross (Idaho), and Eugene Talmadge (Ga.), to FDR, 12 Mar. 1933, FDRL:PPF 200B; David B. Stoltz (Fla.) to Herbert H. Lehman (N.Y.), 12 Mar. 1933; Lehman to Woodin, 12 Mar. 1933; Woodin to Lehman, n.d.; Frank Altschul to Arthur Ballantine, 12 Mar. 1933—all in Lehman Papers, Governorship Papers, microfilm reel 8; *New York Times*, 13 Mar. 1933.

59. Memorandum, 10 Mar. 1933, Lehman Papers, Governorship Papers, microfilm reel 8.

60. Federal Reserve Board, Minutes, 11 Mar. 1933.

61. Ibid.; R. Dana Skinner (Emigrant Industrial Savings Bank) to FDR, 13 Mar. 1933, FDRL:OF 230; New York State Banking Board, Memorial to the Congress, *New York Times*, 31 Mar. 1933.

62. *Congressional Record*, 73d Cong., 1st Sess., 9 Mar. 1933, pp. 52–67.

floor leader, introduced a resolution whereby, for one year, a state nonmember bank might apply directly to the Reserve banks for loans of currency on collateral made eligible for member banks by the Glass-Steagall Act of 1932 and the Emergency Banking Act. The Senate passed the Robinson bill.

The Federal Reserve Board vigorously opposed such direct loans to nonmember banks. Further legislation in that area was unnecessary, the Board contended, since the RFC already had "ample authority to make advances to all kinds of banking institutions including non-member State banks." Or, if nonmember banks desired Federal Reserve money, they could borrow from member banks that would be more aware of their loan status than the district Reserve banks which had little or no information on the financial condition of nonmembers.[63]

Since Congress seemed determined to pass this legislation, however, the Board at least hoped to obtain some safeguards. They demanded three changes: loans would be made only at the discretion of the district banks, Reserve banks would lend only "after inspection and approval of the collateral and a thorough examination of the applying bank or trust company," and security offered to back such loans must meet requirements set for collateral submitted by member banks. The president rapidly agreed to these revisions, and Senator Glass took the recommendations to the Senate, where they were included in a new version of the bill. Representative Henry Steagall introduced a similar measure into the House and the bill passed both chambers.[64]

The Robinson-Steagall Act of March 24, 1933, amended the Emergency Banking Act to include nonmember state banks. The new law authorized Federal Reserve banks to make loans to such institutions on security approved by the Reserve bank and after thorough examination of the borrowing institution. During the time it was indebted to the Reserve bank, the nonmember had to comply with all requirements exacted of state member banks, including the

63. Woodin, Statement, 13 Mar. 1933, Federal Reserve Bulletin, Mar. 1933, p. 130.

64. Federal Reserve Board, Minutes, 14, 15, 16, 17, 21 Mar. 1933; Hamlin, Diary, 14–18 Mar. 1933; Eugene Meyer to Glass, 14 Mar. 1933, Glass Papers, box 5; New York Times, 16–24 Mar. 1933.

maintenance of a reserve balance; the borrower did not have to sub-scribe to stock in the Reserve bank, however.[65]

The Reserve banks accepted the new authorization without enthusiasm. In practice, they stressed the safeguards and reacted cautiously to loan applications. Their directors, particularly in New York, continued to believe that the Reserve banks should support only their own members; the RFC could care for nonmember banks. They proposed that Congress legalize the president's commitment to indemnify Reserve banks for losses incurred in reopening and sustaining member banks, and at the same time broaden the cat-egories of collateral on which the RFC could lend to nonmembers.[66] The plan was stillborn, however, in a Congress caught up in debates over deposit guarantee features of the Glass and Steagall banking bills, alternative ways to insure the reopened banks against failure.[67]

Recovery from the banking crisis proceeded rapidly and efficiently. In the first month of licensing, 12,817 institutions re-sumed operations. This group included 4,789 national banks hold-ing $16,494,549,000 in deposits; 636 state member banks with $9,491,634,000; and 7,392 nonmembers with $5,020,061,000. During the rest of 1933, many of the remaining institutions received li-censes; 452 of the 1,108 national banks, 60 of the 148 state member banks, and 1,393 of 2,959 nonmember banks reopened after re-organization. By the middle of 1934, only 114 member and 509 non-member banks remained closed, tying up deposits of $114,381,000 and $234,234,000 respectively. In the same period, federal and state authorities liquidated 496 member and 509 nonmember banks with deposits of $1,872,013,000.

Even rapid licensing produced relatively sound judgments. Few banks licensed at the end of the moratorium later suspended; by the end of 1933, only 9 national, 6 state member, and 206 non-

65. *Federal Reserve Bulletin*, Apr. 1933, p. 247, Federal Reserve Board, *An-nual Report, 1933*, pp. 38–39.

66. Federal Reserve Board, Minutes, 29 Mar., 27 Apr. 1933; Harrison, mem-orandum of meeting, Board of Directors, New York Federal Reserve Bank, 18 May 1933, Harrison Papers, binder 50, vol. 3:192–95.

67. Harrison, memorandum of meetings, Board of Directors, New York Fed-eral Reserve Bank, 15 May, 1 June 1933, Harrison Papers, binder 50, vol. 3: 197–200, 205–06.

member banks had closed again. To be sure, Reserve rediscount and RFC stock purchases had rescued many shaky institutions because federal authorities felt an obligation to keep licensed banks open.

In retrospect, the Roosevelt administration produced a creditable banking record. In addition to sorting out the chaos of the crisis, the first two terms saw deposits in national banks reach an all-time high; fewer national banks closed than in any other administration; and in 1936—for the first time in fifty-nine years—not a single national bank closed its doors.[68]

The crisis had been met, the banks had reopened. It remained to make sure that it would not happen again.

68. "Number and Deposit of Licensed and Unlicensed Banks as of Close of Business, August 30, 1933," and memorandum on deposits in closed national banks as of 11 Sept. 1933, FDRL:OF 21B; "Extent of Recovery," 9 May 1934, Harrison Papers, box 12, miscellaneous folder; O'Connor to FDR, 27 Sept. 1933; Henrietta S. Klotz to LeHand, 1 Oct. 1936; M. A. LeHand to Treasury Department, 1 Oct. 1936—all in FDRL:OF 230; Federal Reserve Bulletin, 1933, pp. 265, 331–33, 413–14; ibid., 1934, pp. 496–97; O'Connor to FDR, 14 Sept. 1938, quoted in O'Connor, Banking Crisis and Recovery, pp. 137–41 and tables, pp. 87, 90–92; Upham and Lamke, Closed and Distressed Banks, pp. 45–48.

CHAPTER IX

The Banking Act of 1933

ON JUNE 16, 1933, President Franklin D. Roosevelt signed into law the Banking Act of 1933, the first serious and partially successful piece of legislation directed at the fundamental causes rather than the symptoms of the American banking collapse. Earlier statutes and edicts had corrected only visible problems. The Emergency Banking Act of 1933, passed on March 9, reopened solvent banks under license and legalized certain categories of aid to reorganize or liquidate closed banks. Other laws, such as the act of March 22 permitting Federal Reserve loans to nonmember banks, also sought to alleviate immediate uncertainties without altering the structure. Even pre-New Deal statutes such as the Reconstruction Finance Corporation Act and the Emergency Relief and Construction Act of 1932 were intended as bailing out rather than reform efforts. Now at the end of the "hundred days," Congress finally enacted legislation intended to eradicate those defects in American banking which had brought on the February crisis.

The lawmakers had deliberated this larger change for three years. Interest in branch and group banking and the failure of earlier corrective legislation prompted the House to authorize hearings for a new law in 1930. Soon afterward the Senate set its Committee on Banking and Currency on a broader investigation which lasted throughout 1931 and 1932. Senator Carter Glass led the fight for banking reform by sponsoring a series of measures known collectively as the Glass bill, which moved in and out of first place in the attention of the Congress from January 1932 until final passage in

June 1933.[1] A catch-all for banking reform, the Glass bill encompassed revisions in the Federal Reserve System's structure and powers, changes in branch banking restrictions on nationally chartered banks, new relationships between commercial and investment banking and between demand and time deposits, and a host of smaller considerations sparked by multiplying bank failures.

Until 1933, however, the Glass bill made scant progress. President Hoover preferred to concentrate administration efforts on short-term emergency relief measures; he did not endorse the Glass measure until January 1933. By then faults in the banking structure had become too serious to be corrected in the time left before a new administration took over. Although the Glass bill passed the Senate in modified form, its equivalent failed in the House, and the Seventy-second Congress left office on March 4, 1933, without a banking law.[2]

Senator Glass reintroduced his bill on March 9, the day the Seventy-third Congress passed the Emergency Banking Act. Eleven days later the Banking and Currency Committee named a subcommittee, chaired by Glass himself, to consider it. The other subcommittee members were Senators Bulkley, McAdoo, Walcott, and Townsend; all save McAdoo were veterans in the Senate. By April 7 the subcommittee had a tentative draft which essentially followed the lines of the old Glass bill. Meanwhile, Representative Steagall sponsored a similar measure in the House.[3]

Simultaneously, the Pecora investigation into the National City Bank, the shock of entire states losing banking facilities, and the nationwide closing itself underscored the need for permanent banking reconstruction. The political complexion had also changed: the lame ducks left Washington; Democrats held both houses of

1. U. S., Congress, House, Committee on Banking and Currency, *Hearings: Branch, Chain and Group Banking*, under H. Res. 141, 71st Cong., 2d Sess., 1930, 2 vols.; U. S., Congress, Senate, Committee on Banking and Currency, *Hearings on S. 71*, 71st Cong., 3d Sess., 1931. The successive versions of the Glass bill were: S. 4723 (71st Cong., 2d Sess., 1930) introduced on 17 June 1930; S. 3215, S. 4115, S. 4412 (72d Cong., 1st Sess., 1932), introduced in Jan., Mar., and Apr. 1932, respectively; S. 245 and S. 1631 (73d Cong., 1st Sess., 1933), introduced on 9 Mar. and 10 May 1933.

2. For provisions and legislative history of the Glass bill under the Hoover administration, see above, pp. 45–50, 67–74.

3. *New York Times*, 8, 12, 13 Apr. 1933; *Commercial and Financial Chronicle*, 8 Apr. 1933, pp. 2343–44.

Congress and the White House with wide mandates; and the first vigorous actions of President Roosevelt in closing the banks and initiating the New Deal excited confidence and enthusiasm which could be used in related areas. The Glass bill might be one of these, if its specific provisions could muster enough support.

In the spring of 1933 the Glass bill included three major areas of reform: 1) banking structure, including changes in the organization of the Federal Reserve System, possible Reserve control of all banks in the nation, and some solution to the ten-year-old debate on branch, chain, and group banking; 2) commercial and investment banks, their proper relationship and control of credit; and 3) guarantee of deposits by the federal government or by a liquidating corporation—the most controversial issue.

During the banking holiday in March 1933, Leon Trotsky, Marxist revolutionary-in-exile, commented that since America's banking structure had become obsolete, the crisis would result in a "grandiose centralization of the banking system, ultimately merely reinforcing United States financial hegemony."[4] In fact, the Senate Banking and Currency Committee had been considering unification of American banking into a single system ever since Governor Eugene Meyer of the Federal Reserve Board testified on March 28, 1932, that "effective supervision of banking in this country has been seriously affected by competition between member and non-member banks" of the Federal Reserve System and that "competition between State and national banking systems had resulted in weakening both steadily."[5] According to this argument, the collapse of more than 10,000 banks in ten years—most of them small, state-chartered, unitary institutions—proved the superior safety of a single inter-related system.

Since 82 percent of the bank failures of the 1920s had occurred in small, state-licensed, rural institutions, bankers and public officials questioned whether the dual system should survive. They argued that "our business of deposit banks is not local in character; it is, and should be national," with the words "member of Federal

4. New York Times, 18 Mar. 1933.
5. U. S., Congress, Senate, Committee on Banking and Currency, Hearings: Operation of the National and Federal Reserve Banking Systems, 72d Cong., 1st Sess., 1932, testimony of Eugene Meyer, 29 May 1932.

Reserve System" on a bank's window as a sign of sound banking. Some called for a "scientific" banking system which would bring all commercial banks under the single aegis of the Federal Reserve System and establish sensible provisions for regional branch banking. In contrast with the maelstrom in the nonmember banking community during the recent crisis, the Reserve banks were twelve "isles of safety, harbors of refuge in the midst of a violent storm," and similar calm was predicted if all American banks could be grouped under them.[6] Bankers themselves questioned whether their regional clearinghouses were adequate to aid banks in trouble, particularly in view of the transfer of business from the clearinghouses to the Federal Reserve banks during the crisis period and the rush to join the Reserve System after the national holiday.[7]

The Banking and Currency Committee, too, considered the feasibility of this unification of direction and asked Walter Wyatt, counsel of the Federal Reserve Board, to prepare a report on the subject. Wyatt submitted the results of his research in December 1932; the report was released three months later. "The problem," he said, "is how to achieve uniformity of corporate powers, regulation and supervision with respect to banks engaged in the commercial banking business and to provide for their safe and effective operation, by eliminating the existing competition between the Federal Government and the 48 states for the privilege of granting charters to banks transacting that type of business." He suggested a single national banking system and urged legislation to confine "the business of receiving deposits subject to withdrawal by check to national banks"; Congress had the power to enact such a regulation, he said.[8] Two weeks later the American Bankers Association endorsed unified banking, specifically "the establishment of a central bank by the Federal Government, with the 12 Federal Reserve Banks as branches and with State chartered commercial and mutual savings banks admitted into the Federal Reserve System."[9] Secre-

6. Owen D. Young and Thomas W. Lamont in "Should America Adopt a Unified Banking System?" *Congressional Digest* 12 (Apr. 1933): 108, 110, 112; *New York Times*, 21 Apr. 1933.

7. *New York Times*, 8, 10, 16 Mar., 28 Apr. 1933.

8. Walter Wyatt, "Constitutionality of Legislation Providing a Unified Commercial Banking System for the United States," 5 Dec. 1932, in *Federal Reserve Bulletin* (Mar. 1933): 166–86; also in *Commercial and Financial Chronicle*, 22 Apr. 1933, pp. 2728–31; summary in *New York Times*, 30 Mar. 1933.

tary of the Treasury Woodin also favored unification but proposed a single central bank bypassing the Reserve banks entirely—one bank, with 20,000 branches.[10]

According to some observers, branch banking might have prevented or lessened the high failure rate of the 1920s. In fact, the House version of the Banking Act of 1933 originated in hearings into the inadequacy of earlier branch banking statutes. It had been in the United States that the unit bank had failed most frequently between 1921 and 1933. In contrast, Canada, which practiced branch banking, had had no failures in ten years, although it had endured economic distress similar to that in the United States. Canada had ten banks, of which one had only two branches and the other nine had from 140 to 880 branches each, for a total of 3,900 in the nation and 172 abroad. These banks operated under government charter and a bank act revised every ten years; they reported monthly to the Department of Finance. Moreover, they were rigidly prohibited from dealing in bank shares, lending over $10,000 to their own employees, or making loans on real estate or bank stock. Banking in Canada had become a rise-from-the-ranks profession with consequent good management and public confidence.[11]

Senator Glass himself admitted that he came to branch banking reluctantly because of his concern for "the little bank." Of 11,000 failures, however, over 80 percent involved banks with capitalization under $25,000, enough suspensions to convince the senator "of the menace they are to sound banking and the curse to their depositors." Moreover, collapse of "the little bank" created a "psychology that eventually topples over the larger and sounder banks because of the fear created in the minds of depositors and the runs that ensue."[12] To counteract failure of the independent unit bank, and to provide adequate banking facilities to communities which lacked them, the Glass subcommittee originally proposed that national banks be allowed to establish statewide branches in all states regardless of local law and to extend fifty miles into adjacent states, where this territory included an "area of trade." This clause, which

---

9. *New York Times*, 13 Apr. 1933; *Commercial and Financial Chronicle*, 13 Apr. 1933, pp. 2524–25.
10. Hamlin, Diary, 8 Apr. 1933.
11. *New York Times*, 12 Mar. 1933.
12. "Adopt Unified Banking?" p. 106.

had provoked Senator Huey Long's ten-day filibuster during the lame-duck session, worried those who felt that the national banks should not enjoy privileges denied to state banks in the same areas.[13] These defenders of state banking believed that locally-organized and state-chartered institutions could best serve the needs and interests of their own communities. They hoped to keep banking within those confines and to avoid contests with larger branched institutions, most of which they associated with the Wall Street "money power." Broader branching by national banks would, according to these critics, result in "the concentration of wealth in too few hands" and create a discriminatory situation in which state banks could be driven out of existence by superior competition. Others condemned branching entirely, asking whether there could be any real safety in a system which also had failures. Critics cited an impressive list of crashes, headed by the fifty-seven-branch Bank of United States. Moreover, if failures came from overbanking, limitations on charters rather than branching offered an effective solution, according to the Associated Independent Banks of America.[14] Many who endorsed this position hailed from Western states which had long enshrined the concept of unit banking.

Some committee members so opposed statewide branching for national banks that Senator Arthur Vandenberg offered an amendment to prevent the extension of branch banks into cities which already had adequate banking facilities, except where the existing banks would be absorbed. Thus the Western defenders of state and unit banking could be satisfied that their small institutions would not have to compete with the stronger and more stable giants of the East. Glass accepted the modification, perhaps hoping that the provision—which at least offered banking to areas which lacked it—could placate his colleagues and free him to try for a strengthening of the banking system elsewhere in the bill. Therefore, he abandoned the idea of making all banks members of a single, unified, national system and changed the branch banking provisions until they varied little from earlier practice.

The rewritten bill permitted national banks to have branches on a citywide or statewide basis within the limitations imposed by

13. Ibid., pp. 109, 111.
14. Ibid., p. 107; R. O. Byerrum of University State Bank of Chicago to Senator James Hamilton Lewis, 30 Dec. 1932, pp. 50–51.

state laws. For greater strength of the national banks themselves, Glass inserted a requirement that no national bank could establish a branch outside its home city unless it had at least $500,000 capital (in states with a population of less than 500,000 and no cities over 50,000, the minimum capital was $100,000) nor could the aggregate capital of parent bank and branches be less than the minimum for an equal number of unit national banks located where parent and branches were situated.[15] Only a few systems, such as the already giant Giannini bank in California, benefited. Under the act, the state Bank of America merged with its parent Bank of America National Trust and Savings Association to form a complex of 423 branches in 225 California communities. As insurance, a state bank with 8 branches was retained.[16]

Minimum capital for new national banks was raised to $50,000, although existing banks were unaffected; extant state banks could qualify for Federal Reserve membership with $25,000 capital, but state banks organized in the future would have to meet the same requirements as national banks.[17]

Glass also secured tighter regulations over the conduct of bank officials. Officers and directors of any member bank could now be removed from office if, in the view of the Comptroller or a Federal Reserve agent, they continued after warning to violate any banking law or conduct the business of their bank or trust company in an unsafe or unsound manner. Clearly this provision sought to satisfy those defenders of the existing structure who charged that banks had failed because of unprofessional conduct and bad bank management. If continuation of unitary banking carried a built-in risk in the character and ability of bank officers and directors, this clause would minimize that jeopardy. In addition to the usual pressures of loss of prestige and possible public disgrace, a recalcitrant banker now faced fines of up to $5,000 and imprisonment for up to five years. The law also prohibited member banks from making loans to their own executives, and in the interests of efficiency limited the maximum number of directors of a national bank to twenty-five.[18]

Although Senator Glass had hoped to revise the banking

15. Sects. 5 (b) and 23.
16. James and James, *Biography of a Bank*, pp. 375–77.
17. Sect. 17.
18. Sects. 12, 31, 32.

system of the United States, he had secured only a minor strengthening, and still primarily of national banks. Competing state institutions continued in operation, and the principle of prior state control remained.

The senator also tried to rehabilitate another facet of the nation's banking structure—the Federal Reserve System. Glass, an originator of the Reserve, hoped to strengthen and reorganize it to prevent a recurrence of its disastrous showing from 1921 to 1933.

The prestige of the Federal Reserve Board had dwindled as the depression lengthened. Not only had the Board, with its great potential of power, failed to hold down the pre-1929 expansion, but its behavior after the 1929 crash was lethargic and self-immobilizing. So low had the "supreme court of finance" fallen that its recommendations and protests during the Glass bill deliberations were pushed impatiently aside. If any power remained in the System, New York had custody, not Washington. Now the banking act offered *more* power to the central board, both in hopes that it might disengage from New York and Treasury Department dominance, and in the expectation that it could provide a nucleus for whatever centralization might result from other provisions of the law. One area in particular in which New York had been most active was open-market operations. The Glass bill removed open-market purchases from the discretion of the twelve Federal Reserve banks individually, lodging it in a permanent, statutory Federal Open Market Committee, but compromised in leaving actual operations in New York.[19] Open-market activities had been coordinated since 1923 but the open-market committee did not enjoy provision under law until 1933. The Banking Act, however, stipulated that no Federal Reserve bank could engage in open-market operations except under regulations established by the Board, although it could refrain from participating in any single transaction on thirty days' notice to the committee and the Board. A vice-president of the New York bank was to manage the system's open-market operations.

The Federal Reserve System also received authority to restrict the use of bank credit for speculation. Earlier, it could only request cooperation from members, but now each Federal Reserve

19. Sect. 8.

bank had to keep informed about loans and investments of member banks to supervise use of bank credit and prevent its falling into speculative channels.[20] The Board could also limit the percentage of individual banks' capital and surplus which might be represented by loans secured by stock or bond collateral, and could direct any member not to increase its loans for the speculative carrying of securities on pain of suspension of rediscount privileges.[21]

Of greater immediate impact, in an effort to reduce competition on interest rates, the law eliminated all payment of interest on demand deposits except where state law required it on deposits of public funds, and gave the Board authority to regulate interest rates on time or savings deposits in member banks.[22] The *New York Times* reported this clause as the first concrete result of the Glass-Steagall Act, and later economists see it as the origin of a "marked decline in the importance of interbank deposits—the demand deposits on which the payment of interest had been most widespread and at the highest rates." New York City banks reported on June 22 that demand deposits had already dropped due to the ban on interest payments, a trend which hit the entire system by August.[23]

Other amendments to the Federal Reserve Act included increasing the term of appointive Board members from ten to twelve years, making the governor chairman of the Board in the absence of the secretary of the Treasury, fixing the Board's offices outside the Treasury Department, and prohibiting Board members from holding office in any banking or other such institution.

In its changes of the banking structure, therefore, the Glass bill accomplished only limited reforms. As with every measure since the beginnings of banking in the United States, proponents of state's rights and unitary banking had prevented the imposition of a single, strong, coordinated approach to the problem of providing American citizens with banking facilities. Senator Glass had rightly identified the major difficulty of the 1920s as the inadequacy of capitalization, management, diversification, and supervision in the small unit bank.

20. Sect. 3.
21. Sect. 7.
22. Sect. 11 (b).
23. *New York Times*, 17, 23 June, 13 Aug. 1933; Friedman and Schwartz, *Monetary History*, pp. 443–45; Federal Reserve Board, Minutes, 20, 23 June 1933.

His efforts to correct these problems, however, were thwarted by those who represented exactly that small-bank constituency. Since they possessed the balance of power in this case, Glass had little choice but to compromise rather than see his bill returned to the limbo in which it had languished for three long years. That he achieved certain changes in the Federal Reserve statute, on the other hand, is probably due less to any overwhelming support for such revisions than to the fact that they did not excite significant opposition.

The sections of the Glass bill dealing with commercial and investment banks, however, represented a curious and timely meeting of minds of the diverse sections of the country and of the banking community. Although this separation had been central to the senator's concept of his bill, until the spring of 1933 it had met with vigorous attack, particularly from Wall Street. The Pecora hearings changed that attitude.[24] The sensational manner of these hearings, as well as their timing, on the eve of the national moratorium, inflamed public resentment. Outrage centered upon the security affiliates, since by 1930 they were sponsoring 54.4 percent of all new securities issues.

Events as much as publicity acted against the affiliates. The banking crisis had already forced a separation of commercial and thrift accounts. Segregation of new deposits so that they would not be used to pay off liabilities of old deposits became a usual procedure in reorganized or reopened banks after the holiday.[25] In the midst of the collapse Winthrop W. Aldrich, new chairman of the Chase National Bank, announced that his bank (controlled by the Rockefeller interests) would completely sever its investment affiliates so that the commercial banks would not be smeared with "the spirit of speculation." Aldrich generously suggested a program whereby the rival house of J. P. Morgan and Company could follow his good example. Aldrich, a lawyer, had been brought in to rehabilitate Chase on the departure of the unfortunate Albert H. Wiggin. Undoubtedly, he saw the separation of affiliates as a gesture

24. For details of the Pecora investigation of the National City Bank and National City Company, see Chapter 5.
25. See Chapter 8.

to restore the prestige of the big banking houses at a time when that particular aspect of their business was under heavy and justified attack. A few days later Aldrich conferred with President Roosevelt and Secretary of Commerce Daniel Roper on permanent banking reform to secure universal divorce of affiliates; Roper sent Aldrich on to Senator Glass, who had already proposed separation of commercial and investment banking in earlier versions of the Glass bill.[26] Other bankers writing to the president at the same time frequently included an announcement that their bank had never been involved in the securities business or that it was now abolishing its affiliate.[27]

Glass welcomed added support for what he regarded as the paramount issue in his bill, and he included in the final draft a provision for complete separation of investment banking from commercial activities of members of the Federal Reserve System. Bankers had one year in which to choose between deposit banking and investing; after that time, bond departments would be allowed to purchase or sell investment securities only on order of, and for the account of, customers; all underwriting of securities by member banks was prohibited. Conversely, firms which sold securities could not receive call or time deposits; there could be no interlocking directorates between member banks and securities companies; nor could a member bank perform correspondent functions for any organization engaged primarily in buying, selling, or negotiating securities. In addition, the law required periodic examinations of national banks and affiliates of any kind.[28]

Separated banking encountered no opposition after March 1933. After the testimony of Charles E. Mitchell before the Banking and Currency Committee, few defended the affiliate. Bankers who had rejected the idea now saw the virtue of the divorce and climbed aboard Glass's bandwagon.

26. *New York Times*, 8 Mar. 1933; "Should America Adopt a Unified Banking System?" p. 120; Pecora, *Wall Street Under Oath*, pp. 140–41; FDR to Aldrich, 9 Mar. 1933; Aldrich to FDR, 12 Mar. 1933; FDR to Aldrich, 16 Mar. 1933–all in FDRL:PPF 54; George Leslie Harrison, memorandum of conversation with Aldrich, 29 Mar. 1933, Harrison Papers, binder 60; Roper to FDR, 28 Mar. 1933, FDRL:OF 230; Arthur M. Johnson, *Winthrop W. Aldrich: Lawyer, Banker, Diplomat* (Boston: Harvard University, Graduate School of Business Administration, 1968), pp. 149–54, 157–61.
27. Thomas P. Beal, Second National Bank of Boston, to FDR, 13 Mar. 1933, FDRL:PPF 183.
28. Sects. 5, 16, 20, 21, 32, 38.

Insurance of bank deposits, however, uncovered a vipers' nest of controversy which almost killed the Glass bill. Advocates of unit banking hoped that a guarantee of deposits in independent banks would make these institutions so secure that there would be no need for other strengthening devices, such as branching or unification of the system. President Roosevelt, on the other hand, suspected the idea of a guarantee because it had failed so often in the past, and he threatened to veto any measure containing it. Senator Glass also disliked a plan for guarantee, preferring a saving fund such as he had outlined in his original bill. In the end, the president and the senator yielded to the inevitable, and the Glass bill included a kind of deposit guarantee which became, in the words of two later economists, "the most important structural change in the banking system to result from the 1933 panic," and "the structural change most conducive to monetary stability since state bank note issues were taxed out of existence immediately after the Civil War."[29]

In April 1932 Representative Steagall had warned Speaker Garner, "You know, this fellow Hoover is going to wake up one day and come in here with a message recommending guarantee of bank deposits, and as sure as he does, he'll be re-elected." Garner agreed and Steagall himself introduced a deposit insurance bill on April 14. It was reported by the Banking and Currency Committee on April 19 and passed the House on May 25 after four hours of debate.[30] There it stopped. Steagall could not convince Senator Glass to sponsor a similar measure and at the end of the Seventy-second Congress the Glass bill passed the Senate without government guarantee of deposits.

With the coming of the new administration, Garner and Steagall pressed Roosevelt and Glass for a guarantee. In fact, Garner as vice-president had his first disagreement with Roosevelt over the guarantee principle. "You'll have to have it, Cap'n," Garner said, "or get more clerks in the Postal Savings banks. The people who have taken their money out of the banks are not going to put it back without some guarantee."[31] Senator William Gibbs McAdoo, who

29. Friedman and Schwartz, *Monetary History*, p. 434.
30. Timmons, *Garner of Texas*, p. 179.
31. Ibid., pp. 178–80; Gardner G. Perry, memorandum, 20 Feb. 1933, Glass Papers, box 305; Timmons, *Jones*, p. 184; Jones, *Fifty Billion Dollars*, pp. 45–46; Moley, *First New Deal*, pp. 318–19.

had fought unsuccessfully for a guarantee plank in the 1932 Democratic platform, added his voice, as did Senator Borah, William Green of the AF of L, and twenty-five House Democrats who signed a caucus petition in favor of government guarantee.[32] Yet despite this urging, Roosevelt remained "amiable but adamant." At his first presidential press conference on March 8, he publicly opposed deposit insurance, although proposals for government guarantee, compulsory reciprocal insurance, bond issues to cover net losses of failed banks, and expansion of the Postal Savings system filled the newspapers and the White House mail.[33]

Roosevelt had good reason to suspect deposit guarantee; complete failure in recent years had discredited the concept. Forms of deposit insurance had existed intermittently in the United States since New York created a safety fund in 1819; but the idea faded after the panic of 1837 and was not revived until after the Civil War, when deposit banking grew rapidly. Between 1886 and 1933, various congressmen introduced 150 proposals for a federal guarantee of deposits; none had been enacted. Eight states, however, reacted to the panic of 1907 by establishing bank deposit guarantees: Oklahoma, Kansas, Nebraska, Texas, Mississippi, South Dakota, North Dakota, and Washington passed laws guaranteeing deposits of all state banks as well as banking departments in trust companies. By 1929, all of these laws were either repealed or inactive. In every case, the experiment collapsed whenever any sizable proportion of banks failed simultaneously, most of them as a result of the agricultural depression of the 1920s. Deposit insurance could not effectively guard the individual against loss; neither could it readily supply money to communities in the event of bank closings.[34]

Big bankers agreed that a national guarantee would be disastrous. Law and banking policy already offered semiofficial safeguards, they said; if a bank failed, depositors could be paid off in

32. New York Times, 9, 13, 15 Mar., 25 Apr. 1933; Stephen Early, memorandum, 12 Mar. 1933, FDRL:OF 230.

33. New York Times, 8, 9, 10 Mar., 6, 16 Apr. 1933; Norman Hapgood, "Protect the Depositor," Nation 136 (15 Mar. 1933): 283; Marriner S. Eccles, Beckoning Frontiers: Public and Personal Recollections (New York: Knopf, 1951), pp. 107–09; James M. Thomson to FDR, 10 Mar. 1933, FDRL:OF 230.

34. For a history of deposit insurance, see Carter H. Golembe, "The Deposit Insurance Legislation of 1933: An Evaluation of Its Antecedents and Its Purposes," Political Science Quarterly 75 (1960): 181–200; John G. Blocker, "The Guarantee of State Bank Deposits," Kansas Studies in Business, No. 11.

bank capital, surplus, undivided profits, stock in reserve banks, and reserves. Moreover, with periodic audits by federal or state examiners and responsible performance by bank officers, no bank should fail. They blamed the 10,000-odd failures of the past decade on inept management and could see no reason why safe and stable banks should have to contribute to a fund to bail out those which had not operated properly. Insurance put a premium on careless methods. This argument carried particular force with the large New York banks; if assessments for the fund were based on deposits, New York (which held over one-fourth of current bank deposits) would subsidize other sections, especially the Midwest, where losses were greatest. Bankers also suspected any plan of less than full coverage since it would discriminate in favor of small depositors; large depositors would not be completely protected and therefore might become sources of runs on the banks.[35] Moreover, such a fund would actually guarantee the cash position of any member bank, underwriting payment to depositors on demand. Yet the February and March runs had proven that depositors could not be paid off if sufficient cash did not exist—and it would not if any sizable number of banks were forced to draw upon the fund simultaneously, either to remain open or to make payments after closing. A test, they feared, would show up the financial weaknesses of the plan.[36]

Throughout their discussions, however, the bankers returned most frequently to their original point: a guarantee of deposits "requires a heavy expense and a heavy burden on the sound institution for the benefit of the weaker institution," thus subsidizing "wild-cat management." Nothing could substitute for honest and sound banking, they thought, and banks which did not enjoy it deserved to go down.[37]

Finally, the solution to the March crisis had been based on the

35. Howard H. Preston, "The Banking Act of 1933," *American Economic Review* 23 (Dec. 1933): 585–607; *New York Times*, 9 May 1933.

36. Leffingwell to Glass, 16, 18 May 1933, Glass Papers, box 147.

37. A. L. Wiggin, in "Should America Adopt a Unified Banking System?" pp. 115, 117; Willis, "The Folly of Deposit Guarantee," *American Mercury* 31 (Jan. 1934): 16–23; *New York Times*, 19, 20, 21, 27 May 1933; Thomas P. Beal to FDR, 27 May 1933; Winthrop W. Aldrich to FDR, 22 May 1933; C. M. Malone, Guardian Trust Co., Houston, Texas, to FDR, 29 May, 1933; H. L. Brazer Second National Bank, Cooperstown, New York, to FDR, 1 June 1933; Board of Directors, Illinois National Bank and Trust Company of Rockford, to FDR, 9 June 1933—all in FDRL:OF 230.

premise that there would be no guarantee. To the participants in that decision—which included Roosevelt—the choice had been made then: a clean-up of the banking situation, not a stopgap guarantee.[38]

Conversely, defenders of deposit guarantee argued that their proposals had taken all of these objections into account and overcome each negative point. The experiments had not always failed, they said; Steagall cited the case of Nebraska, where the law had operated for twenty years before it was declared unconstitutional. Failures occurred only "in a period of panic" because of "bad banking, lax enforcement, and weak regulation"—all of which could be eliminated in a national fund. Steagall pointed out that in Nebraska "confidence in the law was such that after one-third of the State banks had closed the total of deposits in the remaining State banks equaled that held by the banks in the boom year of 1920. Until the constitutionality of the law and the sufficiency of the guaranty fund was attacked there was no runs on the banks insured under the State guaranty law, nor did fall in deposits show loss of confidence by the people of the State."[39] Examinations before admission and periodic supervision could assure that banks would not have to close and thus use the fund. Moreover, if banks closed because of runs, the placing of the United States government itself behind the banks would eliminate much of the fear which had precipitated those runs in earlier months. And, in particular, such a fund could provide usable money to depositors whose currency was locked in suspended banks, thus assuring a circulating medium and a solution to the Great Depression.

These arguments failed to convince the administration. Throughout the deliberations of the spring of 1933, Roosevelt repeatedly let the Glass subcommittee know that he opposed deposit guarantee. Although the senators had a draft of the bill on April 13, they waited to send it to the full committee until they could confer with the secretary of the Treasury. Woodin had already written to Glass expressing some negative ideas, and he outlined the administration's position in an executive session with the subcom-

38. George Leslie Harrison, memorandum of meeting of Executive Committee, Federal Reserve Bank of New York, 10 Apr. 1933, Harrison Papers, binder 50, vol. 3:153–57. For the debates of 6–8 Mar. over guarantee, see above, pp. 164–75.

39. "Should America Adopt a Unified Banking System?" pp. 114, 116, 118.

mittee on April 21. Towards the bill in general he was neither hostile nor enthusiastic, but he did express strong displeasure with deposit insurance. It seems likely that Woodin was speaking for Roosevelt rather than for himself or the Treasury, since the secretary's chief concern with the Glass bill involved saving his own place on the Federal Reserve Board, a point which he eventually won. Moreover, he took his arguments from officials of the Federal Reserve Bank of New York, suggesting that Roosevelt was willing to endorse the big banker stand against a guarantee.[40] Three days later, the president himself met with the subcommittee and specifically opposed the Steagall plan for total insurance. Governor Harrison reported that the president asked for a two-week delay in the subcommittee's report while he considered deposit insurance and other key features.[41] By the beginning of May, Glass, Steagall, and Roosevelt announced that they had agreed "in principle" on the bill, and the president appeared to support it, but he did not clarify his terms, especially on the insurance program.[42] Woodin backed the bill when Glass agreed to permit the secretary of the Treasury to remain as an *ex officio* member of the Federal Reserve Board.

On May 10, Glass in the Senate and Steagall in the House introduced the bank reform bills. Glass included a plan for insurance under a sinking fund similar to the one he had included in his original bill; he hoped, however, to oblige banks to join the Federal Reserve System in order to benefit from it. Steagall, on the other hand, wrote in a guarantee fund to which all banks could have free access. In these two versions of the bill lay the alignment of large and small banks, branched and unitary institutions. Glass's program, the more conservative, would win whatever support was available from the big banks. The Economic Policy Commission of the Executive Council of the American Bankers Association, for example, had approved of the liquidating corporation in principle, although they

40. W. Randolph Burgess of the New York Federal Reserve Bank drafted the letter to Glass, which Woodin signed without reading; the letter reflected the views of New York rather than those of the Federal Reserve Board in Washington, which caused some resentment in the latter agency. Charles Sumner Hamlin bitterly regarded it as an attempt to wreck the Glass bill and lay a trap for Roosevelt which the president did not see. Hamlin, Diary, 15, 17, 18, 20 Apr., 16 June 1933; *New York Times*, 18 Apr. 1933.
41. *New York Times*, 22, 25, 27 Apr. 1933; Hamlin, Diary, 12 Apr. 1933.
42. *New York Times*, 30 Apr., 2, 5, 6 May 1933.

did not wish to subscribe to its capital fund.[43] Steagall's bill represented the broader guarantee position of the small-bank men, who hoped that such a fund would provide sufficient reinforcement to prop up their banks against threats of branching or compulsory membership in a national system.

The Senate Banking and Currency Committee reported the Glass bill to the Senate on May 15. Debate concentrated on the deposit insurance proposal. Four days later Republican Senator Arthur Vandenberg introduced an amendment to the Glass bill providing for insurance of bank deposits up to $2,500 at once.[44] The Vandenberg amendment appeared made to order for those like Vice-President Garner who had long favored a guarantee. It passed with the support of the Midwestern senators and went to conference committee. Meanwhile, thousands of telegrams and letters, many from depositors in closed banks, inundated the politicians with pleas for a guarantee.[45] The Steagall bill passed the House by a vote of 262 to 19 on May 23, and the Senate, *viva voce*, two days later; only deposit insurance remained open.[46]

Rumor said that Roosevelt would kill the Glass bill if it contained deposit guarantee provisions. So far as the press knew, the president approved the bills in general terms and even said that some form of bank insurance was probably inevitable, but he was trying to "have it made as sound as possible."[47] Yet in private he insisted that the Vandenberg amendment or any modification of it must go; he would veto the entire bill if it did not, he said.[48]

From June 1 through June 7, conferences at the White House tried to resolve the guarantee conflict. The president remained in almost constant communication with Woodin (who agreed with any outcome so long as he retained his Federal Reserve Board member-

43. Charles W. Collins to Marvin McIntyre, 14 Apr. 1933, with report, FDRL:OF 230; "American Bankers Association Position on Glass Bill," mimeographed statement, n.d., Rogers Papers, box 124; *New York Times*, 13 Apr. 1933.

44. Timmons, *Garner*, p. 180; Timmons, *Jones*, pp. 194–95.

45. For a sample, see 1,500 favorable telegrams, Glass Papers, box 259; James W. Wadsworth, COHC, p. 417.

46. *New York Times*, 24, 26 May 1933; *Business Week*, 31 May 1933, p. 20; *Commercial and Financial Chronicle*, 27 May 1933, pp. 3633–35.

47. FDR to Arthur Iselin, 6 June 1933, FDRL:PPF 566.

48. J. F. T. O'Connor, Diary, microfilm copy at FDRL (original at University of California, Berkeley), 2 June 1933.

ship), Senator Glass (who still favored his liquidation corporation plan), Representative Steagall (who spoke for total guarantee), Comptroller J. F. T. O'Connor (who supported insurance), and a host of others. Roosevelt objected to a 100 percent guarantee. On June 12, however, he accepted a modified and delayed plan of insurance.[49] He wisely recognized that the banking crisis and the Pecora findings had heightened the popular demand for bank reform and that the Glass bill provided the best response then available; to sacrifice the entire bill would be a political mistake, even though he might have preferred to wait until a later time for more far-reaching legislation.[50] At least the Glass bill fulfilled the Democratic campaign pledges of 1932 and could be supplemented later if needed. Roosevelt still would not accept an across-the-board guarantee of deposits, but he agreed to a less than 100 percent insurance plan. Therefore, the final version of the Glass-Steagall Act included a Federal Deposit Insurance Corporation established to underwrite deposits on a graduated scale; a temporary insurance plan would cover the period until permanent insurance went into effect.

Under the temporary plan all members of the Federal Reserve System had to participate; nonmember state banks could join if certified solvent by the state banking authorities and examined by the Corporation. Deposits up to $2,500 would be covered out of funds raised by assessments on participants of one-half of 1 percent of their insured deposits, half to be paid in cash and the remainder subject to call, with one additional assessment to be levied if needed and any balance as of July 1, 1934, refunded to the member banks.

On that date, the Federal Deposit Insurance Corporation, managed by the Comptroller of the Currency and two other directors appointed by the president, would become effective. Its capital depended on a $150 million appropriation from the United States

49. O'Connor, Diary, 1 June 1933; Hamlin, Diary, 2 June 1933; O'Connor to Glass, O'Connor to Steagall, 2 June 1933, FDRL:OF 21B. Three years later in a radio address Senator Vandenberg claimed that the president "wrote a letter to the legislative conferees demanding that my amendment be stricken from the Banking Bill"; in response O'Connor commented, "We can not permit erroneous impressions to get out regarding the President's opposition to bank deposit insurance." In 1936 O'Connor said that Roosevelt had opposed insurance of $50,000 and greater amounts only. O'Connor to Marvin McIntyre, memorandum on Vandenberg broadcast, 6 June 1936, FDRL:OF 21B.

50. Ernest K. Lindley, "Wall Street under the New Deal," *Literary Digest*, 22 July 1933, pp. 4–5, 31.

Treasury, one-half of the surplus of the Federal Reserve banks as of January 1, 1933 (approximately $139 million), and one-half of 1 percent of deposits of participating banks (approximately $200 million). As the bankers had feared, New York City banks would bear 28 percent of all members' share in the FDIC, with Chase, National City, and Guaranty alone carrying 12 percent.[51]

All members of the Federal Reserve System were obliged to join; nonmember banks had two years (July 1, 1934, to July 1, 1936) during which they might enjoy the benefits of the FDIC by subscribing to its stock and meeting its standards, but at the end of that time they must qualify for Federal Reserve membership.[52]

The FDIC insured deposits up to $10,000 fully, guaranteed deposits from $10,000 to $50,000 75 percent, and underwrote 50 percent of deposits above $50,000. If a bank should fail, the FDIC would immediately organize a new national bank to assume its deposit liabilities and make available a sum equal to the insured deposits of the old banks so that depositors could withdraw their money at once. The new bank would then either continue in operation by the sale of capital stock, merge with the existing bank, or be liquidated within two years.

After Roosevelt had agreed to the bill, it went back to the Congress. Despite threats of yet another Huey Long filibuster,[53] and on the verge of adjournment, the House and Senate on June 13 accepted the conference report. Glass claimed that the bill remained 97 percent as it had passed the Senate, altered only in the Vandenberg amendment, but Vandenberg called it a "grudging surrender on the part of Secretary Woodin and Wall Street to the irresistible mid-continent revolution typified by my immediate temporary deposit amendment."[54] He was at least partially right. Woodin had taken no personal stand on the bill, speaking throughout as Roosevelt's agent. But the White House had agreed with the large bankers in their concern over the deposit guarantee. The final compromise was more the president's than the bankers', since the American Bank-

51. *New York Times*, 18 June 1933.

52. Comptroller O'Connor had lobbied vigorously for this provision. O'Connor, Diary, 7 June 1933.

53. O'Connor, Diary, 13 June 1933.

54. *Commercial and Financial Chronicle*, 24 June 1933, pp. 4343–44; *New York Times*, 13, 14, 15 June 1933.

ers Association launched a vigorous campaign for a veto, but another group of banking interests, particularly in the Midwest, which Vandenberg had cited, favored the bill, especially in its guarantee forms.[55]

On June 16, President Roosevelt signed the Banking Act of 1933, lauding it as the "second most important banking legislation enacted in the history of the country."[56] For all of its provisions, the president claimed full credit, to the amusement or outrage of contemporary and hindsighted observers.[57] Yet, had it not been for the more radical proposals of a federal government guarantee of all depositors' money in every bank, the FDIC provision might not have been accepted, and without the FDIC, the entire measure would have foundered.

Ironically, the controversial issue of insurance succeeded for exactly the reasons that its bitterest critics condemned it to failure: it made strong banks responsible for the losses of the weak. As a result, the more stable members of the system compelled their less sound colleagues to reform before disaster forced them to seek refuge in the fund. "Bad" banks were seldom permitted to go under but were reorganized under new management or merged with a good bank; thus the FDIC had only to assume responsibility for losses on depreciated assets, not the collapse of an entire institution. Moreover, small depositors felt sure that they would get their money

55. O'Connor to FDR, 15 June 1933, FDRL:OF 21B; O'Connor, Diary, 15 June 1933.

56. *New York Times*, 17 June 1933.

57. When Roosevelt later reviewed the success of deposit insurance, saying that the record justified his earlier confidence, Garner could only wink and comment wryly, "I see Roosevelt is claiming credit for the guarantee of bank deposits." Timmons, *Garner*, p. 180. John T. Flynn, perennial critic of all things Rooseveltian, carped in 1948 that both the Glass bill and the insurance program "were passed without the movement of a finger by him to assist them." Flynn, *Roosevelt Myth*, p. 61. *Business Week* in 1933 and Richard Hofstadter in 1948 felt that Roosevelt deserved no laurels for the measure, that persistent senators, particularly Vandenberg, had wrung concessions from the administration, using "the letters from back home piled high on Congressional desks." "Best Banking Law," *Business Week*, 17 June 1933, p. 17; Hofstadter, *American Political Tradition*, p. 327. Even the singling out of Vandenberg seemed unjust to Steagall, who bristled when Vandenberg claimed credit for deposit insurance in a 1936 radio speech. Steagall noted that he had been introducing deposit guarantee bills for ten years as a minority congressman and that the insurance provision in the final Glass-Steagall Act was his. Steagall, radio address, [1936], FDRL:OF 21B.

even if one bank experienced financial difficulties; therefore, a single failure no longer led to runs which might force sound banks to suspend. Consequently, the FDIC did well: from 1921 to 1933, depositors lost an average of $156 million per year or $.45 per $100 in commercial banks; from the establishment of the FDIC until 1960, losses averaged only $706,000 per year or less than $.002 per $100, with more than half of those losses occurring in 1934.[58]

The Banking Act of 1933 represented a series of compromises in order to secure reform. In branch banking and unification of banks into a single national system, state nonmember banks successfully prevented an overwhelming gift of power to large national banks. On deposit guarantee, conservative Eastern bankers had had to grant the general principle but obstructed efforts to place the federal government itself entirely behind their weaker counterparts. Only on separation of affiliates did the bankers agree, and then merely because the Pecora revelations had showed them the wisdom of cooperating with the inevitable. For politicians such as Glass and Roosevelt, the law also meant giving in—Glass in the sacrifice of fuller reform as it had appeared in earlier versions of his bill, Roosevelt in endorsing banking legislation before he was ready to have it enacted.

In each case, however, bankers and politicians acted in the aftermath of the February and March disasters. Their response constituted the first long-range answer to the demand of those critical days: Something must be done! If, therefore, the Glass-Steagall Act was a partial measure, if it pales when compared with later banking legislation, such as the Banking Act of 1935, it was the first major banking law to achieve passage in almost twenty years, the product of three years of fighting by Senator Glass and a well-intentioned effort to deal with the structural defects revealed by almost 15,000 bank failures.

58. Friedman and Schwartz, *Monetary History*, pp. 434–42. Jackson Reynolds felt that the mere fact that the FDIC "was going to be organized built up confidence in the little people all over the country. These are the people who cause a stampede usually, and it was a great bulwark from them." Reynolds, COHC, p. 172.

CHAPTER X

Conclusion

FUNDAMENTAL flaws in American banking underlay the crisis of 1933. Had the structure itself been sound, the nation's banks might have withstood those human failings of greed and bad management, as well as the pressures of economic decline, which added to the disaster. As it was, however, the system suffered in too many areas from undercapitalization, overbanking, inadequate supervision, and faulty organization. When tested, it could not muster the necessary strength, and it suffered a series of bank failures so great as to threaten every financial institution in the country.

The history of banking in the United States reveals constant resistance to both unification and controls. A multiple system of state-chartered institutions existed simultaneously with efforts at central banking from 1791 to 1811 and again from 1816 to 1836. That dual system continued even after the banking act of 1864 authorized nationally-chartered banks. Thereafter, each state had institutions answerable separately to the state banking commissioner and to the federal Comptroller of the Currency, with no uniformity of rules except for the national banks. The coming of the Federal Reserve System in 1914 did not supersede this complex structure, and, in fact, added to its diversity, for the System exercised only limited powers over the national banks and such state institutions as chose to join it. Those among the framers of the Federal Reserve Act who hoped for centralization of banking were thwarted by the defenders of the small, independent bank; the latter continued to resist measures which would allow larger and stronger banks to establish branches where they would compete with the local unitary banks. In the same way, the directing Board of the Federal Reserve System quickly became the instrument of the twelve Reserve banks and their members rather than a strong controlling body. Thus, the Federal Reserve Board could only hope that the member banks would respond to its requests and influences; so long as those banks met the minimum requirements of capitalization and reserves to remain in the System and passed periodic audits of their accounts, they could operate with relatively little attention to Board proposals.

The defects of this organization became most evident after World War I. Federal Reserve policies, intended to assist European countries in sustaining or restoring their monetary standards, created easy money at low interest rates which encouraged member banks to borrow from the Reserve in order to lend to their own customers at only slightly higher rates. Commercial banks had financed the rise of large corporate enterprises during the war; after 1923, however, they favored more profitable investments in bonds. Resources continued to expand, and the banks had still more money available to lend. Many newer houses and even enlarged older firms decided to take advantage of the great profits to be made from the large volume of demand for mortgage loans and advances to stock market speculators. Thus, they supported the swelling of those markets and the boom of the 1920s. At no time before 1929 did the Federal Reserve Board warn against speculative loans; in fact, the Reserve banks, especially New York, continued their easy money policies which made the spiral possible.

Early in 1929, the Federal Reserve tried to arrest these expansive lending trends. The Reserve banks reversed their open-market operations, and the Board warned against speculation. However their cautions had practically no effect, since those who were supposed to respond to Reserve influence chose instead to continue their own highly profitable business, and the System had no way to force cooperation of its members or even to reach nonmember banks. In the few cases where banks did comply, the money they removed from the markets was quickly replaced by corporations eager for high-yield investments of their excess profits. The break came in October 1929, despite the Federal Reserve's anemic countermeasures.

Even before 1929, good times had not extended to all banks, however. Many small units collapsed during the 1920s when their lending policies turned sour. Banks whose loans supported agriculture, for example, suffered when the postwar agricultural depression prevented farmers from meeting mortgage payments. Most of these failed banks were concentrated in areas which had long resisted banking consolidation and Federal Reserve membership. Hence, they could not draw on the support of reserves or rediscounts when trouble struck.

As the crash of 1929 became the Great Depression of the 1930s, bank failures spread. Money loaned into the speculative markets could not be repaid; economic decline made it impossible for borrowers to pay off even the interest on their mortgages and other loans. Thus, the assets of commercial banks shrank. At the same time, foreign depositors removed their gold and further reduced reserves. When creditors decided to withdraw funds, many banks lacked liquid assets to pay out cash. Some institutions failed, and an epidemic of suspensions followed. Depositors, panicked at the closing of one local bank, rushed to salvage their money from the others, thus creating pressures which the banks could not meet. In 1893 and 1907, conversion of deposits into currency had been restricted by the banks themselves, but in 1930 the Federal Reserve had no authority to prevent withdrawals of cash, and could not arrest bank suspensions which arose from lack of liquidity. Moreover, the stronger banks, which had led the movement for restriction in the past, could now go to the Reserve for discounts to support their own positions and, at the same time, could assume that the System would take care of its weaker members.[1] Few considered the fate of the state nonmember banks, whose capital structure, supervision, and geographic location generally made them most vulnerable to runs. These banks had to dump their assets on the markets to obtain funds, thus driving values down, so that their holdings declined even further.[2]

In their desire for liquidity, the larger and more stable banks

1. Milton Friedman and Anna Jacobson Schwartz, *The Great Contraction, 1929–1933* (Princeton: Princeton University Press, 1965), pp. 15–16.

2. Ibid., pp. 58–59; Federal Reserve Board, *Annual Report, 1933*, p. 4; Maurice Lee, *Economic Fluctuations: An Analysis of Business Cycles and Other Business Fluctuations* (Homewood, Ill.: Irwin, 1955).

believed they could not afford to support renewed credit expansion. Recovery might have come much sooner if business had requested and the commercial banks had agreed to offer sustaining loans in order to renew operations. Even bank failures could have been reduced significantly if stronger institutions had been willing to make temporary loans to smaller, troubled colleagues. President Hoover pleaded with the bankers to fight contraction, but their National Credit Corporation failed to save banks, railroads, or industries because its directors proved too conservative in their lending policies. The Reconstruction Finance Corporation, which replaced it, was somewhat more liberal, but its performance during the first year (February 1932 to February 1933) was clearly limited to stopgap measures. The Federal Reserve, too, tried to swell credit briefly in 1931 and again in 1932, but few member banks chose to follow the leads it set by open-market and discounting operations. The best hope of the Federal Reserve rested on expansion of securities eligible for rediscount under the Glass-Steagall Act of 1932; but these loans proved to be emergency measures which saved few banks. The Reserve System still suffered from the lack of means to compel member banks to accept its policy decisions, in this case freer lending to counteract the depression.[3]

Meanwhile, bank suspensions increased. From 1865 to 1929, a total of 8,599 commercial banking institutions with $2,506,045,000 in deposits failed. During the period from January 1, 1930, to March 15, 1933, 5,790 banks with deposits of $3,456,708,000 suspended: 886 national banks holding $775,644,000; 4,698 state institutions with $2,631,554,000; and 206 private banks having $49,510,000 in deposits. In 1921, the United States had more than 31,000 banks; in 1929, 25,000; and by 1933, 18,000. The failure rate for banks rose above that for other businesses in 1921 and stayed there until 1933. Nearly all banks which closed during the 1920s were small; only 12 percent had a capitalization over $100,000 and 40 percent started with less than $25,000. By 1930, however, size, pace, and average losses to depositors, creditors, and stockholders had accelerated. The first series of post-crash failures, late in 1930, hit Kentucky,

3. Mable T. Wallich and Henry C. Wallich, "The Federal Reserve System during the 1930's," in *The Federal Reserve System*, edited by Herbert V. Prochow (New York: Harper, 1960), pp. 318–23; Friedman and Schwartz, *Great Contraction*, pp. 26–28, 51–53, 88–93, 95–103.

Tennessee, Arkansas, and North Carolina. A second wave, from the middle of 1931 through February 1932, started in Chicago and spread to Ohio and other Midwestern states before it moved into Pennsylvania, New York, and eventually New England. During most of 1932, the RFC was able to stave off major disasters, but in November, Nevada had to declare a banking holiday in order to save a crucial group of banks which held 80 percent of the state's assets. Suspensions increased again in December and during the first six weeks of 1933, when volume of deposits in suspended banks was particularly large in southern New Jersey, the District of Columbia, Tennessee, Illinois, Iowa, Missouri, Nevada, and California. Publication of RFC loans further undermined public faith. Finally, on February 14, 1933, Michigan proclaimed a statewide moratorium to protect its largest banking groups from complete ruin.[4]

Depositors contributed to these suspensions by converting their accounts to cash or transferring funds to banks in which they had more faith. Confidence melted further in the light of the Pecora revelations, which showed that prominent bankers had been greedy, self-serving men with little sense of public responsibility. During the last two weeks of February, this waning of belief in the banks came close to hysteria in many cities, causing the hard-pressed institutions to draw heavily on the great banking centers of Chicago and New York for funds.[5]

President Hoover believed that the panic arose out of fears for the future. He charged that President-elect Roosevelt had deliberately withheld any indication of his policies, particularly on banking and sound money. Worse, in Hoover's eyes, Roosevelt had rejected his predecessor's appeals for an affirmation of his faith in the existing banking system and a pledge not to tamper with the currency. Hoover concluded that the New Deal constituted a "fountain of fear" from the day following Roosevelt's election.[6] From Roosevelt's point

---

4. Federal Reserve Board, *Annual Report, 1933*, pp. 3–4; O'Connor, *Banking Crisis and Recovery*, pp. 94–95; Smolensky, *Adjustments to Depression and War*, pp. 41–45; Jones, *Fifty Billion Dollars*, pp. 13–14.

5. Federal Reserve Board, *Annual Report, 1933*, pp. 5–6; John Foster Dulles, quoted in *New York Times*, 10 Mar. 1933.

6. Hoover, *Memoirs*, 3:215–16; Hoover, *Addresses upon the American Road: 1933–1938*, pp. 115, 203–04, 222; idem, *Further Addresses upon the American Road: 1938–1940*, p. 49; "Chronological Summary of Banking Collapse" and "True Causes of the Banking Panic of 1933," Hoover Papers, West

of view, Hoover's pleas for a public statement actually meant an endorsement of the defeated administration. He would have been foolish to tie himself to plans which the nation had repudiated in November; nor did he feel any obligation to reveal his own intentions before he assumed office. Thus, he remained silent until March 4.

Because Hoover chose to lay so much of the burden of the interregnum on Roosevelt, he himself did little during that period. He refused to take the initiative in measures to save the banks. Each time Hoover considered action, he held back, seeking Roosevelt's cooperation. While he did not wish to share the powers of the presidency, he did hope to spread its responsibilities. When aides prepared instruments whereby he might close the nation's banks or limit withdrawals, Hoover refused to use them unless Roosevelt would countersign every move. Even in the most desperate days of the panic, the president asked the Federal Reserve Board to request him to act. When these endorsements were not forthcoming, he did nothing. The United States suffered a fatal lack of leadership while its bank problems mounted.

State banking holidays increased. Although a moratorium prevented further drains within a given state, it increased pressure outside, as banks withdrew emergency funds from their larger correspondents, particularly in New York. By March 3, the New York Federal Reserve Bank felt that its reserves could no longer sustain the local banks. Since President Hoover would not act, at the last minute Governor Herbert Lehman closed the New York banks; Illinois's governor followed suit.

Herbert Hoover left the presidency and Franklin Roosevelt entered it on March 4, 1933, with the banking system of the United States on the verge of total collapse. Only bank holidays in thirty-four states kept their banks from wholesale failures. All energy seemed directed toward bringing down the banks. If they were to be saved, some strong countermeasure would be necessary.

On Monday morning, March 6, by order of President Roosevelt, the banks of the *entire* country remained closed; they would not open for at least a week—some never again. Roosevelt had called on holdovers from the Hoover administration to devise a plan

---

Branch, Iowa; Meyer, COHC, pp. 617–18; William Starr Myers, Diary, 4 Mar. 1933, Myers Papers, Princeton University; Joslin, *Hoover Off the Record*, p. 11.

for saving the banks, and they gave him exactly the tool offered to Hoover earlier: a proclamation temporarily suspending banking activities and all dealings in gold, under authority of the 1917 Trading-with-the-Enemy Act. Hoover had questioned the validity of this authorization, fearing that a hostile Congress might repudiate his action under it. But Roosevelt accepted the power and confidently called on the nation and the new Congress in emergency session to endorse his stand. His inaugural address had made clear that he, too, would use confidence as a weapon in the war against the depression.

Thus, Roosevelt became the voice and spirit of hope on March 4, 5, and 6, willingly taking up a policy prepared by and for the old order but transforming it into his own optimistic instrument to rescue the banking system. If his handling of the banking crisis was not part of a predetermined New Deal program, it did indicate how this new administration intended to deal with the problems of the Great Depression: Roosevelt would use any solution, from any source, so long as it promised a practicable answer to an immediate difficulty he had to face. He provided the framework—the desire to preserve the existing system and a rejection of radical solutions— and the tone—a triumphant belief that the economic paralysis of three and a half years had been conquered. Insofar as the banking crisis offered a keynote to the New Deal, it was in this: the end of the era of drift and the beginning of hope under new and vigorous leadership.

The dramatic gesture of a national banking holiday broke the back of the panic. Depositors showed relief that action had finally been taken, and Americans got through the days without banks in good spirit. Meanwhile, the Treasury Department supervised skeleton banking services and worked on plans for reopening.

Again, the men of the old order provided the mechanism and the men of the new put it into operation. Continuous meetings at the Treasury showed that the great bankers were still powerless to help themselves; they could not agree on any proposal to resume banking business. Nor could Roosevelt's advisers, new to their offices, devise an acceptable solution. For a while, scrip seemed the answer; banks could pay depositors in pseudo-money issued against their sound assets. But, as Hoover's officials pointed out, the Federal Reserve

Act already provided for just such a situation and made scrip unnecessary; Federal Reserve notes, an elastic currency, could be issued against a member bank's good assets, providing real money when the banks reopened. At the same time, former Secretary of the Treasury Ogden Mills submitted an effective resumption plan. Banks would be classified into three groups—wholly sound, questionable, and hopeless. The safe and liquid banks could open immediately; unsound institutions would be closed and liquidated; and those of uncertain or partially safe condition might be rehabilitated and reopened later. Roosevelt took this solution and made it into another instrument of confidence. Speaking to the nation in a fireside chat on Sunday evening, March 12, he explained that banks would be reopening during the next three days. Only totally sound banks would be opened, he pledged, and they would have enough cash to meet all demands. Others would resume as they became safe. The next day when banks began to reopen, they took in more money than they paid out. The banking crisis was over; the hoarding peril had been reversed.

Although the banking moratorium took its toll on the nation's banks, it was resolved with surprising efficiency. Nearly 18,000 commercial banks had been operative at the beginning of 1933; 17,300 remained at the end of the holiday, but the vast majority of the failures had taken place in January and February. During the first three days after the suspension, the Treasury licensed 4,507 national and 571 state member banks, approximately 75 percent of all banks in the Federal Reserve System, holding some 90 percent of all resources of member banks. By April 12, state banking authorities had licensed over 7,400 nonmember banks, about 71 percent of the existing institutions in that category. At the end of the year, 6,011 member and approximately 8,200 nonmember banks were operating without restrictions; only 512 member and about 1,400 nonmember institutions remained unlicensed. Of the banks which opened gradually after the first great licensing, most were reorganized and many received additional funds from local investors and the Reconstruction Finance Corporation. Some, such as the Detroit banking groups, were taken over by new institutions; others were strengthened by merger. In areas where the law allowed, such as the District of Columbia, banks were brought under closer federal supervision. The RFC also used its power contingent upon its loans and stock purchases to establish better management and operating techniques.[7] These measures completed the action begun by the president's closing proclamation.

The crisis of 1933 proved how badly the American banking system needed reform. Most failures took place in areas which had too many small unitary institutions with inadequate capitalization and poor management. They did not belong to the Federal Reserve System and hence lacked the protection of even minimal requirements and supervision; nor could they call upon a Reserve bank for emergency cash or rediscounts. Banks which did belong to the System were better off in these respects, but the powers of the organization were still insufficient to correct conditions which might contribute to failures or to stopping failures in progress. The Federal Reserve could suggest policies to its members but could not compel their cooperation; for example, it could not prevent loans to speculators. Moreover, the information uncovered by the Pecora probe showed that even national member bankers had been able to indulge their own interests to the detriment of customers, so long as they complied with the formal requirements of the law. While the timing of these revelations undoubtedly contributed to the panic and epidemic of failures, public shock converted many, even bankers, to the cause of reform.

Senator Carter Glass had been urging fundamental banking changes since 1931. Even at the height of the crisis, in February 1933, however, his bill only got through the Senate; it bogged down in the House. Both the Hoover administration and the organized banking community withheld support until too late. Glass resumed his efforts for reform as soon as the new administration took office. He did not win President Roosevelt's support until it seemed almost sure that the Glass-Steagall bill would become law. And in the end, the senator had to be satisfied with a compromise measure, watered

7. O'Connor, Banking Crisis and Recovery, pp. 80–83, 89; Federal Reserve Board, Annual Report, 1933, pp. 14–17, 22; Friedman and Schwartz, Monetary History, pp. 423–25, 427; Jones, Fifty Billion Dollars, pp. 40–45; Harrison, "Review of Business and Financial Developments since March, 1933," Harrison Papers, box 12, miscellaneous folder; Marriner Eccles, speech before American Bankers Association convention, New Orleans, 14 Nov. 1935, FDRL:PPF 1820.

down to get the support of the traditional defenders of the small, unsupported bank.

The Glass-Steagall Act of 1933 achieved partial changes in Federal Reserve powers, branch banking, commercial and investment banking, and the insurance of deposits. Reserve banks could now control members' lending for speculation. In a very small step toward centralization, the law began to shift open-market operations from the Reserve banks, dominated by New York, to the Board in Washington. Branch banking also expanded slightly, although this feature suffered major cutbacks in a compromise with opponents of the large banks. Investment affiliates were permanently divorced from commercial banks. Any institutions which chose might join the Federal Deposit Insurance Corporation to protect their deposits.

More extreme advocates of banking reform had proposed a variety of vigorous measures, ranging from compulsory membership in the Federal Reserve System for every bank in the country (including savings banks), to trade-area branching even beyond state borders, to across-the-board guarantee of all deposits in all commercial banks. These and others who desired a stronger and more integrated banking system found the Banking Act of 1933 disappointing. But it was a greater step in the direction of reform than any since 1914.

The lessons of the crisis of 1933 were not lost with the passage of the compromise banking act. Some bankers, such as Marriner Eccles of Utah, realized even before the panic that the nation's banking system suffered from fatal defects, not the least of which was decentralization of supervision and controls. Although the old decentralizers prevented concentration in 1933, two years later new support emerged for a "radical revision of the Federal Reserve System,"[8] with a definite shift in power to Washington.

Eccles had been named governor of the Federal Reserve Board in November 1934; an innovator in his approach to banking, he admitted that he had suffered a great shock at the conduct of his fellow bankers in 1930 and 1931. It was not surprising, therefore,

8. Leuchtenburg, *Roosevelt and the New Deal*, p. 158.

that he and a colleague submitted a memorandum on banking reform early in 1935 which suggested centralization of control, new
powers for the Federal Reserve Board, and lessening of the influence
of private bankers. These proposals became the banking bill introduced to Congress in February 1935.

A few years before, the Eccles measure would have met heavy
opposition from the farm states and small bank advocates in the
West and Southwest, as well as spenders, monetary reformers, and
antitrusters. After 1933, however, these groups had little choice but
to acknowledge the problems inherent in unit banking, and while
they still distrusted branch, chain, and group banking, they recognized that the United States already had a powerful financial capital
in New York. Better to move that center away from Wall Street to
Washington, if it had to exist at all, they reasoned. Hence, in the
spring of 1935 the banking bill could call for support on exactly
those groups which had opposed centralization two years earlier,
when they had not yet come to appreciate the lessons taught by the
panic of 1933.

Opposition remained formidable. It included the few who
had hoped for full nationalization and thus believed the new bill,
like the old law, did not go far enough, as well as the traditional
defenders of localism and states rights, and, in this case, large
Eastern bankers, who claimed that the Eccles proposals would
subjugate the Federal Reserve Board, and hence the System, to a
politically-dominated financial dictatorship which would force individual banks to underwrite government securities. These latter
groups were also aware of the implications of the bill—to shift
financial power from New York to Washington.[9] The loss of Western, Southwestern, and farm bloc votes, however, cut substantially
into the power of the opposition. The Eccles bill passed the House
of Representatives in May 1935 essentially as written.

In the Senate, however, the measure encountered Carter
Glass. Senator Glass had led the bank reform forces since before
1913, when he sponsored the Federal Reserve and claimed a propri-
etary fatherhood over the System. Most recently, he had invested

9. Ellis W. Hawley, The New Deal and the Problem of Monopoly: A Study
in Economic Ambivalence (Princeton: Princeton University Press, 1966), pp.
312–13.

three years in the fight for the Glass-Steagall Act of 1933, which owed its passage in large part to the crisis and holiday. Yet in 1935, the senator tried, unsuccessfully, to break up the Eccles reform bill into separate measures and thus defeat objectionable provisions. He did, however, succeed in wringing a number of concessions before the bill came to a final vote in August. For example, Eccles at first desired to place control of the Federal Reserve System in the White House, but many of Glass's friends objected on the grounds of excessive political influence; Glass was able to have the bill amended to delete the president's power to remove the chairman and vice-chairman of the Reserve Board. Glass also hoped to eliminate Treasury influence, and in 1935 achieved what he had traded away in 1933: the removal of the secretary of the Treasury as an ex-officio member of that Board. (The secretary at that time, Henry Morgenthau, secured the elimination of the Comptroller of the Currency as well.) And, in order to give the bankers some voice along with the political appointees, Glass obtained banker representation on the new open-market committee.

Yet Eccles's primary objectives survived and the Banking Act of 1935 accomplished greater centralization of banking and of the Federal Reserve System than they had ever before enjoyed. Title II of the measure amended the Federal Reserve Act in four areas, all giving more power to the Board. First, the Federal Reserve Board itself underwent reorganization; it became the Board of Governors of the Federal Reserve System, now with seven members appointed by the president for fourteen-year overlapping terms. The head of the Board, now called the chairman, would be chosen by the president from among the members for a four-year term. Second, the act designated as president the operating head of each Federal Reserve bank. Although the directors at each of the twelve banks could still elect these presidents, the central Board now had the power of confirmation, giving the governors greater influence over the twelve presidents, in order to counteract the decentralization of authority of the 1920s, and in particular to establish Washington's prerogatives over the New York bank. Third, the 1935 law made permanent an emergency power granted in the Thomas amendment to the Agricultural Relief Act of 1933, namely, authority to the Board of Governors to vary reserve requirements of member banks. The longstanding ratios of 7, 10, and 13 percent for nonreserve, reserve, and central reserve cities could be as much as doubled. Fourth, the Board would dominate the Federal Open Market Committee because all seven governors became permanent members of the twelve-man committee, although the New York bank would continue to perform the actual open-market operations with a great deal of discretion in acting for the System.

The Banking Act of 1935 incorporated other changes which arose out of the 1933 collapse. The law made permanent the eligibility provisions of the Glass-Steagall Act of 1932, which allowed government securities to be used as backing for Federal Reserve notes and permitted Reserve banks to lend on any collateral they considered sound. In addition, it introduced a permanent plan of deposit protection under the Federal Deposit Insurance Corporation, now including all Federal Reserve member banks and any others which chose to participate; large state banks were forced into the program by 1942. (By 1961, 97 percent of all commercial banks, holding 98 percent of all deposits, were insured.)

If these reforms were still incomplete, they, like those of the Glass-Steagall Banking Act, represented another step away from the chaos which had brought on the crisis of 1933.[10]

10. Barger, *Management of Money*, pp. 119–21, 360; Robertson, *History of American Economy*, pp. 501–20; Leuchtenburg, *Roosevelt and the New Deal*, pp. 158–61; Hawley, *New Deal and Monopoly*, pp. 312–15; Marriner S. Eccles, *Beckoning Frontiers: Public and Personal Recollections* (New York: Knopf, 1951), pp. 166–75, 179–81, 187, 196–229, 267; Tugwell, *Democratic Roosevelt*, pp. 368–69, 373; John M. Blum, *From the Morgenthau Diaries* (Boston: Houghton Mifflin, 1959), pp. 344–53; Pecora, *Wall Street Under Oath*, pp. 237–38; Frederick A. Bradford, "The Banking Act of 1935," *American Economic Review* 25 (Dec. 1935): 663–72; A. D. Gayer, "The Banking Act of 1935," *Quarterly Journal of Economics* 50 (Nov. 1935): 97–116; *Congressional Record*, 74 Cong., 1st Sess., pp. 1501, 1514–24, 6792–93, 6800–04, 6813–20, 6908–09, 6916–19, 6923–25, 6952, 6971–72, 7183–86, 7251–71, 11776–79, 11824–27, 11840–41, 11906, 11935, 13655, 13688–711, 14768.

SELECTED BIBLIOGRAPHY

"THE BANKING CRISIS OF 1933" appears in virtually every account of the Great Depression, the Hoover administration, and the New Deal. Yet few details have been revealed about this momentous event. In 1933, C. C. Colt and N. S. Keith published *28 Days: A History of the Banking Crisis*, an outline which did not go beyond the version available in the larger newspapers, such as the *New York Times*. The same year, Marcus Nadler and Jules I. Bogen added an economic review, *The Banking Crisis: The End of an Epoch*, and in 1934 the Brookings Institution brought out Cyril B. Upham's and Edwin Lamke's *Closed and Distressed Banks: A Study in Public Administration*, which concentrated on bank failures and reopenings. But political reporter Ernest K. Lindley, in *The Roosevelt Revolution: First Phase*, expressed the belief that the true story could not be told; those in charge, fearing loss of public confidence, had withheld reliable information from the press, and "the main participants in the drama were too numerous and they emerged from long days and nights of tension with blurred and conflicting memories."

In fact, those who handled the crisis added little for many years. Secretaries of the Treasury Ogden Mills and William Woodin left no published accounts and few relevant papers. Acting Comptroller of the Currency F. Gloyd Awalt waited twenty-five years to draft a manuscript, which he has not made public. His successor, J. F. T. O'Connor, limited himself to the reopening procedures in *The Banking Crisis and Recovery under the Roosevelt Administra-*

tion, which appeared in 1938, after he had resigned. Ten years later, Undersecretary of the Treasury Arthur A. Ballantine gave the fullest version then available, in an article entitled, "When All the Banks Closed." Even the two presidents shed little light on the crisis. Roosevelt mentioned the holiday in passing in *On Our Way* in 1934 and in an introduction to the second volume of his *Public Papers* four years later. Hoover's *Memoirs*, published in 1952, reiterated the account in *The Hoover Administration: A Documented Narrative*, compiled by two of his aides, William Starr Myers and Walter H. Newton, in 1936. Not until Raymond Moley wrote *The First New Deal* in 1966 did readers have any detailed information on the inception and handling of the banking crisis. Relying heavily on Awalt's unpublished account, as well as his own recollections, Moley reconstructed the tense days of February and March 1933, emphasizing activities at the Treasury Department, where he spent the hours of decision.

Economic historians could not go much further, due primarily to limited materials. In 1937 the Federal Reserve System summarized "Bank Suspensions, 1921–1936," but only recently have Federal Reserve records become available. Moreover, until very recently, researchers suffered from the lack of uniform statistics for state banking systems, which accounted for over 80 percent of commercial bank failures. Newly available studies of Arizona, by William H. Jervey, and of Iowa, by Lynn Muchmore, have begun to offer necessary analysis at the state level, but these accounts are still limited by uneven classification of banks and criteria for bank examinations, a problem only partially resolved with the use of Milton Friedman's and Anna Jacobson Schwartz's *Monetary Statistics of the United States*.

Manuscript collections are now available which illuminate the national picture. The Comptroller of the Currency collected the files of all federal participants in the banking crisis and deposited them in the Comptroller's official manuscript at the National Archives. Agencies such as the Federal Reserve Board and the Reconstruction Finance Corporation kept minutes of their operations during the crisis period. And several men, including George Leslie Harrison of the New York Federal Reserve Bank and Charles Sumner Hamlin of the Federal Reserve Board, maintained careful records of their roles in the proceedings. Oral history projects, such as that at Columbia University, have also collected the reminiscences of those, such as Eugene Meyer, Ferdinand Pecora, and Jackson Reynolds, who were involved in the banking panic. Wider aspects of banking problems and solutions appear in such files as the Carter Glass and H. Parker Willis papers, as do political considerations in manuscripts of members of the Hoover and Roosevelt administrations and state leaders such as Herbert H. Lehman.

The following is a more complete listing of materials which provided the basis for the present study.

MANUSCRIPT COLLECTIONS

Ballantine, Arthur Atwood. Letterpress Books: Official Files. Herbert Hoover Presidential Library, West Branch, Iowa.

Baruch, Bernard M. Princeton University, Princeton, N. J.

Chapin, Roy D. Michigan Historical Collections, University of Michigan, Ann Arbor.

Comstock, William A. Michigan Historical Collections, University of Michigan, Ann Arbor.

———. Gubernatorial Papers. Michigan State Archives, Lansing.

Couzens, James. Library of Congress, Washington, D. C.

Dodge, Joseph M. Burton Historical Collection, Detroit Public Library, Detroit, Mich.

Fisher, Irving. Yale University, New Haven, Conn.

Frankfurter, Felix. Library of Congress, Washington, D. C.

Glass, Carter. University of Virginia, Charlottesville.

Hamlin, Charles Sumner. Library of Congress, Washington, D. C.

Harrison, George Leslie. Columbia University, New York, N. Y.

Hoover, Herbert C. Hoover Institution on War, Revolution, and Peace, Stanford, Calif.

———. President's Papers: Official File; Personal File; White House Secretaries' Files; Post-Presidential Papers. Herbert Hoover Presidential Library, West Branch, Iowa.

House, Edward M. Yale University, New Haven, Conn.

Howe, Louis McHenry. Franklin Delano Roosevelt Memorial Library, Hyde Park, N. Y.

Irwin, D. Maitland. Michigan Historical Collections, University of Michigan, Ann Arbor.

Jenks, William L. Michigan Historical Collections, University of Michigan, Ann Arbor.

Jones, Jesse Holman. Library of Congress, Washington, D. C.

Kent, Fred L. Princeton University, Princeton, N. J.

Krock, Arthur. Princeton University, Princeton, N. J.

Lacy, Arthur J. Michigan Historical Collections, University of Michigan, Ann Arbor.

Lehman, Herbert H. School of International Affairs, Columbia University, New York, N. Y.

McAdoo, William Gibbs. Library of Congress, Washington, D. C.

Miller, Adolph. Federal Reserve Board, Washington, D. C.

Mills, Ogden L. Library of Congress, Washington, D. C.

Murphy, Frank. Mayor's Papers. Burton Historical Collection, Detroit Public Library, Detroit, Mich.

Myers, William Starr. Princeton University, Princeton, N. J.

New York State Banking Department. Records of the Office of the Governor of New York, 1928–1932. Franklin Delano Roosevelt Memorial Library, Hyde Park, N. Y.

Norbeck, Peter. University of South Dakota, Vermillion.

Norris, George W. Library of Congress, Washington, D. C.

O'Connor, J. F. T. Diary (microfilm copy). Franklin Delano Roosevelt Memorial Library, Hyde Park, N. Y.

O'Laughlin, John Callan. Library of Congress, Washington, D. C.

Pittman, Key. Library of Congress, Washington, D. C.

Reconstruction Finance Corporation. National Archives, Washington, D. C.

Reichert, Rudolph. Michigan Historical Collections, University of Michigan, Ann Arbor

Rogers, James Harvey. Yale University, New Haven, Conn.

Roosevelt, Franklin D. Official File; President's Personal File; President's Secretaries' File. Franklin Delano Roosevelt Memorial Library, Hyde Park, N. Y.

Rosenman, Samuel I. Franklin Delano Roosevelt Memorial Library, Hyde Park, N. Y.

Stimson, Henry L. Yale University, New Haven, Conn.

Taylor, Orla Benedict. Michigan Historical Collections, University of Michigan, Ann Arbor.

Tugwell, Rexford Guy. Diary. Franklin Delano Roosevelt Memorial Library, Hyde Park, N. Y.

United States, Department of the Treasury. Correspondence of the Secretary. National Archives, Washington, D. C.

United States, Federal Reserve Board. Washington, D. C.

United States, Office of the Comptroller of the Currency. Correspondence. National Archives, Washington, D. C.

Vanderlip, Frank A. Columbia University, New York, N. Y.
Walsh, Thomas J. Library of Congress, Washington, D. C.
Willis, Henry Parker. Columbia University, New York, N. Y.

ORAL HISTORY MEMOIRS

All in Columbia Oral History Collections, Columbia University, New York, N. Y.

Bruère, Henry.   Swope, Gerard.
Gavagan, Joseph Andrew.   Tugwell, Rexford G.
Krock, Arthur.   VanSchaick, George S.
Meyer, Eugene.   Wadsworth, James Walcott.
Pecora, Ferdinand.   Whitney, George.
Reynolds, Jackson.

BOOKS

Allen, Frederick Lewis. *The Lords of Creation.* New York: Harper, 1935.
————. *Only Yesterday: An Informal History of the Nineteen-Twenties.* New York: Harper, 1931.
————. *Since Yesterday: The Nineteen-Thirties in America.* New York: Harper, 1939.
Alsop, Joseph, and Kintner, Robert. *Men around the President.* New York: Doubleday, Doran, 1939.
American Bankers Association, Economic Policy Commission. *Banking after the Crisis.* New York: American Bankers Association, 1934.
Babson, Roger W. *Washington and the Revolutionists.* New York: Harper, 1934.
Barger, Harold. *The Management of Money: A Survey of the American Experience.* Chicago: Rand McNally, 1964.
————. *Money, Banking, and Public Policy.* Chicago: Rand McNally, 1968.
Barnard, Harry. *Independent Man: The Life of Senator James Couzens.* New York: Scribner's, 1958.
Beard, Charles A., and Beard, Mary R. *America in Midpassage.* New York: Macmillan, 1939.
Beard, Charles A., and Smith, George H. A. *The Future Comes: A Study of the New Deal.* New York: Macmillan, 1934.
————. *The Old Deal and the New.* New York: Macmillan, 1941.
Bellush, Bernard. *Franklin D. Roosevelt as Governor of New York.* New York: Columbia University Press, 1955.
Bendiner, Robert. *Just around the Corner: A Highly Selective History of the Thirties.* New York: Harper and Row, 1967.

Bingay, Malcolm W. *Detroit Is My Own Home Town.* Indianapolis: Bobbs-Merrill, 1946.

Bining, Arthur C., and Cochran, Thomas C. *The Rise of American Economic Life.* New York: Scribner's, 1964.

Bird, Caroline. *The Invisible Scar.* New York: McKay, 1966.

Blackorby, Edward C. *Prairie Rebel: The Public Life of William Lemke.* Lincoln: University of Nebraska Press, 1963.

Board of Governors of the Federal Reserve System. *Banking and Monetary Statistics.* Washington, D. C.: National Capital Press, 1943.

————. *The Federal Reserve System: Purposes and Functions.* Washington, D. C.: Board of Governors of the Federal Reserve System, 1963.

Braeman, John; Bremner, Robert H.; and Walters, Everett, eds. *Change and Continuity in Twentieth Century America.* Columbus: Ohio State University Press, 1964.

Bremer, C. D. *American Banking Failures.* New York: Columbia University Press, 1935.

Brogan, Denis W. *The Era of Franklin D. Roosevelt: A Chronicle of the New Deal and Global War.* New Haven, Conn.: Yale University Press, 1950.

Brooks, John: *Once in Golconda: A True Drama of Wall Street, 1920–1938.* New York: Harper and Row, 1969.

Burns, James MacGregor. *Roosevelt: The Lion and the Fox.* New York: Harcourt, Brace and World, 1956.

Byrnes, James F. *All in One Lifetime.* New York: Harper, 1958.

Caldwell, Stephen A. *A Banking History of Louisiana.* Baton Rouge: Louisiana State University Press, 1935.

Carosso, Vincent P. *Investment Banking in America: A History.* Cambridge, Mass.: Harvard University Press, 1970.

Carter, Paul A. *The Twenties in America.* New York: Thomas Y. Crowell, 1968.

Chandler, Lester V. *Benjamin Strong: Central Banker.* Washington, D. C.: Brookings Institution, 1958.

Chapman, Charles C. *The Development of American Business and Banking Thought: 1913–1936.* New York: Longmans Green, 1936.

Chase, Stuart. *A New Deal.* New York: Macmillan, 1932.

Coben, Stanley, and Hill, Forest G., eds. *American Economic History: Essays in Interpretation.* Philadelphia: J. B. Lippincott, 1966.

Cochran, Thomas C. *The Great Depression and the World War II, 1929–1945.* Glenview, Ill.: Scott, Foresman, 1968.

————, and Brewer, Thomas B. *Views of American Economic Growth.* Vol. 2, *The Industrial Era.* New York: McGraw-Hill, 1966.

Cole, David M. *The Development of Banking in the District of Columbia.* New York: William-Frederick, 1959.

Colt, C. C., and Keith, N. S. *28 Days: A History of the Banking Crisis.* New York: Greenberg, 1933.

Conklin, Paul K. *The New Deal.* New York: Thomas Y. Crowell, 1967.

Connally, Thomas, with Steinberg, Alfred. *My Name Is Tom Connally.* New York: Crowell, 1954.

Crane, Milton, ed. *The Roosevelt Era.* New York: Boni and Gaer, 1947.

Daniels, Jonathan. *The Time between the Wars: Armistice to Pearl Harbor.* Garden City, N. Y.: Doubleday, Doran, 1966.

Day, Donald, ed. *Franklin D. Roosevelt's Own Story.* Boston: Little, Brown, 1951.

Delano, Daniel W., Jr. *Franklin Roosevelt and the Delano Influence.* Pittsburgh: James S. Nudi, 1946.

Dexter, Walter Friar. *Herbert Hoover and American Individualism: A Modern Interpretation of a National Ideal.* New York: Macmillan, 1932.

Divine, Robert A., ed. *The Age of Insecurity: America, 1920–1944.* Reading, Mass.: Addison-Wesley, 1968.

Dorfman, Joseph. *The Economic Mind in American Civilization.* Vol. 5: *1918–1933.* New York: Viking, 1959.

Eccles, Marriner S. *Beckoning Frontiers: Public and Personal Recollections.* New York: Knopf, 1951.

Einaudi, Mario. *The Roosevelt Revolution.* New York: Harcourt, Brace, 1959.

Farley, James A. *Behind the Ballots: The Personal History of a Politician.* New York: Harcourt, Brace, 1938.

———. *Jim Farley's Story: The Roosevelt Years.* New York: McGraw-Hill, 1948.

Faulkner, Harold U. *From Versailles to the New Deal: A Chronicle of the Harding-Coolidge-Hoover Era.* New Haven, Conn.: Yale University Press, 1950.

Feis, Herbert. *1933: Characters in Crisis.* Boston: Little, Brown, 1966.

Fischer, Gerald C. *American Banking Structure.* New York: Columbia University Press, 1968.

Fisher, Irving Norton. *My Father, Irving Fisher.* New York: Comet, 1956.

Fite, Gilbert Courtland. *Peter Norbeck: Prairie Statesman.* Columbia: University of Missouri Press, 1948.

———, and Reese, Jim E. *An Economic History of the United States,* 2d ed. Boston: Houghton Mifflin, 1965.

Flynn, Edward J. *You're the Boss: The Practice of American Politics.* New York: Viking, 1947.

Flynn, John T. *Country Squire in the White House*. Garden City, N. Y.: Doubleday, Doran, 1941.

———. *The Roosevelt Myth*. New York: Devin-Adair, 1948.

Freedman, Max, ed. *Roosevelt and Frankfurter: Their Correspondence, 1928–1945*. Boston: Little, Brown, 1967.

Freidel, Frank. *Franklin D. Roosevelt: The Apprenticeship*. Boston: Little, Brown, 1952.

———. *Franklin D. Roosevelt: The Ordeal*. Boston: Little, Brown, 1954.

———. *Franklin D. Roosevelt: The Triumph*. Boston: Little, Brown, 1956.

———. *The New Deal and the American People*. Englewood Cliffs, N. J.: Prentice-Hall, 1964.

Friedman, Milton, and Schwartz, Anna Jacobson. *The Great Contraction, 1929–1933*. Princeton, N. J.: Princeton University Press, 1965.

———. *A Monetary History of the United States, 1867–1960*. Princeton, N. J.: Princeton University Press, 1963.

———. *Monetary Statistics of the United States*. New York: Columbia University Press, 1970.

Fusfeld, Daniel R. *The Economic Thought of Franklin D. Roosevelt and the Origins of the New Deal*. New York: Columbia University Press, 1956.

Galbraith, John Kenneth. *American Capitalism: The Concept of Countervailing Power*. Boston: Houghton Mifflin, 1952.

———. *The Great Crash: 1929*. Boston: Houghton Mifflin, 1954.

[Gilbert, Clinton W.] *The Mirrors of 1932*. New York: Brewer, Warren and Putnam, 1931.

———. *The Mirrors of Wall Street*. New York: Putnam's, 1933.

Gosnell, Harold F. *Champion Campaigner: Franklin D. Roosevelt*. New York: Macmillan, 1952.

Graff, Robert D., and Ginna, Robert Emmett. *F.D.R.* New York: Harper and Row, 1963.

Graham, Otis L., Jr. *An Encore for Reform: The Old Progressives and the New Deal*. New York: Oxford University Press, 1967.

Greenleaf, William, ed. *American Economic Development since 1860*. Columbus: University of South Carolina Press, 1968.

Greer, Thomas H. *What Roosevelt Thought: The Social and Political Ideas of Franklin D. Roosevelt*. East Lansing: Michigan State University Press, 1958.

Guilfoyle, James H. *On the Trail of the Forgotten Man: A Journal of the Roosevelt Presidential Campaign*. Boston: Peabody, 1933.

Gunther, John. *Roosevelt in Retrospect: A Profile in History*. New York: Harper and Brothers, 1950.

Gurko, Leo. *The Angry Decade*. New York: Harper and Row, 1947.

Haberler, Gottfried. *Prosperity and Depression: A Theoretical Analysis of Cyclical Movements*. Cambridge, Mass.: Harvard University Press, 1937.

Hacker, Louis M. *American Capitalism*. New York: Van Nostrand Reinhold, 1957.

Halasz, Nicholas. *Roosevelt through Foreign Eyes*. Princeton, N. J.: D. Van Nostrand, 1961.

Hallgren, Mauritz A. *Seeds of Revolt: A Study of American Life and the Temper of the American People during the Depression*. New York: Knopf, 1933.

Hawley, Ellis W. *The New Deal and the Problem of Monopoly: A Study in Economic Ambivalence*. Princeton, N. J.: Princeton University Press, 1966.

Henry, Laurin L. *Presidential Transitions*. Washington, D. C.: Brookings Institution, 1960.

Hicks, John D. *Republican Ascendancy, 1921–1933*. New York: Harper and Row, 1960.

Himmelberg, Robert F., ed. *The Great Depression and American Capitalism*. Boston: D. C. Heath, 1968.

Hinshaw, David. *Herbert Hoover: American Quaker*. New York: Farrar, Straus, 1950.

Hinton, Harold B. *Cordell Hull: A Biography*. Garden City, N. Y.: Doubleday, Doran, 1942.

Hofstadter, Richard. *The American Political Tradition and the Men Who Made It*. New York: Knopf, 1948.

Holbrook, Stewart H. *The Age of the Moguls*. Garden City, N. Y.: Doubleday, 1954.

Hoover, Herbert. *Addresses upon the American Road: 1933–1938*. New York: Scribner's, 1938.

———. *Addresses upon the American Road: 1940–1941*. New York: Scribner's, 1941.

———. *The Challenge to Liberty*. New York: Scribner's, 1934.

———. *Further Addresses upon the American Road: 1938–1940*. New York: Scribner's, 1940.

———. *The Memoirs of Herbert Hoover*. 3 vols. New York: Macmillan, 1951–1952.

———. *The State Papers and Other Public Writings of Herbert Hoover*. 2 vols. Edited by William Starr Myers. Garden City, N. Y.: Doubleday, Doran, 1934.

Hoover, Irving Hood. *Forty-Two Years in the White House*. Boston: Houghton Mifflin, 1934.

Horan, James D. *The Desperate Years: A Pictorial History of the Thirties.* New York: Bonanza, 1962.

Hoyt, Edwin P. *The Tempering Years.* New York: Scribner's, 1963.

Hull, Cordell. *The Memoirs of Cordell Hull.* New York: Macmillan, 1948.

Hurd, Charles. *When the New Deal Was Young and Gay.* New York: Hawthorn Books, 1965.

Ickes, Harold L. *The Autobiography of a Curmudgeon.* New York: Reynal and Hitchcock, 1943.

————. *The Secret Diary of Harold L. Ickes: The First Thousand Days, 1933–1936.* New York: Simon and Schuster, 1953.

James, F. Cyril. *The Growth of Chicago Banks: The Modern Age, 1897–1938.* New York: Harper, 1938.

James, Marquis. *Mr. Garner of Texas.* Indianapolis: Bobbs-Merrill, 1939.

————, and James, Bessie Rowland. *Biography of a Bank: The Story of Bank of America N.T. and S.A.* New York: Harper, 1954.

Johnson, Arthur M. *Winthrop W. Aldrich: Lawyer, Banker, Diplomat.* Boston: Harvard University, Graduate School of Business Administration, 1968.

Johnson, Gerald W. *Roosevelt: Dictator or Democrat?* New York: Harper, 1941.

Jones, Jesse H., with Angly, Edward. *Fifty Billion Dollars: My Thirteen Years with the RFC (1933–1945).* New York: Macmillan, 1951.

Josephson, Matthew. *Infidel in the Temple: A Memoir of the Nineteen-Thirties.* New York: Knopf, 1967.

Joslin, Theodore G. *Hoover Off the Record.* Garden City, N. Y.: Doubleday, Doran, 1935.

Keller, Morton, ed. *The New Deal: What Was It?* New York: Holt, Rinehart and Winston, 1963.

Kirkland, Edward C. *A History of American Economic Life.* 3d ed. New York: Appleton-Century-Crofts, 1951.

Krock, Arthur. *In the Nation: 1932–1966.* New York: McGraw-Hill, 1966.

————. *Memoirs: Sixty Years on the Firing Line.* New York: Funk and Wagnalls, 1968.

Leach, Paul R. *That Man Dawes.* Chicago: Reilly and Lee, 1930.

Lee, Maurice. *Economic Fluctuations: An Analysis of Business Cycles and Other Business Fluctuations.* Homewood, Ill.: Richard D. Irwin, 1955.

Leuchtenburg, William E. *Franklin D. Roosevelt: A Profile.* New York: Hill and Wang, 1967.

————. *Franklin D. Roosevelt and the New Deal: 1932–1940.* New York: Harper and Row, 1963.

————. *The New Deal: A Documentary History.* New York: Harper and Row, 1968.

————. *The Perils of Prosperity, 1914–1932.* Chicago: University of Chicago Press, 1958.

Lillard, Richard G. *Desert Challenge: An Interpretation of Nevada.* New York: Knopf, 1949.

Lindley, Ernest K. *Franklin D. Roosevelt: A Career in Progressive Democracy.* Indianapolis: Bobbs-Merrill, 1931.

————. *Half Way with Roosevelt.* New York: Viking, 1937.

————. *The Roosevelt Revolution: First Phase.* New York: Viking, 1933.

Lippmann, Walter. *Interpretations: 1931–1932.* Edited by Allan Nevins. New York: Macmillan, 1932.

————. *Interpretations: 1933–1935.* New York: Macmillan, 1936.

Long, Huey P. *Every Man a King.* New Orleans: National Book Co., 1933.

Long, John Cuthbert. *Roy D. Young.* N.P.: by the author, 1945.

Looker, Earle. *The American Way: Franklin Roosevelt in Action.* New York: John Day, 1933.

Lyons, Eugene. *Herbert Hoover: A Biography.* Garden City, N. Y.: Doubleday, 1964.

————. *Our Unknown Ex-President: A Portrait of Herbert Hoover.* Garden City, N. Y.: Doubleday, 1948.

McCormick, Anne O'Hare. *The World at Home: Selections from the Writings of Anne O'Hare McCormick.* Edited by Marion Turner Sheehan. New York: Knopf, 1956.

McGee, Dorothy Horton. *Herbert Hoover: Engineer, Humanitarian, Statesman.* New York: Dodd, Mead, 1959.

Major, John A. *The New Deal.* New York: Barnes and Noble, 1967.

Malburn, William P. *What Happened to Our Banks.* Indianapolis: Bobbs-Merrill, 1934.

Mann, Arthur. *LaGuardia: A Fighter against His Times, 1882–1933.* Philadelphia: Lippincott, 1959.

Martin, Ralph G. *Ballots and Bandwagons.* Chicago: Rand McNally, 1964.

Maurois, André. *From the New Freedom to the New Frontier: A History of the United States from 1912 to the Present.* Translated by Patrick O'Brien. New York: David McKay, 1962.

Meyer, Agnes E. *Out of These Roots: The Autobiography of an American Woman.* Boston: Little, Brown, 1953.

Michelson, Charles. *The Ghost Talks.* New York: Putnam's, 1944.

Minton, Bruce, and Stuart, John. *The Fat Years and the Lean.* New York: Modern Age Books, 1940.

Mitchell, Broadus. *Depression Decade: From New Era through New Deal, 1929–1941*. New York: Holt, Rinehart and Winston, 1947.

Mitchell, Wesley Clair. *Business Cycles and Their Causes*. Berkeley: University of California Press, 1963.

Moley, Raymond. *After Seven Years*. New York: Harper, 1939.

————. *27 Masters of Politics: In a Personal Perspective*. New York: Funk and Wagnalls, 1949.

————, with Rosen, Elliot A. *The First New Deal*. New York: Harcourt, Brace and World, 1966.

More Merry-Go-Round. New York: Liveright, 1932.

Morris, Joe Alex. *What a Year!* New York: Harper, 1956.

Mowry, George E. *The Urban Nation, 1920–1960*. New York: Hill and Wang, 1965.

Mullen, Arthur F. *Western Democrat*. New York: Wilfred Funk, 1940.

Myers, William Starr, and Newton, Walter H. *The Hoover Administration: A Documented Narrative*. New York: Scribner's, 1936.

Nadler, Marcus, and Bogen, Jules I. *The Banking Crisis: The End of an Epoch*. New York: Dodd, Mead, 1933.

Nash, Gerald D., ed *Franklin Delano Roosevelt: Great Lives Observed*. Englewood Cliffs, N. J.: Prentice-Hall, 1967.

Neville, Howard Ralph, *The Detroit Banking Collapse of 1933*. East Lansing: Bureau of Business and Economic Research, Michigan State University, 1960.

Nevins, Allan. *Herbert H. Lehman and His Era*. New York: Scribner's, 1963.

————, and Hill, Frank Ernest. *Ford: Decline and Rebirth, 1933–1962*. New York: Scribner's, 1962.

North, Douglass C. *Growth and Welfare in the American Past: A New Economic History*. Englewood Cliffs, N. J.: Prentice-Hall, 1966.

Noyes, Alexander Dana. *The Market Place: Reminiscences of a Financial Editor*. Boston: Little, Brown, 1938.

O'Brien, P. J. *Forward with Roosevelt*. Chicago: John C. Winston, 1936.

O'Connor, Harvey. *Mellon's Millions: The Biography of a Fortune*. New York: Blue Ribbon Books, 1933.

O'Connor, J. F. T. *The Banking Crisis and Recovery under the Roosevelt Administration*. Chicago: Callaghan, 1938.

Ostrander, Gilman M. *Nevada: The Great Rotten Borough, 1859–1964*. New York: Knopf, 1966.

Palmer, James E. *Carter Glass: Unreconstructed Rebel*. Roanoke, Va.: Institute of American Biography, 1938.

Pecora, Ferdinand. *Wall Street under Oath: The Story of Our Modern Money Changers*. New York: Simon and Schuster, 1939.

Peel, Roy D., and Donnelly, Thomas C. *The 1932 Campaign: An Analysis*. New York: Farrar and Rinehart, 1935.

Perkins, Dexter. *The New Age of Franklin Roosevelt, 1932–1945*. Chicago: University of Chicago Press, 1957.

Perkins, Frances. *The Roosevelt I Knew*. New York: Viking, 1946.

Powell, Frederick. *Depositors Paid in Full*. New York: Arbitrator, 1931.

President's Research Committee on Social Trends. *Recent Social Trends in the United States*. New York: McGraw-Hill, 1933.

Prochow, Herbert V., ed. *The Federal Reserve System*. New York: Harper, 1960.

Prothro, James Warren. *The Dollar Decade: Business Ideas in the 1920's*. Baton Rouge: Louisiana State University Press, 1954.

Rauch, Basil. *The History of the New Deal: 1933–1938*. New York: Creative Age Press, 1944.

Richberg, Donald R. *My Hero: The Indiscreet Memoirs of an Eventful but Unheroic Life*. New York: Putnam's, 1954.

Robbins, Lionel. *The Great Depression*. New York: Macmillan, 1934.

Robertson, Ross M. *History of the American Economy*. 2nd ed. New York: Harcourt, Brace and World, 1964.

Robinson, Edgar Eugene. *The Roosevelt Leadership: 1933–1945*. Philadelphia: Lippincott, 1955.

Rodkey, Robert G. *State Bank Failures in Michigan*. Ann Arbor: University of Michigan Press, 1935.

Rollins, Alfred B., Jr. *Roosevelt and Howe*. New York: Knopf, 1962.

———, ed. *Depression, Recovery, and War: 1929–1945*. Vol. 7 of *A Documentary History of American Life*. New York: McGraw-Hill, 1966.

Romasco, Albert U. *The Poverty of Abundance: Hoover, the Nation, the Depression*. New York: Oxford University Press, 1965.

Roosevelt Eleanor. *The Autobiography of Eleanor Roosevelt*. New York: Harper, 1937.

———. *This I Remember*. New York: Harper, 1949.

Roosevelt, Elliott, ed. *F. D. R.: His Personal Letters, Early Years*. New York: Duell, Sloan and Pearce, 1950.

Roosevelt, Franklin D. *Looking Forward*. London: Heinemann, 1933.

———. *On Our Way*. New York: John Day, 1934.

Roosevelt, James, with Shalett, Sidney. *Affectionately, F. D. R.: A Son's Story of a Lonely Man*. New York: Harcourt, Brace, 1959.

Roper, Daniel C., with Lovette, Frank H. *Fifty Years of Public Life*. Durham, N. C.: Duke University Press, 1941.

Rosenau, James N., ed. *The Roosevelt Treasury*. Garden City, N. Y.: Doubleday, 1951.

Rosenman, Samuel I. *Working with Roosevelt*. New York: Harper, 1952.
———, ed. *The Public Papers and Addresses of Franklin D. Roosevelt*. 2 vols. New York: Random House, 1938.
Rozwenc, Edwin C., ed. *The New Deal: Revolution or Evolution?* Boston: Heath, 1959.
Sann, Paul. *The Lawless Decade*. New York: Crown, 1957.
Schlesinger, Arthur M., Jr. *The Age of Roosevelt: The Coming of the New Deal*. Boston: Houghton Mifflin, 1958.
———. *The Age of Roosevelt: The Crisis of the Old Order, 1919–1933*. Boston: Houghton Mifflin, 1957.
———. *The Age of Roosevelt: The Politics of Upheaval, 1935–1936*. Boston: Houghton Mifflin, 1960.
Schwarz, Jordan A. *The Interregnum of Despair: Hoover, Congress, and the Depression*. Urbana: University of Illinois Press, 1970.
Scott, V. E. *60 Days with Franklin Delano Roosevelt*. New York: Walters and Mahon, 1933.
Seldes, Gilbert. *The Years of the Locust: America, 1929–1932*. Boston: Little, Brown, 1933.
Shannon, David A. *Between the Wars: America, 1919–1941*. Boston: Houghton Mifflin, 1965.
———, ed. *The Great Depression*. Englewood Cliffs, N. J.: Prentice-Hall, 1960.
Sherwin, Mark, and Markmann, Charles Lam. *One Week in March*. New York: Putnam's, 1961.
Simonds, William Adams. *Henry Ford: His Life, His Work, His Genius*. Indianapolis: Bobbs-Merrill, 1943.
Slosson, Preston William. *The Great Crusade and After: 1914–1928*. New York: Macmillan, 1931.
Smith, Rixey, and Beasley, Norman. *Carter Glass: A Biography*. New York: Longmans, Green, 1939.
Smolensky, Eugene. *Adjustments to Depression and War, 1929–1945*. Atlanta: Scott, Foresman, 1964.
Sobel, Robert. *The Big Board: A History of the New York Stock Market*. New York: Macmillan, 1965.
———. *The Great Bull Market: Wall Street in the 1920's*. New York: Norton, 1968.
Sorenson, Charles E., with Williamson, Samuel T. *My Forty Years with Ford*. New York: Norton, 1956.
Soule, George. *Prosperity Decade: From War to Depression, 1917–1929*. Vol. 8 of *The Economic History of the United States*. New York: Holt, Rinehart and Winston, 1947.

Sperling, John. *Great Depressions: 1837–1844, 1893–1898, 1929–1939.* Glenview, Ill.: Scott, Foresman, 1966.

Sternsher, Bernard. *Rexford Tugwell and the New Deal.* New Brunswick, N. J.: Rutgers University Press, 1964.

————, ed. *Hitting Home: The Great Depression in Town and Country.* Chicago: Quadrangle Books, 1970.

————, ed. *The New Deal: Doctrines and Democracy.* Boston: Allyn and Bacon, 1966.

Stiles, Lela. *The Man behind Roosevelt: The Story of Louis McHenry Howe.* Cleveland: World, 1954.

Storke, Thomas M. *California Editor.* Los Angeles: Westernlore, 1958.

Studenski, Paul, and Kroos, Herman. *Financial History of the United States.* New York: McGraw-Hill, 1952.

Sullivan, Lawrence. *Prelude to Panic: The Story of the Bank Holiday.* Washington, D. C.: Statesman Press, 1936.

Sward, Keith. *The Legend of Henry Ford.* New York: Holt, Rinehart and Winston, 1948.

Timmons, Bascom N. *Garner of Texas: A Personal History.* New York: Harper, 1948.

————. *Jesse H. Jones: The Man and the Statesman.* New York: Holt, 1956.

————. *Portrait of an American: Charles G. Dawes.* New York: Holt, 1953.

Tipple, John. *Crisis of the American Dream: A History of American Social Thought, 1920–1940.* New York: Western, 1968.

Tugwell, Rexford Guy. *The Brains Trust.* New York: Viking, 1968.

————. *The Democratic Roosevelt: A Biography of Franklin D. Roosevelt.* Garden City, N. Y.: Doubleday, 1957.

————. *F. D. R.: Architect of an Era.* New York: Macmillan, 1967.

————. *How They Became President: Thirty-five Ways to the White House.* New York: Simon and Schuster, 1964.

————. *Mr. Hoover's Economic Policy.* New York: Day, 1932.

Tull, Charles J. *Father Coughlin and the New Deal.* Syracuse, N. Y.: Syracuse University Press, 1965.

Tully, Grace. *F. D. R.: My Boss.* New York: Scribner's, 1949.

Upham, Cyril B., and Lamke, Edwin. *Closed and Distressed Banks: A Study in Public Administration.* Washington, D. C.: Brookings Institution, 1934.

Warner, Emily Smith, and Daniel, Hawthorne. *The Happy Warrior: A Biography of My Father, Alfred E. Smith.* Garden City, N. Y.: Doubleday, 1956.

Warren, Frank A., and Wreszin, Michael, eds. *The New Deal: An Anthology.* New York: Crowell, 1968.

\ Warren, Harris Gaylord. *Herbert Hoover and the Great Depression.* New York: Oxford University Press, 1959.

Wecter, Dixon. *The Age of the Great Depression: 1929–1941.* New York: Macmillan, 1948.

^ Wehle, Louis B. *Hidden Threads of History: Wilson through Roosevelt.* New York: Macmillan, 1953.

Werner, M. R. *Little Napoleons and Dummy Directors: Being the Narrative of the Bank of United States.* New York: Harper, 1933.

———. *Privileged Characters.* New York: McBride, 1935.

Werstein, Irving. *A Nation Fights Back: The Depression and Its Aftermath.* New York: Messner, 1962.

Whalen, Richard J. *The Founding Father: The Story of Joseph P. Kennedy.* New York: New American Library, 1964.

Wicker, Elmus R. *Federal Reserve Monetary Policy, 1917–1933.* New York: Random House, 1966.

\ Wilbur, Ray Lyman, and Hyde, Arthur Mastick. *The Hoover Policies.* New York: Scribner's, 1937.

Wilcox, U. V. *The Bankers Be Damned.* New York: Daniel Ryerson, 1940.

Williams, T. Harry. *Huey Long.* New York: Knopf, 1969.

Willis, H. Parker, and Chapman, John M. *The Banking Situation: American Post-War Problems and Developments.* New York: Columbia University Press, 1934.

Wilson, Edmund. *The American Earthquake: A Documentary of the Twenties and Thirties.* Garden City, N. Y.: Doubleday, 1958.

———. *Travels in Two Democracies.* New York: Harcourt, Brace, 1936.

Wolfe, Harold. *Herbert Hoover: Public Servant and Leader of the Loyal Opposition.* New York: Exposition, 1956.

Woods, John A. *Roosevelt and Modern America.* New York: Macmillan, Collier Books, 1962.

Woodward, George Walter. *The Detroit Money Market.* Ann Arbor: Bureau of Business Research, University of Michigan, 1932.

Young, James C. *Roosevelt Revealed.* New York: Farrar and Rinehart, 1936.

Zinn, Howard, ed. *New Deal Thought.* Indianapolis: Bobbs-Merrill, 1966.

UNPUBLISHED MATERIALS

Bellush, Jewel. "Selected Case Studies of the Legislative Leadership of Governor Herbert H. Lehman." Ph.D. dissertation, Columbia University, 1959.

Burns, Helen M. "The American Banking Community and New Deal

Banking Reform, 1933–1935." Ph.D. dissertation, New York University, 1966.

Condy, W. C. "The Banking Crisis." M.B.A. thesis, University of Pennsylvania, 1939.

Cowperthwaite, Lowery LeRoy. 'A Criticism of the Speaking of Franklin D. Roosevelt in the Presidential Campaign of 1932." Ph.D. dissertation, State University of Iowa, 1950.

Curlee, Joan Ethelyn. "Some Aspects of the New Deal Rationale: The Pre–1936 Writings of Six of Roosevelt's Advisers." Ph.D. dissertation, Vanderbilt University, 1957.

Halteman, Theodore Smith. "The Economic Philosophy of Herbert Clark Hoover: An Analysis of His Administration in the Light of It." M.A. thesis, Wharton School, University of Pennsylvania, 1934.

Jenkinson, Acis. "Banking Developments Leading to the Crisis of March, 1933." M.A. thesis, University of Pennsylvania, 1937.

Leibell, Vincent L. "The Banking Act of 1935." M.B.A. thesis, University of Pennsylvania, 1936.

Levin, David Saul. "Regulating the Securities Industry: The Evolution of a Government Policy." Ph.D. dissertation, Columbia University, 1969.

Neville, Howard Ralph. "An Historical Study of the Collapse of Banking in Detroit, 1929–1933." Ph.D. dissertation, Michigan State University, 1956.

Schwarz, Jordan. "The Politics of Fear: Congress and the Depression during the Hoover Administration." Ph.D. dissertation, Columbia University, 1967.

GOVERNMENT DOCUMENTS

United States, Board of Governors of the Federal Reserve System, *All-Bank Statistics, United States, 1896–1955*. Washington, D. C.: Government Printing Office, 1959.

State of New York, Executive Department. "In the Matter of the Investigation into the Department of Banking of the State of New York, as affecting the business and affairs of the City Trust Company of the City of New York, pursuant to section 8 of the Executive Law of the State of New York; Hon. Robert Moses, Moreland Act Commissioner, presiding, May 20, 1929–June 28, 1929." Franklin Delano Roosevelt Memorial Library: Record of the Office of the Governor of New York, 1928–1932.

United States, Congress, House, Committee on Banking and Currency. *Hearings: Branch, Chain and Group Banking*. Under H. Res. 141. 71st Cong., 2d Sess., 1930.

United States, Congress, House, Committee on Banking and Currency (*continued*)

————. *Hearings: Liberalizing the Credit Facilities of the Federal Reserve System.* On H. R. 9203. 72d Cong., 1st Sess., 1932.

————. *Hearings: Reconstruction Finance Corporation.* On H. R. 5060 and H. R. 5116. 72d Cong., 1st Sess., 1932.

————. *Report on Banking Act of 1933,* to accompany H. R. 5661. 73d Cong., 1st Sess., 1933.

————, Subcommittee. *Hearings: Creation of a System of Federal Home Loan Banks.* On H. R. 7620. 72d Cong., 1st Sess., 1932.

United States, Congress, Senate, Committee on Banking and Currency. *Hearings: Amendments to the Federal Reserve Act.* On S. 4454 and S. 4550. 72d Cong., 2d Sess., 1933.

————. *Hearings: Consolidation of National Banking Association.* On S. 1782 and H. R. 2. 69th Cong., 1st Sess., 1926.

————. *Hearings: Operation of the National and Federal Reserve Banking Systems.* On S. 4115. 72d Cong., 1st Sess., 1932.

————. *Hearings: Stock Exchange Practices.* On S. Res. 84. 72d Cong., 2d Sess., 1932–1933; 73d Cong., 1st Sess., 1933.

————. *Hearings: Unemployment Relief.* On S. 4632, S. 4727, S. 4755, and S. 4822. 72d Cong., 1st Sess., 1932.

————. *Hearings on S. 71.* 71st Cong., 3d Sess., 1931.

————, Subcommittee. *Hearings: Creation of a Reconstruction Finance Corporation.* On S. 1. 72d Cong., 1st Sess., 1932.

ARTICLES

Adams, James Truslow. "Presidential Prosperity." *Harper's Magazine* 161 (August 1930): 257–67.

Albjerg, Victor L. "Hoover: The Presidency in Transition." *Current History* 39 (October 1950): 213–19.

Anderson, Paul Y. "The Money Changers Linger." *Nation* 136 (29 March 1933): 339–40.

Angel, James W. "Gold, Banks and the New Deal." *Political Science Quarterly* 49 (December 1934): 481–505.

Angly, Edward. "The New Deal in Banking." *New Outlook* 161 (April 1933): 27–31.

————. "Our Banks." *New Outlook* 161 (February 1933): 13–16.

————. "Our City Banks." *New Outlook* 161 (March 1933): 33–36.

Atkins, Paul M. "The National Credit Corporation." *Review of Reviews* 85 (January 1932): 48–49, 68.

Ballantine, Arthur A. "When All the Banks Closed." *Harvard Business Review* 26 (March 1948): 129–43.

"The Bank Holiday Fever." *Literary Digest* 140 (11 March 1933): 9–10.
"Banking and Other Reforms." *Bankers Magazine* 126 (April 1933): 305–10.
"Bankless Prices." *Business Week,* 15 March 1933, p. 8.
"The Banks Fold Up." *New Republic* 74 (15 March 1933): 116–17.
"The Banks Reopen." *Business Week,* 22 March 1933, pp. 3–4.
Barsalou, F. W. "The Concentration of Banking Power in Nevada: An Historical Analysis." *Business History Review* 29 (December 1955): 350–62.
Barton, Bruce. "Is There Anything Here that Other Men Couldn't Do?" *American Magazine* 95 (February 1923): 16–17, 128.
"Baruch Kills Currency Inflation:" *Business Week,* 22 February 1933, pp. 3–4.
Beard, Charles A. "Roosevelt's Place in History." *Events* 3 (February 1938): 81–86.
Bellush, Jewel. "Roosevelt's Good Right Arm: Lieut. Governor Herbert H. Lehman." *New York History* 41 (October 1960): 423–43.
Berlin, Isaiah. "President Franklin Delano Roosevelt." *Political Quarterly* 26 (December 1955): 336–44.
"Best Banking Law." *Business Week,* 17 June 1933, p. 19.
"Big Bankers' Gambling Mania." *Literary Digest* 115 (11 March 1933): 11–12.
"Big Banks for a New Deal in Banking." *Literary Digest* 115 (25 March 1933): 9.
Bird, Caroline. "The Day the Money Stopped." *Look* 26 (12 March 1963): 84–91.
Blocker, John G. "The Guarantee of State Bank Deposits." *Kansas Studies in Business,* No. 11.
Brown, E. Francis. "America Meets the Emergency." *Current History* 38 (May 1933): 202–11.
———. "How Real Is American Recovery?" *Current History* 38 (December 1932): 335–39.
———. "The Lame Duck Congress at Work." *Current History* 38 (February 1933): 589–95.
Burck, Gilbert, and Silberman, Charles. "What Caused the Great Depression." *Fortune* 51 (February 1955): 94–99, 204.
———. "Why the Depression Lasted So Long." *Fortune* 51 (March 1955): 84–88, 189.
Burgess, R. L. "Where Did All the Money Go?" *American Magazine* 114 (September 1932): 65–66.
Burke, Robert E. "The Roosevelt Administrations." *Current History* 39 (October 1950): 220–24.

"Business Joins Consultation on the Ills of the Banks." *Business Week*, 6 July 1932, p. 4.

"Business on a Holiday." *Business Week*, 15 March 1932, pp. 6–7.

Carosso, Vincent, "Washington and Wall Street: The New Deal and Investment Bankers, 1933–1940." *Business History Review* 44 (Winter 1970): 425–45.

Chambers, Clarke. "F. D. R.: Pragmatist-Idealist." *Pacific Northwest Quarterly* 52 (1961): 50–55.

"Chase Bank's New Chief." *Business Week*, 4 January 1933, pp. 13–14.

"Chicago Pays Another Installment on Rugged Banking Individualism." *Business Week*, 6 July 1932, p. 6.

"Closed Banks." *Business Week*, 24 June 1933, p. 23.

Cornwell, Elmer E. "The Presidential Press Conference: A Study in Institutionalization." *Midwestern Journal of Political Sciences* 4 (November 1960): 370–89.

Crump, Norman. "The American Banking Crisis." *Nineteenth Century and After* 113 (April 1933): 407–16.

Daiger, J. M. "Bank Failures: The Problem and the Remedy." *Harper's Magazine* 162 (April 1931): 513–27.

———. "Confidence, Credit, and Cash." *Harper's Magazine* 166 (February 1933): 279–92.

———. "Did the Federal Reserve Play Politics?" *Current History* 37 (October 1932): 25–32.

———. "Toward Safer and Stronger Banks." *Current History* 37 (February 1933): 558–64.

Degler, Carl N. "The Ordeal of Herbert Hoover." *Yale Review* 52 (Summer 1963): 563–83.

Dennis, Lawrence. "Can the Banks Be Made Safe?" *Nation* 136 (15 March 1933): 280–82.

"Deposit Insurance." *Business Week*, 12 April 1933, p. 3; 26 April 1933, p. 5; 31 May 1933, p. 20.

"Destroy the Money Power." *Nation* 136 (22 March 1933): 306–07.

"Detroit Gets a Bank." *Business Week*, 5 April 1933, pp. 5–6.

Ebersole, J. Franklin. "One Year of the Reconstruction Finance Corporation." *Quarterly Journal of Economics* 47 (May 1933): 464–92.

"Emergency Pool to Help Banks May Serve to Stop Deflation." *Business Week*, 14 October 1931, pp. 5–6.

Epstein, Abraham. "How Real Was Our Prosperity?" *Current History* 36 (August 1932): 550–56.

Flynn, John T. "The Bankers and the Crisis." *New Republic* 74 (22 March 1933): 157–59.

———. "The Dangers of Branch Banking." *Forum and Century* 39 (May 1933): 258–62.

———. "Inside the R.F.C." *Harper's Magazine* 166 (January 1933): 161–68.

———. "Michigan Magic." *Harper's Magazine* 168 (December 1932): 1–11.

———. "Wanted: Real Banking Reform." *Current History* 39 (January 1934): 394–401.

"For Public Relief, the R. F. C.; For Industry, Federal Reserve." *Business Week*, 20 July 1932, pp. 3–4.

Frisch, Morton J. "Roosevelt the Conservator: A Rejoinder to Hofstadter." *Journal of Politics* 25 (May 1963): 361–72.

"Full Scope of Hoover Plan for Recovery Now Is Revealed." *Business Week*, 24 August 1932, pp. 3–4.

Galbraith, John Kenneth. "On the Economics of F. D. R.: What a President Ought to Know." Review of *The Economic Thought of Franklin D. Roosevelt*, by Daniel R. Fusfeld. *Commentary* 22 (August 1956): 172–75.

Gilbert, Clinton W. "Andrew W. Mellon, Secretary of the Treasury." *Current History* 34 (July 1931): 521–26.

Glass, Carter. "The Need for Banking Reform." *Review of Reviews* 138 (January 1933): 20–22.

"Glass Bill Cracked." *Business Week*, 1 February 1933, p. 14.

Golembe, Carter H. "The Deposit Insurance Legislation of 1933: An Evaluation of Its Antecedents and Its Purposes." *Political Science Quarterly* 75 (1960): 181–200.

"A Good Start." *Business Week*, 22 March 1933, p. 32.

Gras, N. S. B. "Do We Need Private Bankers?" *Current History* 38 (August 1933): 547–52.

Greer, Guy. "Why Canadian Banks Don't Fail." *Harper's Magazine* 166 (May 1933): 722–34.

Hammond, Bray. "The Worst Banking in the World." *New Republic* 73 (1 February 1933): 313–15.

Hapgood, Norman. "Protect the Depositor." *Nation* 136 (15 March 1933): 283.

Harris, S. E. "Banking and Currency Legislation, 1932." *Quarterly Journal of Economics* 46 (May 1932): 546–57.

"Highlights of Michigan Banking History since the Turn of the Century." *Michigan Investor* 50 (26 July 1952): 12–15, 106, 127, 130–32.

Hoarder, George J. [Pseud.] "In Defense of Hoarding." *Nation* 136 (22 March 1933): 318–19.

"Hoover Builds His Program for Using New Relief Power." *Business Week*, 10 August 1932, pp. 5–6.

Ickes, Harold L. "My Twelve Years with F. D. R." *Saturday Evening Post* 220–21 (June, July 1948).

"The Ideal Bank." *Business Week*, 19 April 1933, pp. 16, 18.

"The Indictment of Charles E. Mitchell." *Nation* 136 (5 April 1933): 357.

Jervey, William H. "When the Banks Closed: Arizona's Bank Holiday of 1933." *Arizona and the West* 10 (Summer 1968): 127–52.

Johnson, Gerald W. "The Average American and the Depression." *Current History* 35 (February 1932): 671–75.

Key, Jack B. "Henry B. Steagall: The Conservative as a Reformer." *Alabama Review* 17 (July 1964): 198–209.

Keynes, John Maynard. "The World's Economic Outlook." *Atlantic Monthly* 149 (May 1932): 521–26.

Kirkendall, Richard S. "Franklin D. Roosevelt and the Service Intellectual." *Mississippi Valley Historical Review* 49 (December 1962): 456–71.

———. "The New Deal as Watershed: The Recent Literature." *Journal of American History* 54 (March 1968): 839–52.

Krock, Arthur. "President Hoover's Two Years." *Current History* 34 (July 1931): 488–89.

———. "Reminiscences." *Centennial Review* 9 (Spring 1965): 222–52.

"Legislating a New Era in Banking." *Literary Digest* 115 (24 June 1933): 7.

Lippmann, Walter. "The Peculiar Weakness of Mr. Hoover." *Harper's Magazine* 161 (June 1930): 1–7.

"Liquidation Corp." *Business Week*, 8 February 1933, p. 20.

McAvoy, Thomas T., C.S.C. "Roosevelt: A Modern Jefferson." *Review of Politics* 7 (July 1945): 270–79.

"Making Merry over Bank Holiday." *Literary Digest* 115 (25 March 1933): 28–30.

Manchester, William. "The Great Bank Holiday." *Holiday* 27 (February 1960): 60–61, 137–43.

Markey, Morris. "A Reporter at Large: Washington Weekend." *New Yorker* 9 (18 March 1933): 44–48.

Merry, Ellis B. "Bank Reorganization and Recapitalization in Michigan." *Michigan Law Review* 33 (December 1933): 137–70.

Meyer, Eugene. "From Laissez-Faire with William Graham Sumner to the RFC." *Public Policy* 5 (1954): 5–27.

"Michigan Moratorium." *New Republic* 124 (8 March 1933): 90–91.

"Michigan's Banking Holiday." *Literary Digest* 115 (25 February 1933): 7.

"Michigan's Grim Holiday." *Business Week*, 22 February 1933, p. 5.

Millis, Walter. "Roosevelt in Retrospect." *Virginia Quarterly Review* 21 (Summer 1945): 321–30.

Mitchell, W. C., and Burns, A. F. "Production during the American Business Cycle of 1927–1933." *National Bureau of Economic Research Bulletin* (1936).

Moley, Raymond. "The Great Bank Rescue of 1933." *Bankers Magazine* 151 (Winter 1968): 9–27.

"Morgan and Co." *Business Week,* 7 June 1933, pp. 5–6.

Muchmore, Lynn. "The Banking Crisis of 1933: Some Iowa Evidence." *Journal of Economic History* 30 (September 1970): 627–39.

Myers, William Starr, and Newton, Walter H. "The Origins of the Banking Panic of March 4, 1933." *Saturday Evening Post,* 8, 15, 22, 29 June 1935. Reprinted. New York: Mail and Express Printing Co., 1935.

Nash, Gerald D. "Herbert Hoover and the Origins of the Reconstruction Finance Corporation." *Mississippi Valley Historical Review* 46 (December 1959): 455–68.

"The National City Bank Scandal." *Nation* 136 (8 March 1933): 247–49.

"The Nation Rallying behind the President." *Literary Digest* 115 (18 March 1933): 6–7.

"A Necessary Step." *Nation* 136 (12 April 1933): 385–86.

Nevins, Allan. "President Hoover's Record." *Current History* 37 (July 1932): 385–94.

"New Bank Bills." *Business Week,* 24 May 1933, pp. 5–6.

"The New Bank Law." *Nation* 136 (22 March 1933): 305.

"New Banks–Model T." *Business Week,* 8 March 1933, p. 5.

"The New Day in American Banking." *Literary Digest* 115 (18 March 1933): 3–5.

"Old Banks and New." *Business Week,* 29 March 1933, pp. 4–5.

Ostrolenk, Bernard. "Inflation Trends in America." *Current History* 35 (March 1932): 773–80.

————. "Why the Banks Collapsed." *Current History* 38 (May 1933): 152–58.

" 'Other People's Money.' " *Business Week,* 5 April 1933, p. 9.

Page, Ralph W. "Bankruptcy or Inflation?" *Current History* 38 (March 1933): 680–84.

"Parade of the Experts." *Business Week,* 1 March 1933, p. 3.

Perkins, Frances. "Franklin Roosevelt's Apprenticeship." Review of *Franklin D. Roosevelt as Governor of New York,* by Bernard Bellush. *New Republic* 132 (25 April 1955): 19–21.

"Permanent Bank Reform." *Business Week,* 29 March 1933, p. 3.

Pontecorvo, Guillio. "Investment Banking and Security Speculation in the Late 1920's." *Business History Review* 32 (Summer 1958): 166–91.

"Portrait of a Policy." *Fortune* 5 (January 1932): 28–29, 114–16.

Potter, David M. "Sketches for the Roosevelt Portrait." *Yale Review* 39 (September 1949): 39–53.

"President Hoover's Farewell Address." *Literary Digest* 115 (25 February 1933): 8.

Preston, Howard H. "The Banking Act of 1933." *American Economic Review* 23 (December 1933): 585–607.

"Private Initiative Takes Over the Drive toward Recovery." *Business Week*, 3 August 1932, pp. 3–4.

"Provisions of the Emergency Banking Act." *Congressional Digest* 12 (April 1933): 103–04.

Ratchford, B. U. "The Progress of Banking Reform." *South Atlantic Quarterly* 33 (January 1934): 47–62.

"Reconstruction Finance Corporation." *Business Week*, 4 January 1933, pp. 1–2.

"The 'Red Plot' to Wreck Banks." *Literary Digest* 114 (13 August 1932): 8–9.

Reeves, Clifford B. "A Brief for the Bankers." *American Mercury* 27 (September 1932): 20–29.

"The RFC." *Fortune* 21 (May 1940): 45–50, 122–44.

"R.F.C. Goes to Michigan." *Business Week*, 1 March 1933, p. 6.

"R.F.C. Operations Diminish Danger of Heavy Treasury Drain." *Business Week*, 2 November 1932, pp. 20, 22.

Ritter, Lawrence. "Official Central Banking Theory in the United States, 1939–1961." *Journal of Political Economy* 70 (Feb. 1962): 14–29.

Rosenman, Samuel I. "What Makes a President?" *Ladies Home Journal* 69 (May 1952): 40–41, 103–23.

Rosner, Henry J. "Nationalize the Banks." *World Tomorrow* 16 (22 March 1933): 279–81.

Rossiter, Clinton L. "The Political Philosophy of F. D. Roosevelt: A Challenge to Scholarship." *Review of Politics* 2 (January 1949): 87–95.

———. "War, Depression, and the Presidency, 1933–1950," *Social Research* 17 (December 1950): 417–40.

Schumpeter, Joseph A. "The American Economy in the Interwar Period: The Decade of the Twenties." *American Economic Review* 36 (May 1946): 1–10.

Schwartz, Jordan A. "John Nance Garner and the Sales Tax Rebellion of 1932." *Journal of Southern History* 30 (May 1964): 162–80.

"The 73d Congress Faces the Banking Problem." *Congressional Digest* 12 (April 1933): 97–104.

"Should America Adopt a Unified Banking System?" *Congressional Digest* 12 (April 1933): 106–20.

Showan, Daniel P. "The Hoover-Roosevelt Relationship during the Interregnum." *Lock-Haven* (Pa.) *Bulletin* 1 (1961): 24–50.

Smith, Alfred E. "The Banking Revolution." *New Outlook* 161 (April 1933): 10–11.

"Some Views on Banking Reform." *Review of Reviews* 136 (April 1933): 48–49.

"State Moratorium Plans Stem Tide of Bank Suspensions." *Business Week*, 7 September 1932, p. 12.

Steele, Walter S. "The Red Bankrupt Racket?" *National Republic* 2 (September 1932): 30–32.

"Strong Medicine for Bank Failures." *Literary Digest* 114 (10 December 1932): 7.

Sullivan, Mark. "The Case for the Administration." *Fortune* 6 (July 1932): 35–39, 83–88.

Thomas, Norman. "The Banks of New York." *Nation* 132 (11 February 1931): 147–49.

———. "A Socialist Program for Banking." *Nation* 136 (22 March 1933): 309; (5 April 1933): 376.

"To Make Banking Safe for Depositors." *Literary Digest* 114 (24 December 1932): 3–4.

"Trends of the Markets in Money, Stocks, Bonds: Banking Situation Stable Though Closings Are High." *Business Week*, 13 July 1932, p. 34.

"Trends of the Markets in Money, Stocks, Bonds: Banks Improve Position But Not Credit Policy." *Business Week*, 10 August 1932, p. 30.

Tugwell, Rexford Guy. "The Compromising Roosevelt." *Western Political Quarterly* 6 (June 1953): 320–41.

———. "Flaws in the Hoover Economic Policy." *Current History* 35 (January 1932): 525–31.

———. "Franklin D. Roosevelt on the Verge of the Presidency." *Antioch Review* 16 (March 1956): 46–79.

———. "The New Deal: The Available Instruments of Governmental Power." *Western Political Quarterly* 2 (December 1949): 545–80.

———. "The New Deal: The Decline of Government." *Western Political Quarterly* 4 (June 1951): 295–312; (September 1951): 469–86.

———. "The New Deal: The Progressive Tradition." *Western Political Quarterly* 3 (September 1950): 390–427.

———. "The New Deal in Retrospect." *Western Political Quarterly* 1 (December 1948): 373–85.

———. "The Preparation of a President." *Western Political Quarterly* 1 (June 1948): 131–53.

Tugwell, Rexford Guy (*continued*)

———. "The Progressive Orthodoxy of Franklin D. Roosevelt." *Ethics* 114 (October 1953): 1–23.

———. "The Protagonists: Roosevelt and Hoover." *Antioch Review* 13 (December 1953): 419–22.

———. "The Sources of New Deal Reformism." *Ethics* 64 (July 1954): 249–76.

———. "Transition: Hoover to Roosevelt, 1932–1933." *Centennial Review* 9 (Spring 1965): 160–91.

Vanderlip, Frank A. "What About the Banks?" *Saturday Evening Post* 205 (5 November 1932): 3–5, 64–66.

Villard, Oswald Garrison. "Issues and Men: James H. Perkins and the National City Bank." *Nation* 133 (15 March 1933): 279.

"Wall Street Probe." *Business Week*, 8 February 1933, p. 18.

"Wall Street vs. Woodin." *Business Week*, 19 April 1933, p. 18.

"Washington and the Banks." *Business Week*, 8 March 1933, pp. 3–4.

"Washington Reads the Signs." *Business Week*, 15 March 1933, pp. 4–5.

"Weak Knees and Strong Banks." *Nation* 136 (8 February 1933): 136–37.

Westerfield, Ray B. "The Banking Act of 1933." *Journal of Political Economy* 41 (December 1933): 721–49.

———. "Defects in American Banking." *Current History* 34 (April 1931): 17–23.

"When Banks Were Closed." *Review of Reviews* 87 (April 1933): 52–54.

"When Europe Cracked, Banks Needed Buttress." *Business Week*, 24 August 1932, pp. 4–5.

White, William Allen. "Herbert Hoover–The Last of the Old Presidents or the First of the New?" *Saturday Evening Post* 205 (4 March 1933): 6–7, 53–56.

"Why Canadian Banks Don't Fail." *Literary Digest* 115 (18 March 1933): 7.

Willis, H. Parker. "Are the Bankers to Blame?" *Current History* 39 (January 1934): 385–93.

———. "The Banking Act of 1933–An Appraisal." *American Economic Review, Supplement, Papers and Proceedings of the American Economic Society* 24 (March 1934): 101–10.

———. "The Folly of Deposit Guarantee." *American Mercury* 31 (January 1934): 16–23.

Willit, Virgil. "The Banks Go Chain-Store." *American Mercury* 20 (June 1930): 144–52.

Wright, Esmond. "The Roosevelt Revolution of 1933–38." *History Today* 12 (December 1962): 821–32.

INDEX